E183.8.S95 M68 2012
Syria and the USA :
33663005173253
EGN

DATE DUE

BRODART, CO.   Cat. No. 23-221

Sami Moubayed is a Syrian University professor, historian, and editor-in-chief of *Forward* magazine. He is an author of numerous books on modern Syria, including *Steel and Silk: Men and Women Who Shaped Syria* (Cune Press, 2005). His articles on the modern Middle East appear weekly in *The Huffington Post, Gulf News,* and *Asia Times.* Moubayed studied at the American University of Beirut (AUB) and currently teaches at the Faculty of International Relations at the University of Kalamoon in Syria. He is co-founder of the Centre for Syrian Studies at the University of St Andrews in Scotland and of www.syrianhistory.com, the first and only online Syrian museum.

'*Syria and the USA* is a well-told and entertaining overview of US–Syria relations from World War I to the formation of the United Arab Republic. Sami Moubayed provides the reader with insight into how Syrians view events that are crucial to their political development. He explains how general Syrian attitudes toward the US government changed from admiration to anger over the first half of the twentieth century and explores how US support for Israeli displacement of Arabs in Palestine and military coups in Syria undermined initial attitudes toward Washington. The author's interest in the history of women and cinema in Syria give this diplomatic history cultural depth and a welcome new dimension.'

Joshua Landis,
Director of the Center for Middle East Studies,
University of Oklahoma

'Sami Moubayed is one of Syria's leading scholars and commentators, and he is uniquely qualified to provide important insights into the history of the Middle East in the twentieth century. Anyone wanting to understand how what was an amicable and respectful US–Syrian relationship early in the twentieth century deteriorated by the 1950s into a confrontational one would do well to read Moubayed's book. He weaves together a scholarly yet entertaining tapestry of information that presents the all-too-often ignored Syrian perspective of its relationship with the United States. The US–Syrian relationship today is still fraught with mistrust and misunderstanding. Moubayed shows in his book that this is not a new phenomenon – it has a rich and interesting history.'

David W Lesch,
Professor of Middle East History,
Trinity University

'The history of relations between Syria and the United States up until the 1960s is little known and understood. Sami Moubayed, one of Syria's leading young historians, now offers us a remarkably comprehensive study that illustrates how a positive start in diplomatic relations in the early part of the twentieth century eventually began to unwind in unfortunate ways by mid-century. Using a variety of sources including the US State Department archives and the private paper collections of Syrian political leaders, Moubayed sheds new light on the political intrigue and shenanigans that were so characteristic of the Cold War era. Scholars and foreign policy experts will appreciate the author's efforts at reconstructing the history of an important chapter in America's relationship with the Middle East region.'

Philip S Khoury,
Ford International Professor of History,
Massachusetts Institute of Technology

SYRIA
AND THE
USA

WASHINGTON'S RELATIONS WITH DAMASCUS
FROM WILSON TO EISENHOWER

SAMI MOUBAYED

I.B. TAURIS

LONDON · NEW YORK

Published in 2012 by I.B.Tauris & Co Ltd
6 Salem Road, London W2 4BU
175 Fifth Avenue, New York NY 10010
www.ibtauris.com

Distributed in the United States and Canada
Exclusively by Palgrave Macmillan
175 Fifth Avenue, New York NY 10010

Library of International Relations Vol 56

ISBN 978 1 84885 705 6

A full CIP record for this book is available from the British Library
A full CIP record for this book is available from the Library of Congress

Library of Congress catalog card: available

Copyedited by Lauren Williams

Typeset by Newgen Publishers, Chennai
Printed and bound by CPI Group (UK) Ltd, Croydon, CR0 4YY

CONTENTS

LIST OF ILLUSTRATIONS

All images courtesy of www.syrianhistory.com

ACKNOWLEDGEMENTS

Research for this book has taken me to the state archives of world capitals, the reading rooms of international libraries, and the attics of Syrian families. I would like to acknowledge the places that made it happen, before moving on to the men and women who, had it not been for their endless support and patience, this book would never have seen the light. I will start with the Jaffet Library at the American University of Beirut (AUB) – my favourite venue in Lebanon – where I have spent days and nights researching modern Syrian history. Other centres include the Assad National Library in Damascus, the Syrian Museum of Historical Documents, the Office of the Historian at the State Department in Washington DC, the official Mandate Archive at Nantes in France, the Mitterrand Library in Paris, the Public Records Office (PRO) in London, and the British Library Newspapers at Colindale.

As for individuals, I would like to thank those who took the time to see me for interviews, shedding light on their political careers during the early years of Syrian–US relations. I start off with the late Munir al-Ajlani, who passed away in Saudi Arabia in 2004, long before this book was complete. For five years I spent long hours with Munir Bey in Beirut and Brummanah, discussing major episodes in his life as parliamentarian, minister and academic in the 1930s, 1940s and 1950s. The invaluable Syrian treasure, HE Abdullah al-Khani, Secretary-General of the Presidential Palace under Presidents Quwatli, Atasi and Shishakli, was also extremely generous with his time and resources. So were the families of Presidents Shukri al-Quwatli, Hashem al-Atasi and Adib al-Shishakli. A special thank-you goes to Ambassador Imad Moustapha and Colette Khoury, granddaughter of Prime Minister Fares al-Khoury, whose family contributed giants – in every sense of the word – to modern Syrian history.

Acknowledgements cannot be complete without the friends who took time to read the manuscript of this book prior to publication, offering their comments and suggestions that helped finalize this book. HE Ambassador Imad Moustapha managed to steal time from his hectic schedule in the US, reading the book from beginning to end and offering valuable comments about an epoch that preceded his tenure in the US during the Bush and Obama Administrations.

This book was the brainchild of a conversation I had over a cup of coffee with my good friend Ibrahim Hamidi, Syria's celebrated journalist from the London-based *al-Hayat*. Ibrahim and I had agreed to co-write a book on Syria, with me covering the early years of the twentieth century and him tackling the post-1970 era. Due to his hectic schedule, Ibrahim dropped out of the project but never hesitated to offer his advice when needed. He saw things from the angle of a seasoned journalist, complementing my views as a historian. A note of appreciation is due here to my good friend Sahban Abd Rabbo who has supported my writing career since I was a 19-year-old political science student at AUB. Sahban read early drafts of all of my previous books on Syria. With Sahban I co-created www.syrianhistory.com back in 2004, the first and only online museum of Syrian history. The two of us have taken the world apart in endless discussions and pieced it back together. We have debated everything there is to discuss under the sun, ranging from politics and philosophy to art and religion. We argued more often than agreed, but at the end of the day, we sought that the truth prevails amongst us.

Finally, my dear friends Sahban Abd Rabbo and Abdulsalam Haykal, who shoulder-to-shoulder and hand-in-hand, have been by my side since I was a 19-year-old political science student at AUB. Abdulsalam and Sahban have edited all of my previous books on Syria. With Sahban I co-created www.syrianhistory.com back in 2004, the first and only museum of Syrian history, an initiative that Abdulsalam joined in 2009. Abdulsalam and I worked together in breathing life into the Damascus Chapter of the AUB Alumni Association, and in establishing *Forward* magazine, Syria's leading English-language monthly back in 2006. The three of us have taken the world apart in endless discussions since our college days, and pieced it back together. We have debated everything there is to discuss under the sun, ranging from politics and philosophy to art and religion. As AUB taught us, at the end of the day, we sought that the truth should prevail amongst us. To them and to other friends, Muhammad A. Agha, Kareem Tabba, Amer al-Hafi, Nourallah Qaddura, Hussam Ramzi, Anas Fakhry, Michel Arcouche and Vahe Hovaguimian, I am eternally grateful.

I would like to wrap up by thanking my family, whose unwavering support never faltered – not for a moment – during my career in academia and journalism. My mother and father, two sisters Leena and Sereen, and brother-in-law Maher Shehadeh were always pillars of support, believing in me from day one. My mother, a saintly figure in every sense of the word, never doubted that one day I would become a professional writer, although it took my father a few years – until after I received my PhD – to begin giving me credit. His belated acknowledgement paid off, since it forced me to work extra hard to obtain his blessing, which is so dear to my heart.

Needless to say, any faults or inaccuracies in this book are strictly my own, and nobody but myself shoulders responsibility for them.

Sami Moubayed

Damascus

FOREWORD

Syria and the USA have never known each other well enough. Both have viewed the relations between them through third-party eyes, ever since the State of Israel was established on the historic land of Palestine in 1948. Almost every US administration tried to find its own policy towards Syria, often bringing the relationship back to square one. World events impacted the assumptions each country had about the other, especially in the many years since the USA enlisted Syria as a state sponsor of terrorism. Since the 'war on terror' became the building block of US foreign policy after the tragic events of 9/11, differences between Syria and the USA seemed irreconcilable. The US occupation of Iraq, the Syrian-backed Lebanese defiance of Israel, and the unworried Syrian–Iranian alliance, all meant that Syria stood in the way of almost every US interest in the Middle East. With Egypt and Saudi Arabia taking more favourable stands towards the USA's intervention in the historically turmoiled region, Syria became the spearhead for the anti-American camp. Dubbed in the media as the 'axis of defiance', the USA called it an 'axis of evil'. Then 2011 came, and the two countries never seemed further apart.

* * *

Until 2011, these were the traditional challenges of the US policy in the region. But this is going to change. A group of US college students who came to Damascus in 2009 asked me whether terrorism was going to remain the main challenge to their country's foreign policy. I thought that while there was still a rise in anti-US sentiment in the region, the main challenge was going to be the new generation of Arabs. The USA would have to accustom itself to dealing with counterparts that considered themselves as peers, and as people who

emerged from the colonial era in the Middle East with a foreign policy cen-
tred around the Arab–Israeli conflict. In my work with the youth and young
entrepreneurs in Syria, I was lucky to meet and was inspired by an empowered
and globalized generation. They were destined to realize that the complacent
'status quo', which seemed to suit the USA and Israel, is standing between
them and their potential. This generation included leaders who believed that
change was within the realms of possibility. The rise of countries like Turkey
was inspiring, the economic crises that shook the world was a demonstration of
how quickly things can change, and clearly opportunities present themselves.
In a few years, the USA will be looking at a very different Arab Middle East:
one with a louder voice.

* * *

A staunch advocate of closer relations between my country and the USA, I
find it damaging that Syria is seen only in the controversial contexts of the
Arab–Israeli conflict, war on terror, and the newly found problems in Iraq and
the region. To many Syrians as well, the USA was the enemy's friend to say
the least. I had countless encounters with Americans over the past ten years,
whether in Syria, the USA or elsewhere. From elected leaders to government
employees, doctors to shopkeepers, investment bankers to the average Joes and
Janes, Americans were always curious to know more about my Middle Eastern
country. I was a witness to the euphoria of American diplomats in Damascus
as they welcomed Nancy Pelosi at the American Residence during her March
2007 visit, which Mr George W. Bush discredited as 'counterproductive'. They
were torn apart between the official line, which they could not depart from,
and the reality which contradicted with labels such as 'axis of evil' and 'rogue
state'. I walked with them in Old Damascus, along the biblical Straight Street,
now Souk Medhat Pasha. Their amazement was evident at a mosque, a church
and a synagogue sitting next to each other in peace and harmony. They always
enjoyed the extra welcome when shopkeepers knew they were American. The
experience was overwhelming, especially when put in contrast with the expec-
tations that the media and politics promoted about Syria.

* * *

So how do the two worlds meet? Not too far from the times we live today was
the middle of the nineteenth century, when a US missionary thought of starting the Syrian Protestant College, now AUB (American University of Beirut).

The impact that AUB had on Lebanon and the region was immense, graduating generation after generation of political, business and social leaders
since 1866. The institution was a bridge between the Arab world and the
USA, even at the most critical of times such as the Lebanese civil war and
the Israeli invasion of Beirut in 1982. The region has changed dramatically
from the days when AUB founder Daniel Bliss came to spread Protestantism.
What was then called 'Syria' is now Syria, Lebanon, Jordan, and Palestine/
Israel. What was then a nation emerging from civil war is now the world's
only superpower. Yet, the USA always had, in the graduates of AUB and
similar institutions, strong champions of the 'American way', becoming quite
unintentionally, as one US diplomat described it, 'one of the most successful
public diplomacy tools for the United States'.

* * *

The 'American dream' was pursued by many, especially in the last years of the
Ottoman empire. The exodus from Syria and Lebanon to the shores of Boston,
Massachusetts, sent to the USA a great number of people who Khalil Gibran,
also an emigrant, called 'contributors to this new civilization'. In a famous poem
recited to young Americans of Syrian origin, Gibran described how his people
should interact with their new home. 'I believe that you have inherited from
your forefathers an ancient dream, a song, a prophecy, which you can proudly
lay as a gift of gratitude upon the lap of America.' Gibran said, 'To be a good
citizen is to stand before the towers of New York and Washington, Chicago and
San Francisco saying in your hearts, "I am the descendent of a people that built
Damascus and Byblos, and I am here to build with you, and with a will".' The
same sentiments were echoed by many leaders and influencers, having found
in the concept of the USA much common ground with a region populated
by people with differing ancestral origins, religious backgrounds and historic
identities.

* * *

Both examples do not go far back in time, but they are too far from the realities of today. There was no Israel back in the nineteenth century, no Taliban
and Osama bin Laden, no superpower and definitely not a uni-polar world. The
judge and foe in the region were not one and the same.

* * *

The election of President Barack Obama represented the American Dream at its best. I was inspired enough to write him a letter, which I handed to President Jimmy Carter in December 2008. I thought of Abraham Lincoln's promise of 'a new birth of freedom', and Obama's promise of 'the change we need'. Indeed, the world needed the USA to change. Syria needed the USA to change. The government and people of Syria who were working very hard to meet the challenges of a rigorous reform programme were faced with international isolation, US sanctions, and continuous threats that materialized in one occasion in an unprecedented US raid on Syrian soil. In the letter to Obama, I tried to explain in what ways the USA and Syria were similar, and how the two countries share intrinsic values that are key to their foundation and existence, such as entrepreneurship, sheltering the persecuted, tolerance of diversity, and secularism. But Obama was in a race on the local and international fronts. Despite the momentum of 'yes we can', promises were easier said than delivered.

* * *

This book could not come at a more opportune time. It could not have been written by someone who understands Syria and the USA better than Sami Moubayed, who has devoted himself to revealing meaningful historical events often overshadowed by the affairs of the day. After all the exposure Syria got during the Bush years, someone had to step up to the plate and tell a story that was always cut short. The history of the relationship between the leader of the old world and the leader of the new world did not start yesterday, and its gradual degradation from mutual accommodation to mutual hostility had to be spelled out. Sami draws the parallels between what is happening today, and what happened early on in the twentieth century. Syria, a pragmatic yet independent country with regional weight and respect, and a leadership capacity in the Arab street, has always been interested in befriending the USA. Understandably, Syria's attempts are never to the liking of others, who are way more influential in US politics than Syria and all the Arabs (and their oil reserves) combined. Sami argues in his captivating anecdotal style that the USA was the 'spoiler' in the region and in Syria. He gives the reader the other side of a story whose plot has been built around Syria being the spoiler.

* * *

Sami and I have been friends for more than 15 years. His career as a writer started in his junior year at AUB, and it was completely unexpected. Sami wrote his first book to prove to someone that he was beyond his 19 years, and indeed he was. While his demonstration of intellect did not help the original cause, he discovered his talent and true passion: Syrian history. Since then, Sami has authored several books, written numerous articles, and deciphered to the world how Syria thinks and what Syria wants, in his unique story-telling approach. He befriended the movers and shakers of the bygone era, spent hours with them talking and understanding the inner workings of Syrian politics, business and society from the years that led to independence. They trusted him and shared details they had never told or documented. There were other historians doing similar research, but few if any were as skilled, well-informed, encyclopedic and prolific as Sami was. His work is in the same league of internationally acclaimed books on modern Syria. What adds distinction to Sami's contribution is that he is Syrian, writing from Syria and from a Syrian perspective.

* * *

How would the world change if Syria, a leader of the old world, and the USA, a leader of the modern world, join forces? How would it change if they became allies? What's the missed opportunity for the USA, economic and otherwise, for the unfavourable image in the Arab World, and how would closer cooperation with Syria open doors for closer links with the Arab World? These were questions I asked of several senior US administration officials at the Presidential Entrepreneurship Summit in April 2010. These questions are even more relevant after 2011, although it is not clear how the events of this year are going to play out in the end. Over dinner at an old Damascene house turned restaurant, I asked one of the USA's most respected veteran diplomats whether he agreed that the USA would be the biggest winner if peace between Syria and Israel was achieved. After all, a peace treaty would put an almost century-long conflict on a one-way track to closure. It would help relieve American politics from the well-known internal pressures of the Israeli lobby. It would boost the efforts of groups like J Street, and the new generation of Arab–Americans that have learnt the lesson that to be able to influence the system you have to be part of it. And it would redraw the map of the USA's alliances to unleash the potential of partnership with 350 million Arabs. The diplomat agreed, and thought that in such a context the questions over Syria's role in Lebanon and Iraq, or relationship with Iran, as significant as they were, seemed futile. He went on to say that without peace with Syria and Israel, the latter would continue to be the spoiler in what could be a relationship that gives a new foundation for

America's position in the Middle East, and thus, probably, a new foundation for the world's order.

* * *

I am confident that Sami's effort will make readers think of the road not taken in the Syrian–US relationship. At a roundtable with a delegation of senior executives from US technology firms visiting Damascus in June 2010, my opening remarks on Syria's position on the relationship with the USA, 'I think the US does not have to do much to win allies here. America, the concept, not the government, has many allies in Syria. America, the institutions, not the policies, has many friends. A grain of goodwill can help bridge differences and certainly can reverse perceived differences', were not well-received by the accompanying team from the State Department. In this book are cues for us to think of the chance that there can be closer, warmer and friendlier relations between Syria and the USA. Syria led the old world, and the USA is leading the modern world. But there is a chance, regardless of how small or futile, to lead a new world, a better world, together.

Abdulsalam Haykal
Young Global Leader at the World Economic Forum (WEF)

PREFACE

At the time of writing, in late 2011, the Arab Spring is entering its ninth month in Syria. We do not yet know whether it will succeed. While we wait, the entire country stands at a crippling halt. Why should it not, with so much history-in-the-making taking place all around us, not only in Syria but throughout the Arab world? Young people currently on the streets of Syria were born in the late 1980s or early 1990s. To them, the era of President Hafez al-Assad is history. Many of them were below the age of ten when he died in June 2000. It is only natural that they would show little interest in bygone historical figures who have been dead for more than 50 years, such as, for example, former Presidents Mohammad Ali-Abed and Taj al-Din al-Hasani. As far as they are concerned, modern history is what they are crafting today with their very own hands not only in Syria but in Tunisia, Egypt, Libya and Yemen.

History – purely for the sake of history – is a necessity for anybody wanting to go into a serious career in academia, literature, art or politics. For ordinary people, however, history is a luxury that they feel does not touch upon their day-to-day lives. I teach modern Syrian history to students at the University of Kalamoun in Deir Atiyya, a college town on the outskirts of Damascus. I see how students interact with events that took place long before their parents were born. Contrary to what many people might think, these students realize how important it is for them to fully digest what democratic Syria was all about. These same students, however, feel that they need to know more about Syria prior to the Baath Party era, which began in March 1963, and is very likely to come to an end in 2012. The 'old Syria' whose green flag is being hoisted in anti-regime protests all over the country, was all about democracy, good citizenship, equal opportunity and the rule of law. It inspires young Syrians, although its founders – men such as Shukri al-Quwatli and Hashem al-Atasi – are all gone.

This is why, more than at any point in recent years, pre-1963 Syria is vital for the future of Syria. We need not copy a bygone era, because that would be uncreative, dull, and ultimately wrong. That era, with all its merits, was riddled with mistakes, if one scratches beneath the surface of what Syrian politics was all about in the 1940s and 1950s. There was a horrific imbalance in the distribution of power and wealth, between Damascus and Aleppo on one hand, and every other Syrian city on another. There were sharp divisions between urban and rural Syria, between officers and civilians, and between Damascus and Aleppo, the two heavyweight political and commercial centres of the young Republic. The patron–client system was at its zenith, and ambitious officers had absolutely no respect for the authority of the democratically elected civilians who had been brought to power by ballots rather than bullets. They gambled with the nation, over and over, crippling its growth with coup after coup during the period 1949–1970.

Now is the time, however, to look back and learn from our mistakes, in order to create a new Syria in 2012. This is where this book, *Syria and the USA*, comes into play – at a time when Syrian–US relations are at their lowest point ever. During the period that is researched in this book, Syrians learned to play politics with the USA the hard way, through trial and error. Good intentions and gentlemanly politics were apparently not enough to create a sound Syrian–US relationship. Syrian politicians back then wanted the Americans to help them achieve independence from France and set up a working democracy once the French colonialists had left the country. That did not come without strings attached, as they quickly discovered, leading to the realization that independence could only be achieved through the will and might of the Syrian people, rather than through the assistance of a foreign power, be it the USA, Great Britain or the USSR. They did it their own way, with no US assistance, and learned from their own mistakes in founding the new Republic after 1946.

Nearly 20 years ago, I was a student at the American School in Damascus. We had to study US history and memorize parts of the US Constitution. I had to learn it the hard way and grew up proud of my strong command of US history. I believed in US principles, democracy, opportunity, and the right to 'life, liberty, and the pursuit of happiness'. As a young teenager, I learned to hate America's enemies and love its friends. I cursed Fidel Castro, Joseph Stalin and Mao Zedong. I defended the Americans vigorously because I had befriended them and been educated by them during childhood and early manhood.

Obviously few people in the Arab world agreed with what I said, but many were willing to listen. This, naturally, was before the Iraq War in 2003.

'You don't know the USA,' I would tell my anti-American friends. The America I knew was not that of George W. Bush. It was the great nation that had achieved milestones in business, industry, literature, art and entertainment. My America was that of Henry Ford and John D. Rockefeller. It was the America of Abraham Lincoln, Franklin Roosevelt and Martin Luther King. It was the America of Walt Disney and Edgar Allan Poe; that of giants such as Buster Keaton who inspired other non-American giants such as Charlie Chaplin.

My defence of the USA has been muted by unfolding events since the 1990s. First came US bias towards Israel during the Second Intifada of 2000. Then came Afghanistan. Then Guantanamo Bay. Then came the occupation of Iraq. Then Abu Ghraib. Then the alleged murder of Yasser Arafat in 2004, which took place under the watchful eyes of the Americans. Then Lebanon in 2006, and Gaza in 2008. By then it no longer even occurred to me – not for a moment – that the USA was right, just, fair, or even good. I could barely remember the America I had grown up with as a child. Things changed, rather significantly, with Barack Obama's rise to power in 2009 and took a completely new turn when the Arab Spring started in 2010.

***

Having said that, I believe that today, the USA is completely irrelevant to what is happening throughout the Arab world. The Obama Administration tried to ride the wave of the Arab Spring, hoping that by doing so it would endear itself to the angry Arab street, which remains furious with its clear bias towards Israel. It did not instigate the Arab Spring and, as a matter of fact failed drastically at meeting the aspirations of young Arabs. It was too slow in 'riding the wave' in Egypt, for example, too timid in dealing with Syria, and was an 'accomplice to crime' in Yemen and Bahrain, where it turned a blind eye to atrocities being committed by pro-US regimes against peaceful demonstrators in Sana'a and Manama.

During a 2005 visit to the Arab world, US Secretary of State Condoleezza Rice lectured Arabs on democracy, reform and peacemaking. Rice appeared before 600 students at the American University in Cairo (AUC) and boasted of the democratic system the USA had created in Iraq, saying that the Iraqis were greatly satisfied with their new-found status, which should inspire the Arab masses. The speech at AUC was symbolic for a variety of reasons. First, it was the first time that a US Secretary of State had pushed so strongly for reforms and had criticized a host country such as Egypt, a good friend of the USA, for its democratic record. As she spoke, members of the Egyptian opposition marched through Cairo, chanting against their President, US-ally Hosni Mubarak, saying: 'Give him a visa Condoleezza – and take him with you!'

The opposition, unimpressed by her remarks, could not ignore that the only reason Mubarak had remained in office since 1981 was that despite his authoritarian measures he had been backed wholeheartedly by every US administration since Ronald Reagan's. Second, her visit carried a startling confession, as Rice said: 'For 60 years, my country, the United States, pursued stability at the expense of democracy in the region. And we achieved neither. Now we are taking a different course. We are supporting the democratic aspirations of the people.'

Rice had grown up in Alabama, one of the states to witness the greatest persecution against blacks, and had certainly been influenced by the Civil Rights Movement of the 1960s. In fact, she was born in 1954 the year education was desegregated in the USA. History-makers in Alabama, such as Rosa Parks and Martin Luther King, certainly had a profound effect on her career. Rosa Parks had laid the cornerstone for national myth in the US by symbolic defiance and refusal to give her bus seat to a white man on that great and fateful day in US history – 1 December 1955. Is her story any different from that of the thousands of Arabs who have become symbols of defiance in Arab society after the Arab Spring erupted in Tunisia in December 2010?

To the Arab street, the new symbols of resistance are young Arabs who are being taken to jail for demanding 'freedom'. Arab intellectuals and activists have read the famous speech by Reverend Martin Luther King and, like him, have often said that he had a dream of emancipation, and they had a dream of emancipation, from Israeli occupation and oppression by Arab regimes. The Arabs had a dream that their children would one day live in a nation where they would not be judged by their leaders as inferior to the powerful elite, 'not by the color of their skin but by the content of their character'. Like King, they had a dream that 'with this faith we will be able to work together, to pray together, to struggle together, to go to jail together, and to stand up for freedom together, knowing that we will be free one day'.

1

WILSONIAN PRINCIPLES AND SHATTERED DREAMS

The Paris Peace Conference opened on 18 January 1919, when international leaders assembled in France to discuss the future of the world. The Ottoman Empire, which had ruled Syria since 1516, had just collapsed. Sharif Hussein, leader of the Arab Revolt against the Ottomans in 1916–1918, was invited to attend, but declined – he was too busy laying claim to the vast deserts of Arabia, which he wanted to bring under the Hashemite Crown. Instead, he sent his 36-year-old son, Sharif Faisal, who, in October 1918, had been proclaimed the first Arab ruler of Syria after 400 years of Ottoman rule.

Young and passionate, yet politically inexperienced, the short and handsome bearded Bedouin headed for Europe, not knowing what to expect from the Occidental world. US President Woodrow Wilson, registered to attend the Paris Conference, had expressed a revised American interest in Europe, and a newborn interest in the Middle East. Before 1919, the word 'Arab' had never been mentioned in public by a US president – and certainly not the word 'Syria'.[1] Apart from second generation Arabs who lived and worked in the USA as Arab–Americans, no American leader had ever met an Arab residing in the Arab world. To the Arabs, the USA was far away – completely detached from the Middle East, its plight, past and future. Apart from Christian missionaries who had come to the region during the nineteenth century, no senior US officials had visited the Arab territories of the Ottoman Empire. The only Americans the Arabs had ever met were nurses, doctors, educators, archeologists and biblical scholars. Wilson – although an educator by training – was the first US president to come into face-to-face contact with an Arab.[2]

Sharif Hussein's son Faisal had triumphantly marched into Damascus on 3 October 1918, aided by the mighty British Army. He had received a hero's welcome, unprecedented since the days of the Umayyad Dynasty. Everywhere he went, flags of the Arab Revolt were perched on balconies, along with photographs of the young Prince and his legendary father, Sharif Hussein Ibn Ali. Faisal knew the Syrians relatively well, having frequently visited Damascus in the early years of the Great War and befriended its prominent Ata Pasha al-Bakri and his son, Nasib. Most Syrians welcomed the Arabian Emir as a breath of fresh air, coming after the ruthless era of Jamal Pasha, the Ottoman Governor of Syria during the Great War. Faisal was young and mirrored the ambitions of young Syrians of his age, who had been dragged to the war front in large numbers to fight for an Ottoman cause that did not concern them, on the part of Germany. He was a Hashemite, scion of a family that descended directly from the Prophet Mohammad, and had plenty of war medals for his military role in the Arabian Revolt. A passionate, bold and decorated war hero, he seemed the perfect ruler for the people hungry for Arab leadership. A few local politicians, however, complained that Faisal was an 'imported' ruler with a social, cultural and political background that was very different from that of most Syrians. Many took great pride in their urban past and saw Faisal as an uncivilized Bedouin, unfit to rule those who had been raised in the grace of great cities like Damascus and Aleppo.[3] From day one, Faisal tried to prove to the handful of his opponents in Damascus that they were wrong about him. He promised to usher in reforms and stability, becoming 'a modern day Mu'awiya!'[4]

Faisal spoke with a Bedouin accent that was strange to many urban dwellers – certainly the residents of his new capital, Damascus. Still inexperienced in politics, he had begged his father not to go to Paris and to send his elder brother Abdullah instead.[5] He needed to spend quality time with the Syrians, he argued, so they would familiarize themselves with their new monarch, while he would learn of their culture, norms and living habits. Blending in did not seem too difficult, for the Syrians showed eagerness to please their new leader. When he declared, for example, that he preferred European bowler hats to the traditional Ottoman fez, hundreds of young people discarded the fez and began to dress to the liking of their new Prince.[6] Faisal had never travelled beyond Arab territory and, although fluent in French, felt that he was not ready to face seasoned world leaders like France's Georges Clemenceau and Great Britain's Lloyd George. It was safer to stay behind in his comfort zone in Damascus and for Abdullah to go instead, given the latter's strong interaction with British officials during the Great War. Hussein, a stern man, curtly refused his son's suggestion, claiming that he needed Abdullah – perhaps the ablest of all his children – by his side for further conquests in Arabia. Hussein's only instructions were verbal; Faisal was to press for an answer from the Great Powers regarding the future of Arab territories liberated from the Ottoman Empire. The British, in their famous correspondence with Sharif Hussein, had promised him a kingdom in the Arab world to be ruled along with his sons Ali, Abdullah and Faisal. Now that the Great War was over, Hussein wanted the British to fulfil their wartime promise. According to Sir Alec Kirkbride, a future British advisor to Abdullah, 'He (Hussein) and his sons agreed that Ali, the eldest, should succeed their father as King of the Hijaz; that Abdullah, the second, should be King of Iraq and that Faisal, a third, should become King of Syria.'[7]

While Faisal had spent the pre-war years dabbling in Ottoman politics with Arab nationalists in Damascus, Abdullah had been instructed to open channels with Great Britain, which attached great importance to the Arab world, due to its presence in Egypt. In February 1914, Abdullah had gone to Cairo, at his father's request, and met with Lord Herbert Kitchener, the British Consul-General in Egypt. Abdullah inquired on the British response should Sharif Hussein – who had recently been appointed Prince of Mecca by the Ottoman Sultan – raise a revolt against the Ottoman Empire. Kitchener initially gave him a cold shoulder, given that war had not yet erupted in Europe and there was no sense in provoking conflict with the Ottomans. When war did break out in August 1914, many European statesmen felt that it would be swift and 'over by Christmas'. In November 1914, however, the Ottoman Empire went to war against Great Britain and France, completely changing the attitude in London. Kitchener's successor, Lord Henry McMahon, famously orchestrated the British–Arab alliance through a series of correspondence carrying his name, and that of Sharif Hussein, in 1915. Hussein made it a condition that in exchange for opening an internal front against the Ottomans, he wanted Palestine, Lebanon, Iraq and Syria to fall under his control. McMahon controversially approved Sharif Hussein's request.

On 11 November 1918, Hussein sent a note to the British that Faisal would attend the Paris Conference in his capacity as the new ruler of Syria. There are no documents available to prove whether Hussein knew beforehand that President Wilson was going to be in Paris, but even if he did it is doubtful that he would have really cared. Hussein came from an older generation of Arab politicians who worried more about what statesmen coming from Paris and London were thinking; Washington was on nobody's radar in 1919. The telegram confirming Faisal's attendance did not reach the British until 19 November.[8] When Faisal arrived at the port of Marseilles on board the British ship, *Gloucester*, nobody in the French government knew what to do with the Arab royal. The young Prince immediately panicked. Lord Derby, the British Ambassador to Paris, swiftly contacted the Foreign Office, asking them to grant him an official reception, and on-the-spot entry permission. The French snapped that they did not recognize Faisal's government in Damascus and could not welcome him as head of state, representing the newly created and yet not internationally recognized Kingdom of Syria. He would be treated as a royal guest, they said, and a friend of Great Britain. He would be allowed to speak at the Paris Conference, which was due to open in six weeks, but would have no say over the decisions made.[9] The British used their considerable influence with the French to take him on a tour of France, while he waited for the conference to begin. Delegates of the Foreign Ministry even escorted him on a night out on the Champs Élysées, then to a Parisian night club where he was given full entertainment with half-naked dancing girls, in complete disregard to his conservative Muslim background. Faisal grumbled to one of his hosts, 'I did not come here for entertainment or fun! I came here to serve my nation!'[10] He was granted an audience with the president of Sorbonne University, and received a delegation of French artists, one of whom expressed enchantment with the Emir, who they claimed 'bore a striking resemblance to Jesus Christ'.[11] Faisal then made a dashing visit to London, where after staying at the Carlton Hotel, he was given an immediate, if ceremonial, audience with King George V and Foreign Minister Arthur Balfour. The meeting was so brief that Faisal was not even given a chance to properly discuss the fate of Jews and Arabs in Palestine, given that the Foreign Minister's signature graced a famous declaration that granted the Jews a national home in Palestine. Recalling the meeting years later, Balfour noted that during his brief encounter with Faisal, the Emir made no mention of Iraq or Palestine and was only concerned with his throne in Syria.[12]

Faisal in Paris

The thing that worried Faisal most while in Paris was the realization that Europe was determined to fulfil the Sykes–Picot Agreement, which carved up the Middle East between French and British mandates, and the Balfour Declaration, granting the Jews a national home in Palestine. The Sykes–Picot Agreement, which was officially named the Asia Minor Agreement, had been signed in February 1916, granting mandates to France and Great Britain on the same territories that had been promised to Sharif Hussein and his three sons. Then came the Balfour Declaration in November 1917, stressing that Great Britain favoured 'the establishment in Palestine of a National Home for the Jewish people'. In Paris, Faisal quickly saw that these two wartime promises would surely hamper his family's ambitions of ruling all Arab territory just liberated from the Ottoman Empire and be likely to bring his political career to an abrupt end. Hussein and Faisal had first heard of the Sykes–Picot Agreement shortly after it was signed, before the full text was first revealed in *Izvestia* and *Pravda*, two Russian newspapers, on 23 November 1917. *The Manchester Guardian* reprinted the text on 26 November 1917, which in turn found its way into the Arab press. The text became public only three weeks after the Balfour Declaration was issued, sending shockwaves throughout the Arab world. Miraculously, the Arabs were persuaded to allay their worries, through British pledges that the Hussein–McMahon correspondence would be honoured, regardless of the Sykes–Picot Agreement. Hussein, aged and apparently naïve, accepted everything the British told him.[13]

With these fears and complications in mind, and a challenge to defeat his opponents in Syria at any cost, Faisal attended sessions of the Paris Conference on 1 January 1919. Initially he stayed at the Continental Hotel, overlooking Tuileries Gardens, just down the block from the American delegation that was registered to attend the Paris Conference.[14] He then switched to a small private hotel, a former mansion to King Louis XVI, on the well-heeled Avenue du Bois, transforming it into his headquarters, complete with an Arab tent, strong Arabic coffee, and full Bedouin uniform, for the remainder of his stay in Paris.[15] Faisal's first surprise was that he was not welcomed as a head of state by the French government, but rather as an envoy for his father, the King of Hijaz, meaning that as far as the Great Powers were concerned, the sovereignty of Syria, and authority of its new Emir, were both in doubt. He took along a trusted aid, Nuri al-Said, who was to become the future Prime Minister of Iraq, and Jamil Mardam Bey, a recent graduate of Paris who was to become the future Prime Minister of Syria, as his private translators. Other members of the Syrian delegation included the Lebanese statesman Rustom Haydar from Baalbek, and the Palestinian nationalist Awni Abdul Hadi. Faisal relied on Haydar, Mardam Bey and Said to convey his messages in French and English to the world leaders assembled in Paris.

On 1 January 1919, Faisal presented a memorandum to the conference, calling for self-government in Syria. On 6 February he addressed the Council of Ten, making similar demands for self-rule.[16] The French thundered back that the young prince had no authority to speak on behalf of the people of Syria. Faisal immediately contacted his younger brother Zayd, who was acting as Regent back in Damascus, asking him to gather the signatures of city notables saying that Faisal Ibn al-Hussein was in Paris with a mandate to speak on behalf of the Syrians. The signatures were gathered by Zayd and Faisal's Prime

Minister Rida Pasha al-Rikabi, and included the Greek Orthodox Patriarch of Antioch and All the East, the Catholic Patriarch, and the Chief Rabi of Syria.[17] Among those to sign the document was Hashem al-Atasi, a senior administrator from the Ottoman Era who was now running for the to-be-created Syrian parliament as a deputy for Homs (and was to become a future three-time president of Syria). Days later, one of Faisal's American friends, Howard Bliss of the Syrian Protestant College, whispered in the Emir's ear that he should give a copy of the declaration to Woodrow Wilson, pointing to the direction of the tall and frail President of the USA.

Although he needed no introduction, Bliss told Faisal that Wilson was the first US president to ever leave his country while in office, and the first to attend an international convention. His country had joined the war in April 1917 and was theoretically fighting on the same side as the Arabs although there had been no Arab–American contact during the war. Wilson's presence in Paris was testimony to the rising role of the USA in world affairs, Bliss added, stressing that if Faisal wanted to be heard in France, he had to knock on the door of the US President. Wilson had first attracted Arab attention in a speech delivered at the US Congress on 8 January 1918. In that speech, he assured Americans that the Great War was being fought for a moral cause and for peace in Europe. Wilson spoke about the four 'great ends for which the people of the world are fighting'. One of them, he added, required that 'the settlement of every question, whether of territory or sovereignty, of economic arrangement, or of political relationship, [should be determined] upon the basis of the free acceptance of that settlement by the people immediately concerned, and not upon the basis of material interest or advantage of any other nation or people which may desire a different settlement for the sake of its own exterior influence or mastery'. The speech, which was translated into Arabic and republished in Arab dailies, came ten months before the armistice. Wilson mentioned his infamous Fourteen Points, which captivated Faisal and ordinary Arabs. A full translation and study of the points was made by Abdul Rahman Shahbandar, Faisal's political consultant, who was to become his Minister of Foreign Affairs in 1920. Shahbandar, who spoke flawless English and like Bliss, always had the Prince's, ear, had greatly admired Wilson since 1912.

To Shahabandar, Bliss and Faisal, Wilson's Points Five and Twelve were of particular interest. They read:[18]

Point Five: A free, open-minded, and absolutely impartial adjustment of all colonial claims, based upon a strict observance of the principle that in determining all such questions of sovereignty the interests of the populations concerned must have equal weight with the equitable claims of the government whose title is to be determined.

Point Twelve: The Turkish portion of the present Ottoman Empire should be assured a secure sovereignty, but the other nationalities which are now under Turkish rule should be assured an undoubted security of life and an absolutely unmolested opportunity of autonomous development.[19]

The Bliss legacy

Thanks to the Fourteen Points, Faisal developed an immediate admiration for Wilson long before meeting him, and by many accounts the two men bonded well in Paris. The US President, then aged 63, was old enough to be Faisal's father, and the young Emir treated him with the respect of an obedient son. Of all the photographs of Faisal from 1916 until his death in 1933, only one is found of him smiling graciously, and it was taken by Edith Wilson, the US First Lady. After his first encounter with Faisal, Wilson remarked, 'Listening to the emir, I think that I hear the voice of liberty, a strange – and I fear stray – voice coming from Asia.'[20]

The sympathy that Wilson developed immediately for Faisal was a result of two influences; the Emir's charm, and Faisal's extensive conversations with American academics, who accompanied Wilson to Paris as part of his official think tank. The US team included William Westermann, a professor at Columbia University who was an expert on the Crusades, George Louis Beer, another professor at Columbia, international historian James Shotwell, and Isiah Bowman, a cartographer and president of the American Geographical Society.[21] During his first encounter with these men, Faisal boasted of his family history, being a direct descendent of the Prophet Mohammad, and of the sacrifices his family had made during the Arab Revolt against the Ottomans. Faisal enchanted them over dinner with stories of his swashbuckling battles in the deserts of Arabia, and the injustices imposed on the Arabs for the past four centuries. Westermann, the most influential among the group, noted in his diary, 'Faisal wanted no ruler over his country, British or French, he wanted independence. He has not freed Syria to make it French'. The man was seemingly easy to win over, since any deep understanding he had on the region ended around 1300. Westermann then scribbled, 'Voila; great is Faisal! I am a converter!'[22] In addition to extensive talks with these men, Faisal also called frequently on Edward M. House, the influential advisor to Wilson, affectionately called 'Colonel House' although he was a politician and diplomat by training, never a military officer. House had played a crucial role in shaping wartime diplomacy, and had helped Wilson outline his Fourteen Points.[23] At one point during the talks, Faisal requested that in order to add weight to his Syrian delegation, Wilson attach an American officer to accompany the Syrians in Paris.[24]

More than any of these men, however, it was Howard Bliss who introduced the Arabs to America, and America to the Arab world. Born in Lebanon in 1860, Bliss was the son of Reverend Daniel Bliss, the founder and first president of the Syrian Protestant College. The college had been chartered in 1864 by New York State and had opened its doors to students on 3 December 1866. The aim was to serve 'all conditions and classes of men without regard to color, nationality, race or religion'. Arabic remained the language of instruction until 1883, when it was replaced by English. Howard Bliss had grown up at the college campus in Beirut but had completed his higher education in the USA, studying at Amherst College, graduating in 1882. After his father's retirement, he returned to Beirut to become second President of the college in 1902. During his stay in the USA, Bliss befriended Wilson's predecessor, President Theodore Roosevelt, and helped internationalize the Syrian Protestant College's standing in US academic circles, obtaining full recognition for its degrees from Ottoman authorities in 1903.[25]

The Great War put the college in trouble; student enrolment dropped sharply and, as famine hit Beirut, so did teacher recruitment. Bliss managed to pull through the difficult years and went with Faisal, who knew the College well, to Paris in 1919. Two of the Emir's top men were graduates of the Syrian Protestant College. His Finance Minister, Fares al-Khoury, had studied there and graduated in 1894, only to return for a two-year tenure to teach mathematics and Arabic.[26] A fiery orator, a brilliant mathematician, a talented poet and a seasoned politician, Khoury was one of the most highly educated officials in Faisal's Arab government, thanks to the Bliss College. Abdul Rahman Shahbandar, one of the most renowned medical doctors in Syria, also studied at the Faculty of Medicine at the college. He too had worked in the Arab underground under the Ottomans before joining Faisal's Arab Revolt in 1916. Under the Ottomans he had helped create the School of Medicine in Damascus, which in 1923 came to be known as the Syrian University. Both Khoury and Shahbandar – friends since college – spoke frequently to Faisal about what the USA had to offer the Arabs, citing the liberalism, tolerance and free speech they had learned as students at the Syrian Protestant College. In the years to come, the two men were to become the loudest advocates of a sound Syrian–US relationship – and were also to suffer terribly for this view. Shahbandar went on to be assassinated in 1940 while Khoury was ejected from the premiership in old age in 1955 for harbouring pro-American sentiment during the cold war. Faisal had also heard plenty of stories about the University's values from T. E. Lawrence, a British colonel fighting alongside the Arabs in the Great Revolt. Lawrence, who developed a sincere friendship with Faisal, would always tell him, 'the Syrian Protestant College teaches revolution!'[27] These revolutionary ideas – liberalism, freedom of speech, religion and conduct – echoed what the Arab Revolt had stood for, and Faisal hoped to find them in Wilson, after hearing his Fourteen Points.

The origins of the Syrian Protestant College, which initiated an entire century of Arab–US relations, can be traced back to the early nineteenth century, when Presbyterians sent missions to the Ottoman Empire. They preached the Christian faith in the Muslim world, but while doing so, opened modern schools, attracting students from every faith. Elie Kedourie described them saying: 'They went out to proselytise, and have stayed to sympathise.' Part of that sympathy was for nationalist sentiments in the Arab world, which included getting rid of the Ottomans and, after 1919, the British and the French. Their ideals, which were viewed with suspicion at first, suddenly made sense in 1918, when Wilson issued his Fourteen Point declaration. The reasoning was: with colleges like these (in reference to the Syrian Protestant College) we can produce men like these (Wilson) who will protect or guarantee, our independence! Wilson's words served the missionaries in Syria more than the Bible had done in nearly 50 years of preaching. It was good deeds, rather than conquests, that endeared America to the Arabs, and Wilson to Prince Faisal.

Howard Bliss did not live long enough to see the Syrian Protestant College change its name to the AUB in 1920. The change of name was significant, however, because it highlighted values, social service and education, which were becoming acceptable – in fact demanded – in the Arab East. The name change took place less than one year after Faisal and Wilson first met in Paris. The educated elite in Syria and Lebanon, enchanted with Wilson, eagerly accepted the new name and, slowly to increasingly, adopted an Anglo-Saxon way of life.

The King–Crane Commission

On 6 February 1919, Faisal walked into the clock room at the Quai d'Orsay. He was greeted with mild applause as he spoke about Arab grievances during the war, and cited Wilson's Fourteen Point declaration, calling for international recognition of his throne in Syria.[28] He deliberately spoke in Arabic, and relied on Howard Bliss and T. E. Lawrence for translation. A few days earlier, on 30 January 1919, the conference had agreed that Armenia, Syria, Mesopotamia, Palestine and Arabia were to be 'completely severed' from the Ottoman Empire. The conference had noted, however, that they were 'inhabited by people not yet able to stand by themselves under the strenuous conditions of the modern world'. That is why they needed to be placed under the mandate of 'advanced nations' in a 'sacred trust of civilization'. Each mandate, the conference added, would be tailored according to the needs and peculiarities of the people on whom it would be imposed.

Thanks to Wilson and Bliss, the four major allied countries, Great Britain, France, Italy and the USA, agreed to form an Inter-Allied Commission to inquire on whether the people of Syria wanted a French mandate in territories recently liberated from the Ottoman Empire. According to Fares al-Khoury, Wilson told Faisal, 'If the people truly want independence, then I will not allow any country in the world to control Syria!'[29] The British, French and Italians, backed out of the commission, seemingly unconvinced by its mission, and as a result it was condensed into an American one, which was sent to Syria under orders from Wilson, in June 1919.[30]

The commission was headed by two Americans, Henry King and Charles R. Crane. King was an educator who taught theology and philosophy at Oberlin College, while Crane was a wealthy philanthropist who knew the Middle East. In 1912 he had heavily contributed to Wilson's presidential campaign, and in 1917 Wilson had appointed him to a special diplomatic mission to Russia. Many years later, he helped finance the first oil explorations in Saudi Arabia and Yemen, and in 1920–1921, served as his country's ambassador to China. The two men died in 1934 and 1939 respectively, shortly before their country became overtly interested in the affairs of Syria and the Oriental East.

The King–Crane Commission spent six weeks in the region, visiting 36 towns, and receiving petitions from 1,520 villages. It reported that 1,863 petitions came from ordinary Syrians, which were all 'against Zionist claims and purposes'.[31] Out of the 260 that came from Palestine, 222 were related to the Zionist programme.[32] Throughout its residency in Syria, the commission asked the same questions: 'What do you think of Great Britain and France?' And, 'do you feel that Syria needs a Western power to help its people march confidently into the twentieth century?' They realized that public opinion matters, and policy imposed without the agreement of the affected people would not work, since it would only generate armed and political resistance.

While in Syria, the commissioners were escorted by Faisal's right-hand man, Abdul Rahman Shahbandar. Born in 1880, Shahbandar came from a middle-class family and had developed strong secularist tendencies during his college years. When the Ottoman Empire collapsed in 1918, he joined Faisal's entourage in Damascus, as a translator and political consultant, before becoming his Foreign Minister in 1920. He taught at the Arab Academy of Medicine and worked on translating all curricula from Ottoman Turkish into Arabic. An educator in his own right, he found plenty in common with the two American visitors. Shahbandar took them of a tour of all major mosques, churches and synagogues in Syria, and made sure that they met with students, women activists and merchants. He was particularly interested in women's rights, a rising trend in Syria, and urged young activists like Naziq al-Abid, a Muslim, and Mary Ajamy, a Christian, to speak their minds in front of King and Crane. Another 'guide' to the American delegation was Khoury, another alumnus of the Syrian Protestant College who had served in the Arab underground during the final years of the Ottoman Empire. Both men – like many of the educated elite in Syria – were enchanted by the American diplomats, and Khoury described Crane as a man 'who loved justice and freedom'.[33] So inspired by Crane was the eminent Arab scholar George Antonious that he dedicated his book, *The Arab Awakening*, to him. The two men mapped out the Syrian population, and presented charts to the US delegation.

The inhabitants of Syria, they roughly estimated, stood at 'around 1.5 million, meaning 25 people per kilometre'. They included 1.2 million Sunnis, 175,000 Christians Orthodox, Catholic and Protestant, 60,000 Druze, 25,000 Shiites, 25,000 Jews and 15,000 Ismailis. The Syrian Consultative Council, or Shura Council, had a long meeting with the two American guests, chaired by its president, Fawzi Pasha al-Azm. They presented the King with a written report, saying: 'We who have signed below, Members of the Shura Council to the Arab Government, in our capacity as notables of the Syrian nation, and our responsibility for the country's financial and moral conditions, and our long experience in running affairs of state in these lands, on which we were raised, and in which we assumed different posts during our careers ... present your excellencies with this report. First we express our heartfelt gratitude for the great Allied Powers, America, England, France, and Italy, for extending a hand of support to us. They gave us money and men to get rid of Ottoman oppression, which has been on our necks for 400-years. During that period, the Ottomans erased what remained of ancient Arab Syrian urbanization.'[34]

The council advised that all peoples controlled unwillingly by the Ottoman Turks should become, 'completely and definitively free'. It recommended, 'serious modification of the extreme Zionist Program for Palestine of unlimited immigration of Jews'. The Syrian recommendations included, 'If the wishes of

Palestine's population are to be decisive as to what is to be done with Palestine, then it is to be remembered that the non-Jewish population of Palestine – nearly nine-tenths of the whole – are emphatically against the entire Zionist programme ... there is no one thing upon which the population of Palestine were more agreed upon than this.' The Commission noted, 'Only two requests – that for a united Syria and independence – had larger support'. On 3 July 1919, Fawzi al-Azm presented a ten-point declaration to the King–Crane Commission. It became known as the Damascus Programme and it called for accepting Faisal as a constitutional monarch of Syria, with full independence. It also strongly denounced Zionist claims in Palestine. The Emir himself met the two Americans, and passionately declared, 'French control [of Syria] would mean certain death to Syrians as a distinguished people. France takes off boldness and manliness from the people and prevents them from progress and development'.[35] The most striking thing the Syrians told the commission was that although they refused a French mandate, they would nevertheless welcome an American one, because the USA would tutor, rather than conquer, people of the East, injecting them with the values outlined in Wilson's Fourteen Points. Of the 1,863 petitions, 1,084 asked for a US mandate in Syria.[36]

One notable statesman who challenged this claim was a young bureaucrat in the Municipality of Damascus, who was yet to become father of his country's independence from the French in 1946: Shukri al-Quwatli. He had worked with the Arab underground in 1916–1918, as a member of the secret anti-Ottoman organization, al-Fatat, and been imprisoned and tortured for his views. He was among the many Syrians who King and Crane met with, and when asked about whether he supported the notion of a US mandate on Syria, replied, 'God forbid ... of course not, Mr Crane. With all due respect to you and President Wilson, we will not move from one disaster to another. The Americans, according to what they say about themselves, can be considered as friends. But if they one day think of coming to these lands as occupiers, they will become enemies for sure. Reduction of sovereignty is non-negotiable. Tell President Wilson that our demand is to be free'.[37] He then suggested 'we cancel the idea of a mandate, and allow the Syrians to build their state and live in peace on their land. To do that, we would need assistance from the American people, because they know the taste of liberty. But for sure, we are not in need of a new occupation'.[38]

Zionism makes and breaks the Syrian–US honeymoon

Arab historians who have tackled Wilson's relationship with Emir Faisal have often glossed over the US president's unwavering support for Zionism. They have tended to see Wilson in black and white frames, failing to realize that his support for Arab aspirations could never have been complete or sincere, because as a devout Christian, he believed in ancient Biblical prophecies, and was bent on helping the Jews return to the Holy Land. As far as Arab concerns went, Arab independence cannot be complete if Palestine – or northern Syria as customarily called by many Syrians back then – was occupied and transformed into a Jewish home. Wilson had absolutely no regard to the 13 centuries of Muslim presence in Palestine. As President of Princeton University in 1902–1910, he had appointed the first Jew to the Faculty, and the first Jew to the New Jersey Supreme Court when he was Governor of New Jersey in 1910–1912. He then brought Louis Brandeis to the US Supreme Court in 1916. Brandeis, and other prominent American Zionists, probably influenced Wilson into delaying, then discarding, the King–Crane Commission findings.[39]

Shahbandar, well-versed in American politics, knew Wilson presented a double-edged sword for the Arabs. His support did not come in one piece – sovereignty in Syria had to be at the expense of the future of Palestine. This was a price both Shahbandar and Faisal seemed willing to pay for the sake of establishing a Hashemite monarchy in Damascus. Having followed the debate among Syrian Americans over the fate of Palestine, Shahbandar realized early on that there was no point in trying to convince Wilson to abandon a concept that was so dear to his heart. Rather, Faisal should use it, to endear himself to Wilson. On 28 November 1918 and again on 15 February 1919, a fellow surgeon from Jaffa named Fouad Shatara had tried in vain to talk the Wilson White House into changing course on Palestine. Writing for the Palestinian Anti-Zionism Society (later named the Palestinian National League) Shatara had communicated with Robert Lansing, Wilson's Secretary of State. He wrote, 'We had faith in European and American governments' sense of justice, and we still believe that finally, however plausible the Zionist pleas may sound, the Powers will not abet a scheme that has for its ultimate aim the usurpation of every right a nation, however small, has'. He added, 'May we therefore be allowed to present at this late hour, our side to the President of the United States, so that with him, our cause may not be left un-championed at the forthcoming Peace Conference'.[40] He added, 'Palestine is our home and in laying our case before the US Government, we feel we can fully rely upon the American sense of justice and fair play'.

Shahbandar knew Shatara well. He had worked as a surgeon in New York and an instructor at the Department of Anatomy at the School of Medicine at Long Island College. Shatara's appeal, as well as that of many Arab–Americans, had gone completely unnoticed in the upper echelons of Washington DC.

Shahbandar warned Faisal that, back in October 1917, Wilson had endorsed the Balfour Declaration, testimony to the amount of support he would grant the Arabs at Paris if they did not follow suit.[41] Shahbandar tried to tell the Emir that he must push for Syria first, and let the Palestinians worry about Palestine. Opposing the Balfour Declaration was unwise, he claimed, calling on the Emir to reach a deal with the Zionist Commission President, Chaim Weizmann, who was representing the Zionists in Paris. Shahbandar was actually the driving force behind the short-lived Faisal–Weizmann Agreement (signed on 3 January 1919) which called for Arab–Jewish cooperation on development of a Jewish homeland in Palestine and a greater Arab one in the lands liberated from the Ottoman Empire. The agreement was more of an attempt at pleasing Wilson, than at reaching any real deal with the Zionists.

Faisal had first met Weizmann in June 1918, shortly before the end of the Great War, in Aqaba in present day Jordan. The idea was for the two leaders to hammer out an agreement that guaranteed Arab support for a Jewish State, in exchange for Jewish support for an Arab one under the Hashemite Crown. Shahbandar reasoned that having one Jewish state within a strong and united Arab world was better than having a Jewish state among divided Arab states, as stipulated by the Sykes–Picot Agreement.[42] Although he did not live long enough to see that happen in 1948, he had seen the writing on the wall since 1919. Both Faisal and Weizmann seemed to have little regard for the wishes of the Palestinians, who Weizmann called 'treacherous', 'arrogant', 'unedu-cated' and 'greedy'.[43] He added that 'there is a fundamental qualitative differ-ence between Jew and Arab' and noted that Faisal was 'contemptuous of the Palestinian Arabs, who he doesn't even regard as Arabs'.[44] During the meeting, Weizmann had assured Faisal that the Jews 'did not propose to set up a govern-ment of their own but wished to work under British protection, to colonise and develop Palestine without encroaching on any legitimate interests'.[45]

Faisal did not leave behind a written account of his encounter with Weizmann, and it is therefore impossible to confirm the authenticity of the future Israeli President's claim. What we do know is that in preparing for the meeting, British diplomat Mark Sykes had written to Faisal about the Jews, saying, 'This race, despised and weak, is universal and all powerful and cannot be put down'.[46] Sykes seemed to be warning the young Emir that they should either support them, or risk their opposition, echoing words spoken to him by Shahbandar. A second meeting took place between Faisal and Weizmann in London, also in 1918, and a third in Paris in January 1919. The agreement, which was initially kept secret from political circles back home in Damascus, mainly concluded that: both sides agree to conduct talks in cordial goodwill and understanding, and to work together to encourage Jewish immigration into Palestine – on a large scale – while protecting the rights of Arab land-owners and farmers, and safeguard the free practice of religion for Muslims, Christians, and Jews; the Muslim Holy Places were to be under Muslim con-trol; the Zionist movement undertook to assist the Arab residents of Palestine and the future Arab state to develop their natural resources and establish a growing economy; the boundaries between an Arab State and Palestine should be determined by a commission after the Paris Peace Conference. The parties committed to carrying into effect the Balfour Declaration, calling for a Jewish national home in Palestine.

Two weeks prior to signing the agreement, Faisal went to great lengths to legitimize his deal with Weizmann, telling a Reuters journalist:

> The two main branches of the Semitic family, Arabs and Jews, under-stand one another, and I hope that as a result of interchange of ideas at the Peace Conference, which will be guided by ideals of self-determination and nationality, each nation will make definite progress towards the reali-sation of its aspirations. Arabs are not jealous of Zionist Jews, and intend to give them fair play and the Zionist Jews have assured the Nationalist Arabs of their intention to see that they too have fair play in their respec-tive areas. Turkish intrigue in Palestine has raised jealousy between the Jewish colonists and the local peasants, but the mutual understanding of the aims of Arabs and Jews will at once clear away the last trace of this former bitterness, which, indeed, had already practically disappeared before the war by the work of the Arab Secret Revolutionary Committee, which in Syria and elsewhere laid the foundation of the Arab military successes of the past two years.[47]

But, just weeks after signing the agreement with Weizmann, Faisal met with reality in Paris, when he realized that no matter how hard he tried, both the Balfour Declaration and the Sykes–Picot Agreement were going ahead. Despite all efforts at pleasing Wilson, he was going to lose both Palestine and Syria and nobody – neither Wilson nor Weizmann – were seriously going to challenge the agreement that gave the French government a mandate in Syria. Upon hearing the news of the agreement, Faisal's father, Sharif Hussein, immediately refused to recognize it, making the Emir look small in front of the world lead-ers he was courting in Paris.[48] To save himself from complete humiliation, the Emir backed out of the agreement, saying that his acceptance was conditional on the fulfilment of British wartime promises to the Arabs.

Collapse of the Arab government

The King–Crane Commission finally published its report, after much delay, in 1922, but by then, it was too late for both Faisal and Syria. French forces began arriving on the Syrian coast in 1919 and on 24 July 1920, they defeated the ill-prepared Syrian Army at the infamous Battle of Maysaloun. On 29 April 1919, Faisal met for the last time with French Prime Minister Georges Clemenceau at the Ministry of the Interior. Clemenceau was fed up with courting the young Arab prince and bluntly told him that no matter how hard he tried, his kingdom in Syria would not last, adding there was no possible way to evade implementing a French mandate in the Levant. Faisal snapped, telling him, 'We Arabs would rather die than accept supremacy of the French' to which the French Premier responded, 'We must have the French flag over Damascus!'[49] 'Never,' snarled the ruler of Damascus, then marched out of the room, went to his hotel, and began preparations to return home. Before heading back to Damascus, however, Faisal made one last attempt to rally world powers behind him, this time heading to Rome for an audience with Pope Benedict XV. Like all his encounters in Europe, the meeting amounted to nothing.[50]

Faisal saw the end coming, and on 8 March 1920, frantically proclaimed himself King of Syria. The Syrian National Congress came out with thundering declarations challenging both the Balfour Declaration and the Sykes–Picot Agreement. This act of defiance – taken without any consultation with world powers – enraged the French, the British and the Americans. And, although Wilson remained at the Oval Office until March 1921, he became incapacitated after suffering a severe stroke in October 1919 and therefore was not present to defend Faisal in the summer of 1920. His illness fell shortly after the King–Crane Commission returned from Syria. No follow-up of the Commission's findings took place, and eager to see an end to the troublesome US president and his anti-colonial agenda, France and Great Britain went ahead with their plans for the Middle East. One of the reasons why publication was delayed was that the Republican-led Senate wanted to first pass the Treaty of Versailles (in the end it never did). Wilson was now useless to Arab dreams, and his successor, Warren Harding, a newspaper publisher and Senator from Ohio, was clearly uninterested in the complex world of the Middle East. There are doubts that Wilson, who by then was confined to a wheelchair, ever even read the report.[51]

Faisal was furious at being ejected from Syria, with little respect or ceremony, having gone to great lengths to please the Americans, by the signing his ill-fated agreement with Weizmann. His army was mercilessly crushed at the Maysaloun Battle and he was sent into exile, heading first to Haifa in Palestine and then to Europe, where he complained to the British at having been left with no throne in Damascus, despite all goodwill gestures by the Americans, the Jews and British. The new French High Commissioner Henri Gouraud gave instructions that Faisal be offered no assistance while leaving Syria, and while making his exodus, military officials refused to even give him fuel for an automobile that until recently had been the royal car of the King of Syria. Speaking to *The Washington Post* in September 1920, Faisal angrily lamented, 'We counted upon America! You laid down the principle of self-determination. You sent a commission to Syria last year and our people flooded to its hearings to record their views. The commission soon found that we desire, passionately, independence!'[52] Speaking to an American diplomat in London, he added, 'You have pushed me into a ditch'.[53]

Conclusion

American officialdom in 1919–1920 saw little to no value in an American–Arab alliance, unlike President Wilson who had somewhat prophetically predicted that within the next 50 years the region's entire fate would shift from the Anglo–French orbit into the American one. That is why, apart from the feeble attempt at change via the King–Crane Commission, nothing serious came from the USA in 1919. Wilson was the only real American visionary, but differed from the likes of T. E. Lawrence, who commented during the Great War that 'We could see a new factor was needed in the East; some power or race which would outweigh the Turks in numbers, in output, and in mental activity'.[54] He added, 'I mean to make a new nation, to restore a lost influence' and worked hard to make that vision a reality, seeing how valuable the Arabs were going to be in the establishment of a new world order. Lawrence saw the Arabs as an added value to the post-war order, while Wilson had nothing but sympathy – at best – for them. The USA only came to that realization much later into the twentieth century, but back in 1919 saw the Arabs as nothing but pawns on a chessboard which they could navigate to achieve US ambitions in the region, with complete disregard to what the Arabs really wanted.

The man to suffer most from his attempted alliance with the USA was undoubtedly Faisal. The experience shattered his reputation at home by those who did not yet grasp how influential the USA was becoming in the post-war era. Before 1919, Faisal was the Arab liberator, hailed as a beloved leader who had helped them do away with 400 years of Ottoman occupation. After 1919, he was transformed into a puppet for world leaders, be they US or British. The Syrians, who eventually heard of his agreement with Weizmann, never forgave him for giving too much away at Paris, and for packing up and leaving them to sort out their own mess with the French after 1920. 'Had he been Syrian', recalled Munir al-Ajlani, a future parliamentarian who was 15 during the Faisal era, 'then he would have stayed behind and died defending Syria!'[55] The two men to push Faisal into the US orbit, Khoury and Shahbandar, remained committed to stronger Syrian–US relations, and were to pay for it. Shahbandar was gunned down during the Second World War, accused of being an agent for imperialism, while Khoury was ejected from office in 1955, after having spent 60 years in the nationalist movement, forced to resign by hard-liners for steering his country towards the USA.

Faisal undoubtedly gave the USA and the British much more than he got in 1919. He was eager to come across as a civilized statesman, rather than a guerilla leader in Bedouin dress. That explains why he went to dramatic lengths at times, such as signing an agreement with Weizmann, or placing flowers on the casket of Mark Sykes – who died in February 1919 while attending the Paris Peace Conference – before it was taken back for burial in his native Yorkshire.[56] This was done despite all the wrongs done to Faisal, his family and the Arabs by the much loathed Sykes–Picot Agreement which was graced with Mark Sykes' signature. At one point in Paris, he even asked one of Wilson's aids that the Americans assume direct control over Syria and appoint him king, while snubbing both the British and the French.[57]

In 1919, no oil had been discovered in Arabia, which explains why nobody took the Arabs very seriously in Paris. All of Faisal's wishes materialized, however, shortly after his death in 1933, when the Americans did assume a more direct role in Syrian affairs, in fact helping bring General Husni al-Za'im to power in 1949, to help protect American economic and political interests in Damascus. By then, they wanted al-Za'im to sign an armistice with Israel, and authorize the usage of Syrian territory for American pipelines running from Saudi Arabia to Lebanon. It took the discovery of oil, the creation of the state of Israel, the diminishing of British and French influence in the region and another 30 years, for Faisal's US agenda to see the light.

2

CRANE IN DAMASCUS AGAIN

Matters changed significantly for the Syrians in the 1921 post-Wilson era. Faisal had fled Syria for Haifa in the summer of 1920, then to Europe, where he complained to the British at having been ejected from his rightful kingdom. In compensation, the British granted him a throne in Baghdad, where he served as monarch until his death at a hospital in Switzerland in 1933. After a revolt erupted against French occupation, on the Syrian coast and in the northern city of Aleppo in August 1920, the new pro-French Prime Minister Ala al-Din Droubi was murdered by angry pro-Faisal Syrians in the Hawran province.

The French High Commissioner Henri Gouraud carved Syria into city states, creating the modern state of Lebanon, the state of Aleppo, the Sanjak of Alexandretta, and the state of Damascus. Addressing Syrians in August 1920, one month after the Battle of Maysaloun, he arrogantly declared, 'I did not make war last month with the inhabitants of Damascus. I made war on a bad government!' Adding insult to injury, Gouraud continued, 'France has always found pleasure in this gift; to see marching by her side her adopted children like her own children. Who could believe that these Moroccans and Senegalese [recruited from French colonies in Africa to serve as soldiers at Maysaloun], after having spilled their blood for four years on the battlefield, would sacrifice themselves again yesterday if France were not a true mother to them?'[1] This was in sharp contrast to what the Syrians had told the King–Crane Commission in 1919. Then, they had made it clear that, given the chance of choosing a mother, they would have picked the USA, certainly not France that came with General Gouraud as their stern father.

Warren G. Harding, a US Senator from Ohio, soon replaced Woodrow Wilson at the White House. He possessed all of Wilson's sympathies towards

Zionism in America, yet none of his towards the Arab world. Under Harding, the USA pursued a policy of isolationism, keeping the country at arm's length from the problems of Europe and the Middle East. The change of leadership in Washington received no more than passing mention in the Syrian press, which had seemingly lost interest in America once Wilson was out of office. Even the Zionists were uncomfortable with Wilson's successor. Stephen Wise, the prominent American Zionist leader, wrote to his wife, '[Harding] is so little fitted to cope with the problems that press ... he represents such a decline from Wilson'.[2]

The American press, however, showed surprising interest in news of the wandering King of Syria. On 28 July 1920, *The New York Times* reported, 'Emir Faisal is no longer King of Syria. General Gouraud, who has captured Damascus, Faisal's capital, has issued a proclamation stating that the Emir is from now a private citizen, and furthermore, the Emir has been invited to leave the country with all his family.' It continued, 'Syria has not gotten a new king, but it has a brand new ministry, handpicked by Gouraud, which has accepted all the French conditions including a fine of 10,000,000 Francs upon Damascus and its vicinity. Faisal has not been heard from since Gouraud's troops entered Damascus.'[3] concluding rather condescendingly, 'Faisal owes the French 80,000,000 Francs they paid him to "feed the hungry Syrians"'.[4]

Realizing that Harding's White House was in no mood to re-engage with Damascus, pro-American Syrians were completely mute in the early years of the mandate but they were suddenly injected with new spirit when their beloved Charles Crane paid a second visit to Damascus in April 1922. This was the same man whose name graced the ill-fated commission report to President Wilson, which recommended abolishing the French mandate and replacing it with an American one. The Syrians received news of his arrival with mixed emotions. Many, like Shahbandar and Fares al-Khoury, saw him as a saviour, eager for Crane to 'come and see what the French had done' to Syria. Others, less seasoned than both men, frowned at Crane, believing that he had sold them nothing but illusions back in 1919. He was accused of having been an 'imposter', and of promising them more than what the USA had been willing – or able – to offer.[5] The fact that he had no government mandate for the visit, travelling instead as a private citizen, added to general suspicion towards his visit, although Crane had informed the State Department of his Syria trip, out of courtesy.[6] Shahbandar snarled at the sceptics: 'He has the ear of influential members of Congress. We must show him around, and he must see the damage done by the French, to convey it to the US government!'[7]

The American in Damascus

Shahbandar received notification of Crane's visit from Edward Nickoley, the acting President of the American University of Beirut, who had replaced Howard Bliss in 1920 when the latter died of tubercular pneumonia.[8] Nickoley told him that Crane, accompanied by his aid Donald Prodi, wished to stop in Syria 'to visit his Syrian friends' on 1 April 1922. A close confident of Shahbandar, Hasan al-Hakim, half-jokingly asked if the proposed visit was an April Fool's prank being pulled by the American diplomat on the Syrians.[9] Crane, however, did indeed arrive in Damascus by train from Haifa, on 5 April, where he was greeted by Shahbandar at the Hejaz Railway Station, under the watchful eye of French intelligence. He checked into the Damascus Palace Hotel in room 23 and stayed in the Syrian capital for two nights. Shahbandar contacted his trusted friend Fares al-Khoury and asked him to arrange for Crane to attend Sunday mass at a church in Bab Touma, the Christian quarter of the Old City of Damascus, to meet Christian leaders and clerics. He then asked four Damascus notables, Hasan al-Hakim, Ismail Tabbakh, Uthman Sharabati, and his in-law, Rashid Bakdounes, to arrange for Crane's visit to the Midan, Shaghour and Qanawat neighbourhoods.[10]

Crane went on a city-wide tour, meeting with community leaders, clerics, politicians and the families of nationalists executed by the Ottomans in May 1916. Everywhere he went he heard uniform grievances; political repression, lack of respect for nationalist sentiment, misuse of public office, corruption and deteriorating economic conditions. In Damascus and Aleppo, over 25 per cent of the male population was unemployed, said Shahbandar, taking him to the popular Quwatli café in Damascus to meet with young men searching for jobs — some of them university graduates. Custom restrictions on trade with Palestine, for example, had killed the once flourishing textile industry in Syria, forcing the Palestinians to import textiles from Egypt.[11] While most Syrians complained of little financial revenue, French-appointed officials, such as the new governor of the state of Damascus Haqqi al-Azm, were getting 360 SP per month. His Education Minister Mohammad Kurd Ali, the Syrians told Crane, was getting 260 SP, the equivalent to 110 Ottoman gold coins. Under the Ottoman Empire, the governor of Damascus (which encompassed far greater territory than the borders of Damascus in the post-Faisal era) received 150 Ottoman gold coins, showing just how much wealth was being spent on French cronies.[12] The Syrians added that their gold was being smuggled by French officers to Paris, begging Crane to help them. Shahbandar angrily added, 'Less developed countries like the Philippines are about to get independence from the United States, while we in Syria might get stuck with the French forever!'[13]

Crane's eventful stay in Syria included two important visits; one to the gravesite of the renowned Muslim scholar, Ibn Taymiyya, the other to the home of Mustapha Pasha al-Abid, an aristocrat from Damascus.[14] A French officer had buried his dog at the Muslim graveyard, next to the tomb of the revered Ibn Taymiyya, arousing a furious response from Muslims in Damascus. The provocative act not only showed complete ignorance and disregard for local traditions, but added to Crane's conviction that allowing the mandate to be imposed on Syria was a gross mistake on behalf of the USA.[15]

At Mustapha Pasha's mansion, the scene was very different. Back in 1919, Crane had met with the Pasha's daughter Naziq, a 19-year-old activist who was lobbying with Faisal to grant women suffrage rights. She was also founder and chair of a humanitarian NGO, the Red Star – a predecessor of the modern Red Crescent – and an active contributor to several Damascus dailies during the Faisal era. Young, passionate and beautiful, she made a very strong impression on Crane, who, in 1922, personally requested that he meet her again. Naziq had studied in Istanbul and spoke flawless Ottoman Turkish, German and French and listed Mary Ajamy, the founder of the late Ottoman-era women's periodical, *al-Arus* as a role model. Ajami had studied nursing at AUB and lobbied Ottoman authorities for women's emancipation, turning bitter after they executed her fiancé in 1916. Under Ajamy's influence, Naziq al-Abid appeared unveiled before Crane both in 1919 and 1922, telling him how she had gone to battle in Maysaloun, uncovering her face for the newspaper cameras and shocking Damascene society out of its stuffy Puritanism. She was the only woman in combat, marching through the streets of Damascus unveiled on her way to battle with Defence Minister Yusuf al-Azma, in full military uniform, with rifle strapped on her shoulder. 'Some were very critical, accusing me of blasphemy,' she told Crane in 1922, 'but most people supported me – I was off to battle, not to a cabaret!' She then confidently added, 'I am now seated before you, with my face showing in front of a complete stranger. Does this make you lose respect for me? I think not!' Unable to conceal his admiration for the bold young girl, who shattered all foreign stereotypes of Muslim women, Crane muttered, 'Of course not Miss Abid!' Abid reportedly smiled and said, 'Good, then go tell that to the Americans that we Syrians, men and women alike, say no to occupation!'

The conversation lasted for more than two hours as the pair drank lemonade in the courtyard of the Abid mansion. While Crane took notes, Abid spoke about her new NGO, Nour al-Fayha (Light of Damascus), which strived to sharpen the skills of women in the Damascus countryside, training them to read, write and master Oriental handicrafts. She then turned towards her US guest and said, 'Mr Crane, you can call me Naziq'. It was Crane's turn to smile,

'I will,' he said, 'if you agree to call me Charles'. In addition to Nour al-Fayha, Abid told him she was about to launch a periodical by the same name, and was co-administering a school for the children of martyrs, located in the Arnous neighbourhood, with another women activist, Subhiyya Tanner. 'We were just given notice to evacuate in 24-hours,' she miserably explained to Crane, 'They treated us as bandits simply because I would not "sell" them my co-operation'. The Governor of Damascus, Haqi al-Azm (appointed by the French), she said, 'wanted to buy my allegiance to the mandate with 100 SP per month. I said "no!"' Crane was speechless. The encounter between Abid and Crane took a comedic turn when he asked her if she was engaged or married. She replied that due to her work load, she was not, and Crane fired: 'Then I have a proposal for you'. Unable to suppress the teenage girl in her, the 23-year old Abid burst into laughter, asking the ageing American guest, 'Do you want to marry me?' Crane's eyes glowed, 'I wish my dear, Naziq. But I am an old man from behind the oceans, and you are a beautiful flower from Damascus! You need a fighter like yourself!' He then turned to Shahbandar, who was watching with great interest, and said, 'If only you were 40-years younger, Doctor!' Crane's proposal was actually to bring Abid, along with a Christian girl from Damascus called Alice Qandalaft, to study in the USA. 'When I first came to Syria I developed an admiration for its people; they love to live and love to work. You the people of Syria are ambitious, reasonable, and very smart. I have visited many European countries and those in the Far East, and am certain that the Syrians in general and the Damascenes in particular are different. I am amazed by the family bonds in this country, the patriotism of those around me, and the low crime rate. What troubles me, however, is that the American people know very little about your part of the world, because of the geographical distance. You would serve as a great ambassador for your country, in my country', he told her.

Abid immediately accepted. Shahbandar asked her to consult with her family, and give the issue some serious thought before responding, 'This is America dear Naziq, not Homs'.[16] Crane added that he would entrust Shahbandar with the scholarship money, $2,000 for him to grant to Qandalaft or Abid, should they accept his offer. The outcome of Crane's second visit was to send two girls to study in the USA. Philanthropic as it was – it spoke volumes on how much sympathy the American statesman had for Syria. Here was the ageing US diplomat, coming to Syria as a grandfatherly figure, dishing out rewards left and right to young Syrians who, if it were not for him, would never dream of studying in the USA. Back then, the state-run Syrian University was still in the making, and the Arab Academy of Medicine and Law, operating since the Ottoman era, did not accept female enrolments. Abid eventually turned down the offer, however, and Shahbandar was clapped in chains the minute Crane left Damascus, charged by French authorities of receiving funds from the USA to topple the mandate in Syria. He was defended by his friend, Fares al-Khoury, one of the finest attorneys in Syria – to no avail. A French court sentenced him to 20 years of hard labour for the $2,000 found on him – ten years for every thousand.[17]

Aftershocks of the Crane visit

Rumours, meanwhile, spread in Europe and the USA that, like Shahbandar, Crane had also been sentenced to 20 years in jail by a French military court in Syria in absentia. *The New York Times* reported in May: 'Considerable surprise developed in official and diplomatic circles today when unofficial reports reached Washington that Charles R. Crane, the Chicago millionaire and former American minister to China, had been sentenced to 20 years in prison on a charge of inciting uprisings in French mandated territory in Syria after a hearing conducted in his absence by a French military court in Damascus.'[18] The French government cabled the State Department, inquiring on Crane's 'precise status', and was informed that he was 'no longer a member of the American diplomatic service,' and that he had visited Syria 'in his own personal capacity and in no way represented the United States Government.'[19] At the House of Representatives in Washington DC, representative Sabath, a Democrat from Illinois, pushed for a resolution, asking Secretary of State Charles Evans Hughes for an inquiry into Crane's adventure in Syria.[20] *The New York Times* reported, 'Confirmation is lacking of reports that Mr Crane has given Miss Abid, a Muslim teacher, a check for USD 1,000 for travelling expenses for completing her education'. Abid disappeared to evade arrest, and the French responded by arresting one of her students, Miss Rahwanji, in a vain effort to force the child to give information they sought. They locked her up for two hours in an empty tomb. She was then taken to prison in a state of collapse.

Crane himself, travelling to France and Switzerland after Syria, commented on the affair saying: 'It would not surprise me if the military authorities of Syria were much aroused over the popularity of the United States throughout Syria.' He added, 'It is true that big demonstrations occurred around my automobile as I was leaving Damascus. Thousands of Syrians gathered around the car and sang the national anthem and cheered the United States.' Crane, the US newspapers noted, 'was believed by the populace to be an official representative of the American government'. Crane's speeches, the paper added, 'resulted in the wildest patriotic fervor. It was supposed that the United States was going to intervene in favour of the Mohammedians to throw out the French!' Crane denied that he had been persecuted by the French in Syria – a claim that was echoed in Beirut from the highest levels, by General Gouraud. He spoke harshly about malpractices, noting that the French 'have a vicious Chief of Police ... (who) used machine guns on unarmed people, and some of the finest men of Damascus were given long terms of imprisonment, without trial'.[21] He added, 'I have been very cordially received by many members of the French senate and others high in the government. There is not the slightest indication that any action has been taken or is contemplated against me.'[22]

One day after Shahbandar's arrest, an estimated 8,000 men gathered at the Umayyad Mosque in the heart of the Old City of Damascus to hear inflammatory speeches in his defence. By the time Friday prayer was over, the crowd had reached 10,000 and broke out of the grand mosque, headed towards the Citadel of Damascus where Shahbandar and his comrades were being held. They marched through the Hamidiya Bazaar, carrying portraits of Shahbandar, and armed with knives, slingshots and sticks, threatened to liberate him by force. A French garrison immediately dispersed the crowd, arresting 46 Damascenes. The same pattern was repeated daily until 10 April, when the demonstrators adopted a new approach. This time, 40 women – headed by Naziq al-Abid and Shahbandar's wife, Sarah Mouayyad al-Azm – took part in the demonstration against the French. Prosperous merchants in the marketplace all shut down their establishments in solidarity with the arrested nationalist. Many women marched unveiled, while some ululated at high pitch, chanting slogans calling for the long life of Shahbandar and Charles Crane. Once again, the French intervened, arresting 36 people.[23] What is interesting about the massive demonstrations in response to Shahbandar's arrest is that people were not suspicious of the man for having taken money from a US diplomat. At a grassroots level, ordinary Syrians did not know of Crane's philanthropy, or that the money was actually set aside to educate two young Syrian girls. What they were told by French-controlled media was that Shahbandar was on the US payroll. Nobody in the Syrian streets, however, accused him of treason. Nobody doubted his intentions or asked 'why America?' Had such a case occurred in the 1960s or 1970s, any politician – even somebody of Shahbandar's calibre and popularity – would have been immediately ruined. His reputation would have been damaged beyond repair, labelled as a spy (*jasous*) or agent (*amil*). But that was not the case in the 1920s. Far from being considered a traitor, Shahbandar was hailed as a patriot, regardless of his relationship with the USA. America back then was still seen as safe haven by ordinary Syrians. Working with it was honourable – in fact welcome – because the USA had no imperial record, no mandate history, and no desire to occupy or mentor the people of Syria. At least that is how grassroots Syrians viewed the USA back in 1922.

Under Crane's urging, on 13 May a petition was sent to the Cairo bureau of *The New York Times*, signed by 'the people of Syria' which claimed to be speaking for 4.5 million Syrians. It read:

> The Syrian people, in their struggle for liberty and independence, have placed all hope and confidence in the liberal American people. Despite the fact that the Government of Washington according to the wishes of the imperialists of Europe, did not publish the Crane Report (in 1919) never for a single day did Syrian confidence in the American people diminish.[24]
>
> Entirely to the contrary, every time French occupation became more severe and administration became more corrupt and cruel, the Syrian people looked towards America. The feeling is exactly as Mr Crane stated after his recent visit to Damascus, where he saw those who shouted 'Long live America' thrown into prisons and massacred by French troops.[25]

Shahbandar and Crane had tried, yet again, to tell the Syrians that the USA held many possible ways forward for Syria. But once again, as in 1919, the USA was completely incapable of saving Syria, or her people, from the French dragnet. Crane went to Paris and spoke to members of the French Assembly about nationalist aspirations in Syria, and even tried calling on Prime Minister Poincaré, with little success.[26] He promised to convey the hopes of Shahbandar and his friends to members of Congress, but there is no recorded evidence that he went so far upon his return to the USA. He did meet with influential politicians in Washington circles, however, saying that American missionary interests in Syria amounted to $60 million, arguing that saving Syria from the French was in America's national interest.

For his part, Shahbandar served 17 months in jail, along with all those who had facilitated Crane's visit. He was released by the new French High Commissioner Maxime Weygand then banished to Egypt in October 1923. Two months beforehand, Warren Harding died in office and was replaced by his vice president, Calvin Coolidge, who also showed no interest in the complex affairs of the Middle East or the plight of the people of Syria. Once out of jail, however, Shahbandar went on a nine-month tour of Great Britain and the USA. In London, Conservative Party politicians invited him to attend a session at Westminster, arousing outcry from the French who now accused him of being both a British and American agent.[27] In the USA, he called on

Crane in Chicago, by then busy planning the establishment of the Institute of Current Affairs in Washington. The Institute, which did not open its doors until 1925, offered fellowships to young Americans below the age of 35 to travel and live in a foreign country for two years. The two men spoke at length about contemporary art; Crane was an avid collector and Shahbandar a keen art appreciator, the situation in Syria, aftershocks of his visit, and the change of leadership in America.[28] According to Munir al-Ajlani, then a teenager in Damascus who went on to become a close ally of Shahbandar in the 1930s, 'When in the US, Shahbandar went to Washington, and met with President Calvin Coolidge at the White House.'[29]

Conclusion

Crane's visit was indeed a turning point in Syrian-US relations, although it was not mandated by the US government. Crane represented a generation of Americans who believed in good deeds and justice for the Third World, regardless of how condescending his philanthropy may have seemed to ordinary Syrians. His interest in Syria was a far cry from isolationist policies of the Harding White House, but it shows how anxious the Syrian elite were for engagement between Damascus and Washington DC. It also reveals how uninformed the Syrians were about the USA. They saw it as a mystical, distant country that could somehow miraculously end all their troubles. Charles Crane was a knight in shining armour, coming to the Oriental East to save the Arabs from European colonialism, seemingly wanting nothing in return. This image of America, no matter how flawed, continued to serve as the guiding force in bilateral relations up until the Second World War. It explains why, against all the odds, pro-American voices continued to be heard throughout the upper echelons of power in Damascus during the 1920s and 1930s. When reality struck in 1939, the Syrians finally understood there was a very different side to US generosity – serious ambitions related to oil, geography and politics. What finally got American officialdom to understand the importance of courting the Syrians, nearly 20 years after Crane's visit to Damascus, was the Nazi craze that took over the Arab world during the Second World War.

3

THE ROCKY 1920s

For the remainder of the 1920s, Abdul Rahman Shahbandar tried, with limited success, to elicit support from top US officials for the Syrian case. Fares al-Khoury became a silent partner in the drive for engagement with the USA, confining his efforts to Syrian domestic pursuits by teaching liberal views to his students at the Faculty of Law at the Syrian University, which was created in 1923. Shahbandar's forced exile gave him the opportunity to adopt a more international approach. He visited the USA, Switzerland and Great Britain, serving as an unofficial ambassador for Syria, before settling as a medical doctor in Cairo. When his travels failed to arouse international sympathy for Syria, Shahbandar directed his efforts to mid level bureaucrats in the US State Department, especially the Division of Near East Affairs.[1] These officials were less than enthusiastic about Zionist aspirations in Palestine – and, just as Shahbandar had used the issue to attract Wilson's attention in 1919 he then attempted to use it in reverse, to win the minds of State Department officials. The belief that a strong anti-Zionist sentiment pervaded the State Department was apparently shared by Chaim Weizmann, who wrote in his memoirs, 'Our difficulties [in the USA] were not connected with the first statesmen. These had always understood our aspirations. It was always behind the scenes and on the lower levels that we encountered an obstinate, devious, and secretive opposition.'[2] This belief was based on earlier experiences with the State Department, which both Shahbandar and Weizmann had observed well during the Great War. Back in 1917, for example, Secretary of State Robert Lansing had repeatedly advised President Wilson 'to go very slowly' when it came to extending public support to Zionist aspirations in Palestine, noting, 'we are not at war with Turkey and should avoid any appearance of favouring taking territory from that Empire by force'.[3]

Shahbandar made a final attempt at eliciting some support from President Harding, through the Syrian–Palestinian Congress he had founded in Geneva in late 1921, which aimed at toppling the French mandate in Syria and the British one in Palestine.[4] A letter was sent to the White House, carrying Shahbandar's name and that of the Executive Council of the Congress, addressed to the US President.[5] Once again he called for US support against the mandate, reminding Harding that against all odds, the Syrians had never lost faith in the USA, stating, 'The imperialists are making mandated people enslaved colonies!'[6] The Harding White House never replied.

The League of Nations Council had approved the French mandate over Syria exactly two years after downfall of the Faisal regime, on 24 July 1922. While Shahbandar was roaming Europe speaking to anyone willing to listen to anything about Syria, France and the USA had signed a convention over Syria and Lebanon on 4 April 1924. The USA agreed that France could have full control over Syria and in return France granted American citizens, especially missionaries, special privileges in Syria such as freedom of worship, liberty to administer their schools without intervention from local authorities, and exemption from customs and tariffs, mandated by Syrian law.[7] No similar right was given to mandate citizens, both Syrians and French, in the USA.

The Revolt of 1925

The USA began to take serious interest in Syrian affairs when a nation-wide military revolt erupted against the French in the summer of 1925, headed by the Druze chieftain, Sultan Pasha al-Atrash. On 18 July, Druze fighters opened fire on a French plane encircling the Druze Mountain, 75 miles south-east of Damascus. Armed fighting followed and by the end of July the French had 10,000 troops stationed at the mountain, whose entire population did not exceed 50,000. General Roger Michaud was sent to Suwayda, capital of the Druze Mountain, to force Sultan Pasha to end the hostilities. On 2 August, his battalion, composed of 3,000 troops, was ambushed by Atrash's men, who killed 14 men, wounded 385 and took 432 hostages, along with 2,000 rifles. Michaud himself fled the scene and in disgrace his commanding officer committed suicide after being defeated by the Syrian forces.[8]

A former ally of Faisal who had fought against the Ottomans during the Great War, Atrash was close to the Hashemite family in Amman, now headed by Faisal's brother Emir Abdullah, and a friend of Faisal himself, who had by then been crowned King of Iraq. Shahbandar had just been pardoned, again, in early 1925 and had founded a political party in Damascus, the first of its kind under the mandate. The party, also loyal to the Hashemites, aimed at liberating Syria from the French and restoring the Hashemite crown to Damascus. Among the party founders was an assortment of politicians who had served in government under Faisal, including Hasan al-Hakim, the former Director of Posts and Telegraphs, Fares al-Khoury, the former Minister of Finance, and Jamil Mardam Bey, Faisal's interpreter at the Paris Peace Conference. The People's Party, as it was named, had no intention of taking up arms against the French. None of its leaders had the money, or the military experience, to engage in such an endeavour. Additionally, the French had ruthlessly crushed two rebellions in Aleppo and on the Syrian coast in 1919 and 1920, temporarily muting all Syrian opposition. Atrash's revolt took the People's Party off guard. It would have been political suicide for Shahbandar to oppose such an uprising, given its popular support. As a result, he closed his clinic in Damascus and took up arms with Atrash, travelling to the Druze Mountain to serve as the revolt's political mastermind. He wrote all of its communications, coordinating with traditional nobles to bring the revolt to Damascus. This was a departure in policy for the seasoned pro-American statesman, who had built his entire career until then on political engagement rather than military force, refusing, for example, to take up arms against the Ottomans during the Great War.

On 18 October 1925, approximately 400 armed horsemen marched into the Syrian capital, taking their cue from Shahbandar, and headed for the Azm Palace in the heart of the Old City. The ancient palace, with all its treasures and artefacts, was home to the eighteenth-century Ottoman governors of Syria and had been used by the French as lodgings for senior personnel since 1920. Shahbandar had fallen prey to a rumour claiming that the new French Commissioner, Maurice Sarrail, would be arriving from Beirut to spend the day at the palace. The rebels had orders to arrest him to be traded for hundreds of Syrian prisoners in French jails. Sarrail did not show up in Damascus, but no sooner had the Syrian rebels landed in the central Hamidiyyeh market than the Old City was sealed off by French forces, and bombs began landing on and around the Azm Palace. The shelling continued for two days, targeting different neighbourhoods of Damascus, with a death toll of around 1,400 civilians and leading to the displacement of nearly 500.[9] Nearly every shop in the old market surrounding the Umayyad Mosque was destroyed either by machine-gun fire or bombing. The Midhat Pasha and Bruziyeh Market, just outside the gates of the Azm Palace, were the worst hit. The roof of the Hamidiyyeh market was completely blown off, and nearly one hundred yards of the market collapsed on the small shops. The streets of the Old City, usually swarming with people busy with commercial activity, were showered with broken glass, destroyed merchandise, and the bodies of civilians. In the area of Bab al-Jabiyeh, al-Kharabeh and Shaghour, 150 homes were destroyed beyond repair.[10] During the raid, three American companies were accidently hit by the French bombs landing from the Citadel of Damascus, Socony Vacuum Oil, Singer Sewing Machine, and the US licorice firm, MacAndrews & Forbes.[11]

Naturally, the USA were furious. US consul general to Syria, Paul Knabenshue, began reporting on the rebellion periodically to the State Department from his headquarters in Beirut. Overnight, the US government developed a sincere interest in Syria.[12] *The New York Times* reported in late October, 'Americans are placing practically the entire blame for the catastrophe upon General Sarrail'.[13] Tensions rose dramatically between the French and the US governments, especially after Knabenshue made it clear that France was responsible for all of the bloodshed, and of having triggered and aggravated violence in the Syrian interior. In one of his memoranda to Secretary of State Frank B. Kellogg, he wrote:

> France, through mal-administration and through following a policy more of colonization than of a truly mandatory regime, has brought a revolution in the country which has caused the ruin of at least one hundred thousand inhabitants, the destruction of ancient and sacred landmarks, and has endangered the lives, property, and potential interests of foreigners (in Syria).[14]

The State Department responded by rushing emergency aid to Syria, through Near East Relief and the Red Cross, and officially demanded compensation for US companies from the French government. It quickly made it clear, however, that this aid was going to Americans based in Syria, not to ordinary Syrians, so that France did not fail in its duties to mend the lives of ordinary Syrians which it had destroyed.[15] So angry was Knabenshue that he requested that the US Navy send two destroyers, Coblan and Lamson, to the shores of Beirut, to serve as a deterrent to the French Army.[16] He wrote to the State Department, 'It is the presence here of American destroyers alone that has given a sense of security to the population.'[17] In explaining his case to superiors at the department, he added, 'We cannot depend on French assurances'.[18]

Knabenshue sent a 60-page report to the State Department entitled, 'Political Situation in Syria' outlining the damage caused by Commissioner Sarrail, and calling on his government to intervene with the British to halt the onslaught in Damascus.[19] He made it clear that a British mandate in Syria would better serve US interests in the Middle East, drawing on recommendations made by the people of Syria six years earlier, to the King–Crane Commission.[20] The French, displeased with the US consul's audacity, contacted his government through their ambassador to Washington, demanding immediate withdrawal of the two ships from Beirut. Secretary of State Kellogg was undaunted, however, replying, 'We will withdraw them when we think we can safely do so'.[21]

USA in Syrian culture

The USA's interest in the affairs of Syria began to disappear as the Great Revolt ended gradually in 1927 and came to a grinding halt with the Wall Street Crash of October 1929. Shahbandar, sentenced to death for his role in the revolt, was forced to flee in 1927 and spent ten years in exile, limiting his ability to influence Syrian public opinion with regard to the USA. Given the magnitude of the financial crisis, nobody in the USA – not even the loudest Arabists – had any tears left to shed for Syria or the Oriental East. The years 1927–1933 were bleak for Syrian–US relations, with very little political development. While the USA was busy struggling with the Great Depression, Syrians themselves were slaving away at attempts to draft a republican constitution for themselves – a project that was rejected by the French because of the legal document's anti-French clauses. Syria's economy was severely dislocated when it sank into the clutches of its own depression in the early 1930s. Between 1930 and 1934, approximately 150,000 were unemployed in Syria and Lebanon, approximately 15–20 per cent of the labour force.[22] The Damascus Chamber of Commerce reported that, due to the collapse of the handicraft industry, nearly 77,000 Syrians were unemployed in the late 1920s and early 1930s.[23] The local tanning and dyeing industries were also in decline, as was the confectionery industry. In 1932, for example, there were between 700 and 750 traders operating in Damascus. One year later, this number had fallen to 400.[24] The value of Syria's total exports in 1929–1933 fell by half, while the value of imports fell by 38 per cent, increasing the trade deficit by 18 per cent. Wool production fell by 86 per cent, raw silk by 81 per cent, and textiles by 56 per cent.[25]

The only relief for ordinary Syrians during these difficult years were the American films showing in the growing cinema industry in Damascus and Aleppo. The first encounter Syrians ever had with the cinema dates back to the French Lumière brothers, sometime around 1897, followed by a film shown at an Aleppo cafe by two entrepreneurs from Anatolia in 1908.[26] Cinemas devoted fully to film did not open until 1914, but all movies shown in Syria were strictly German-made, due to the complicated alliances of the Great War. That changed after the War, when American and French films invaded the cultural scene, and cinemas mushroomed in important cities like Damascus, Beirut, and Aleppo.[27] Movies were still silent, much to the pleasure of ordinary Syrians who spoke only Ottoman Turkish. That, along with cheaper rent of American films, explains why Syrians went for American movies, which contained plenty of action – not talk – mainly cowboy Westerns, or the slapstick comedies of Charlie Chaplin.[28]

Throughout the 1920s and 1930s, Charlie Chaplin appeared everywhere in Syria – in newspapers and magazines, on cinema billboards, and in any intellectual discussion at local cafes in the Syrian capital. So popular was the 'Little Tramp' in Damascene society that he even made a publicity stop in Syria, before heading to Egypt in 1929.[29] This was right after Chaplin's classic *The Circus* had topped box-office sales throughout the country, drowning all French productions. The fact that Chaplin was actually a British citizen did not really matter to ordinary Syrians – who only cared for his role as an extremely funny clown, coming from the faraway studios of Hollywood in California. He took them to an imaginary world, where there were no French soldiers regulating their lives, no revolts against occupation, and no economic hardships. His hallmark appearance, oversized shoes, tight coat, derby hat, cane and small moustache remained hugely popular in Syrian culture for the next ten years.[30] As one retired officer of the 1920s put it, 'Chaplin literally looked like thousands of Syrians who were forced to dress in a funny way, because of the difficult economic conditions Syria was going through. Funny indeed, he reminded them of themselves and relieved them of the misery of occupation and economic hardships, with laughter.'[31] In addition to *The Circus*, two of the Little Tramp's classics, *The Kid* (1921), a feature film, and *The Gold Rush* (1925), were both box-office hits in Syria.[32]

Ticket prices in Syria were not cheap, however, costing ten US cents towards the end of the 1920s – an entire day's wage – meaning that only a certain privileged class could visit the cinemas. Most ordinary Syrians relied on the majestic voice of the Egyptian diva Um Kalthoum for entertainment through the radio shows every Thursday. By the early 1930s, most major newspapers had a cinema column in them, and there were 40 cinemas in Syria and Lebanon, holding approximately 22,000 seats and selling 2.3 million tickets per year.[33] Other prominent American films that kept up momentum in Syrian–US relations were Gary Cooper's 1929 first sound film, *The Virginian*, and a series of Tarzan films, notably, *Tarzan the Mighty* and *Tarzan and the Golden Lion*, produced in 1928 and 1929.[34] Also topping the charts was another remarkable novelty, the motion-picture cartoon, which first came to Syria via Walt Disney's 1928 black-and-white, *Steamboat Willie*. Charlie Chaplin, Mickey Mouse and Tarzan, it could be argued, did more for bilateral relations between Washington and Damascus in the 1920s than Presidents Harding, Coolidge and Herbert Hoover combined.

Roosevelt: another Charles Crane

Franklin Roosevelt, the first Democrat to reach the White House since Woodrow Wilson, initially seemed no better than any of his predecessors in answering Syria's desperate calls. Far from being interested in affairs of the Middle East, he had plenty of troubles awaiting him at the White House, which he had an elected mandate to resolve. He had come to power in March 1933 promising economic activism, optimism and a 'New Deal' for the US people, to relieve them from the haunting Great Depression. The New Deal, which received mixed coverage in the Syrian press, was a complex package of economic programmes carried out in 1933–1935, with the goal of achieving what Roosevelt termed the '3Rs' – being relief of the unemployed, reform of business and financial practices, and recovery of the US economy. The pro-Shahbandar daily al-Shaab, for example, carried a headline, 'Roosevelt: A breath of fresh air in America!'[35] Shahbandar, who had followed FDR's (Franklin Delano Roosevelt) 1932 campaign from his exile in Egypt, predicted early on that incumbent Herbert Hoover was doomed to fail in the presidential elections. When accepting the Democratic nomination, Roosevelt had famously declared, 'Throughout the nation men and women, forgotten in the political philosophy of the Government, look to us here for guidance and for more equitable opportunity to share in the distribution of national wealth. I pledge you, I pledge myself to a new deal for the American people. This is more than a political campaign. It is a call to arms!'[36] In one editorial, Shahbandar quoted the speech at length in Arabic, calling on elected Syrian politicians – whom he disliked for being too soft on the French – for a new deal with the Syrian people, emphasizing 'redistribution of national wealth's a must in Syrian society'.[37] A socialist at heart who came from a humble background, Shahbandar had great faith in FDR, who as predicted, won 57 per cent of the popular vote in all but six US states.

Syrian journalists such as Nasuh Babil, a doyen of the journalist community in Damascus, admired FDR's resolve, and wrote affectionately of him in his mass circulation daily al-Ayyam. By that time, Syria had a parliament, constitution and a newly elected president – the first in his country's history – Mohammad Ali al-Abid. An aristocrat from Damascus, Abid's father Ahmad Izzat Pasha had been a close confident of the Ottoman Sultan Abdulhamid II and reportedly the richest man in Ottoman Syria. In reward for the Pasha's numerous services to the Imperial Court in Istanbul, Abdulhamid had appointed his son, Mohammad Ali, as Ottoman Ambassador to Washington DC, in the summer of 1908.[38] Franklin Roosevelt had just dropped out of Columbia Law School, after passing the New York State Bar exam, to take a job with the prestigious Wall Street firm, Carter Ledyard & Milburn. Although the two men never met, President Abid was well acquainted with FDR's predecessor (and fifth cousin), Theodore Roosevelt, who held office in 1908.[39] In his capacity as Imperial Ambassador, Mohammad Ali al-Abid was received at the Oval Office by Theodore 'Teddy' Roosevelt, briefing him of a coup against the Ottoman Sultan only weeks after his arrival in Washington. Aged only 50 in 1908, Teddy was the youngest President in US history, with an abundance of energy, wit and a variety of interests that included boxing, horseback riding, tennis, hiking, travel and writing. Abid was enchanted by the 'cowboy' spirit of the US president and his love of knowledge, two traits that remained imprinted in his mind until FDR came to the White House, 24 years later, in 1933.[40] Upon reading news of FDR's election, President Abid sent a congratulatory cable to the new US leader, 'on behalf of the people of Syria'.[41]

The Syrian president tried, with no luck, to nurture relations with the USA during his years in power in 1932–1936, recognizing the huge potential of the USA and how much influence it could yield if it decided to intervene once again in the affairs of the Arab world. Two months after FDR's election, the government of Saudi Arabia signed a concessionary agreement with Standard Oil of California (SOCAL) allowing the company to explore for Arab oil, news that immediately attracted the attention of the Syrian President and Shahbandar.[42] The concession was assigned to California–Arabian Standard Oil, but it was quickly announced that no oil had been found in Arabian Desert. Drilling continued until after President Abid left the presidential palace in Damascus, with no success. Oil was finally found – to the delight of the USA, in Dammam, a few miles north of Dhahran, in 1938. The well was quickly developed and began producing over 1,500 barrels per day, while the company changed its name in 1944 to Arabian American Oil Company (ARAMCO). Washington considered oil companies as instruments of its foreign policy, and control of Arab oil laid a solid foundation for the USA to pursue wider political, economic and strategic involvement in the Muslim and Arab world. Shortly after the discovery of oil in Saudi Arabia, prominent oilmen wrote to FDR, firmly drawing his attention to the fact that, 'the center of the world's petroleum output was shifting to the Gulf'.[43] As a result of this finding, the USA opened its first embassy in Saudi Arabia in 1933, having previously administered its affairs in the Arabian Desert, from its premises in Cairo. It did not send a resident ambassador to

Riyadh, however, until 1943, when it became certain that oil was gushing in the Kingdom – plenty of it – which was vital for the USA and the Allied war efforts. Between 1941–1945, the USA supplied 6 out of 7 billion barrels of oil consumed by the Allies, thanks to friendly states, such as Saudi Arabia. Interest in Saudi oil produced an interest in Arab affairs at large, for FDR and senior officials at the State Department. It paved the way for a new friendship between Syria and the USA during the years of FDR, although its prime advocate, Abdul Rahman Shahbandar, did not live long enough to see it materialize. After returning to Syria from over ten years in exile, he was gunned down by French agents in the summer of 1940. Mohammad Ali al-Abid, another enthusiast of lower calibre, died shortly after leaving the Syrian presidency, in 1939.

Perhaps unsurprisingly, the man to take Syrian–US relations to new heights was Saudi Arabia's best friend in Damascus, Shukri al-Quwatli, who would become the President of Syria during the middle of the Second World War, in August 1943.

4

THE ROAD TO WASHINGTON RUNS THROUGH BERLIN

While oil may have jump-started US interests in the Arab world, so did a variety of other factors, including the USA's entry into the Second World War, Roosevelt's proclaimed commitment to a democratic world free of tyranny, and fear of rising Nazi influence in Damascus. Many historians, especially in the Arab world, wrongly argued that Israel and ARAMCO were the real reasons for US interests in Syria, claiming that bilateral relations only kicked-off in 1947–1948. But more than Zionism and certainly more than oil (which was not yet tapped in Syria) the USA came knocking on the doors of Damascus when they felt that Syria was on its way to becoming a Nazi satellite. The Nazi option – just as the Soviet option would become during the cold war – was always available for the leaders of Syria when the gates to the White House were sealed off to them. In the post-war era, the Syrians had tried in vain to cement a relationship with Washington, which became very difficult under Presidents Harry Truman and Dwight Eisenhower. When all attempts failed, Syrian politicians began snuggling up to the Russians in the mid-1950s, in a replica of what had happened between Syria and the USA in the years leading up to the Second World War, when all attempts at befriending Presidents Harding, Coolidge and Hoover, ended in vain. Under Wilson, the USA had viewed Syria with plenty of sympathy but never as a real partner who could advance US interests in the regional or international community. Back then, Syria was a weak, underdeveloped and poor country, with a hapless monarch, who was being tossed around in the ongoing political football between the Great Powers after the Great War. Apart from a moral obligation, Wilson saw no need to go out of his way to protect Syrians or help them achieve independence. Simply put, there was nothing in it for the USA. By the 1940s, things had changed, when all world powers – headed by Nazi Germany – began competing for power and influence in Syria, as part of the balance of power. Syria suddenly became valuable.

The USA was startled out of its slumber – and self-imposed isolation – when at 7.45 am on 7 December 1941 the Japanese attacked Pearl Harbor, forcing President Roosevelt to declare war on the Axis Powers. Four days later, on 11 December, Adolf Hitler declared war against the USA. France and Great Britain had entered the war against Germany after Hitler ordered the invasion of Poland in 1939. The Allies had then lost the subsequent Battle of France and the Nazis had marched into Paris on 14 June 1940. As a result, France fell under German occupation and Syria became part of Hitler's growing Empire. Three days after the fall of France, a Franco–German armistice was signed, and Henri Pétain, a decorated officer from the First World War, was propped up as head-of-state by the Nazis, establishing the Vichy regime, and cancelling the constitution of the Third Republic. From day one, the Vichy government tried to convince France's colonies, including Syria, that it had no interest in maintaining territories outside of Europe. It promised to do away with the despised mandate system if the Syrians cooperated for what remained of the Second World War.

Nazi influence in Syria

The Second World War had an immediate and direct effect on Syria, because of the French mandate. At a grassroots level, the people of Syria were enchanted with Adolf Hitler, united in a desire to defeat the French. Crowds gathered in the old cafes of Damascus to listen to Hitler's inflammatory speeches while his autobiography *Mein Kampf* became a national best-seller in Syrian bookstores, after being translated into Arabic.[1] The Syrians even provided transit facilities for 106 German planes being sent to the East through Damascus, Aleppo and Palmyra.[2] True, the Third Reich was a dictatorship – no different perhaps from what France had brought to Syria in 1920 – but so long as it was willing to help the Syrians achieve independence, they did not really care what kind of system it imposed on Europe. Prominent nationalists in Syria took up Hitler's cause, notably the youth leader Fakhri al-Barudi, and the Damascus notable Shukri al-Quwatli, aided by King Farouk of Egypt, who was also vehemently pro-Nazi. One vehicle for advancing Nazi goals in Syria was *al-Nadi al-Arabi* (The Arab Club) a secular organization that preached Arab nationalism and emancipation from European control.[3] It was founded by Said Fattah al-Imam, a young Syrian educated in Berlin during the inter-war years, who was close to both Quwatli and Barudi. In 1936, Imam travelled twice to Germany, once even meeting personally with Hitler to try to talk him in to shipping arms to the Palestinians and Syrians so they could use them to fight off the British and the French. In December 1937 Hitler dispatched his youth leader Balder von Schirach to Damascus to single out potential allies for Nazi Germany in the Middle East. Accompanied by a delegation of 15 Nazi officials, he met with Imam, Quwatli and Barudi, hammering out an alliance between them and the Third Reich.[4] In June 1938, Hitler sent another official, Walter Beck, to Damascus to offer 70 scholarships to Syrian students wanting to pursue their college education in Berlin.[5] In February 1939, a third Nazi, von Hentig, came to Syria to request that 'friends of Germany' assist in spreading Nazi propaganda in the Arab world.[6] A paramilitary organization called the Steel Shirts was set up in Syria by Fakhri al-Barudi in the mid-1930s, inspired by the disciplined armies of Hitler and Mussolini in Europe. It trained young men to become 'three-dimensional citizens,' similar to Renaissance men like Leonardo da Vinci.[7] They were drilled in sports, music, maths, sculpture, art, poetry and tools of combat. They were also given a military uniform, which looked hauntingly like the Nazi uniform, and an armband with a torch-bearing hand, similar to the Nazi swastika.[8] In the absence of a national army (the French had abolished the Syrian Army in 1920) the Steel Shirts were mandated to protect the different neighbourhoods of Damascus from crime, theft and French malpractice.

One of the prime figures who helped orchestrate the Syrian–Nazi relationship was Hajj Amin al-Husseini, a Palestinian nationalist who had served in the 1920s as Grand Mufti of Jerusalem. Like Said Fattah al-Imam, he too was a close friend of both Quwatli and Barudi. In 1933, only weeks after Hitler rose to power in Germany, Husseini, who hailed from one of the most prominent families in Palestine, met the German Consul-General in Jerusalem, Heinrich Wolff, saying that Muslims around the Middle East were enthusiastic about the Nazi Party and wanted to befriend the new master of Berlin.[9] Husseini then went to the US Consul George Wadsworth (who was to become the USA's first ambassador to Syria) in August 1937, noting that because of the USA's distance from imperialist ambitions, it could understand that Zionism, 'represented a hostile aggression directed against an inhabited country', expressing fears, however, that because of an influential Jewish lobby in Washington DC, the White House might be persuaded to side with the Zionists in Palestine.[10] Husseini, aided by Syrian money and recruits, headed a nationalist uprising against the British and the Zionists in Palestine in 1936–1939.[11] When his rebellion was

crushed, he fled to Rome, on 11 October 1941, and met with Fascist authorities, pledging to support the Axis Powers if they 'recognise in principle the
unity, independence, and sovereignty of an Arab state, including Iraq, Syria,
Palestine, and Transjordan'. The Italian Foreign Ministry approved his plan,
recommending a grant of 1 million lira, and referred him to Benito Mussolini,
who granted him an audience on 27 October.[12] In close collaboration with his
Syrian colleagues, he presented a draft for German–Arab cooperation, containing a clause:

> Germany and Italy recognise the right of the Arab countries to solve
> the question of the Jewish elements, which exist in Palestine and in the
> other Arab countries, as required by the national and ethnic interests
> of the Arabs, and as the Jewish question was solved in Germany and
> Italy.[13]

The proposal was signed by Mussolini and forwarded to the German Embassy
in Rome. On 6 November, Husseini arrived in Berlin where he met Joachim
von Ribbentrop, Hitler's Foreign Minister, finally meeting the Fuhrer himself
on 28 November.[14] He asked Hitler for a public declaration that 'recognised and
sympathised with the Arab struggles for independence and liberation, and that
would support the elimination of a national Jewish homeland'.[15] According to
Maarouf al-Dawalibi, a friend of the Mufti who was to become Prime Minister
of Syria in the 1950s, 'Hitler told the Mufti that when the German Army
entered Paris, they found confidential documents at the Quai d'Orsay related
to Syria. Apparently, the Zionist organisation had sent several urgent appeals
to the French government back in 1936, asking them to refrain from signing
an independence treaty with Syria, unless Syrian leaders support Zionist aspirations in Palestine.'[16]

   That single piece of news was enough to send Syrian emotions souring
against France in favour of Nazi Germany, much to the displeasure of the USA.
The Allies were watching developments in Syria uneasily, given Syrian support
for the Mufti's Nazi adventure. They tried hard to curb Nazi influence in Syria,
to no avail. Prior to creation of the Vichy regime, the French had tried to arrest
Syrians with declared Nazi sympathies, placing Quwatli under house arrest
and banishing Fakhri al-Barudi to Amman, where he was kept under 24-hour
surveillance by British Intelligence. They also outlawed his Steel Shirts, claiming the group was a 'vehicle for Nazi penetration in Syria'.[17] French Intelligence
even spread a rumour aimed at defaming Hitler in Syria, saying that the Fuhrer
saw no difference between Arabs and apes, and once through with his war

in Europe, would direct his armies towards the Middle East to conquer the Arabs.[18] The more war raged on in Europe, the more pro-Nazi ordinary Syrians became, much to the dismay of pro-Allied statesmen like Khoury. He was among the few who argued against a Nazi victory, warning his colleagues in the National Bloc, 'You have no idea what kind of a world we will have if the soldiers take control of Europe'.[19] The US Consulate reported on these strong and contradictory trends in Syrian society, sending daily dispatches to the US State Department, strongly advising the Roosevelt White House 'to take action before the Arab East turns Nazi'. The US Consul in Syria, Theodore Marriner, had been shot dead in Beirut on 13 October 1937 by an Armenian angered at being denied a visa to the USA.[20] While the case was initially written off as an isolated incident back in 1937, it suddenly took on added meaning after the outbreak of the Second World War: the Syrians were radicalizing because world powers had failed to help them achieve their national aspirations. If the West wanted to prevent Syria from becoming a Nazi satellite, countries such as Great Britain and the USA had to act fast to counterbalance French influence in the Levant. Time apparently was not on their side.

Franklin Roosevelt eventually responded to numerous calls by his advisors, delivering his famous 'Four Freedoms' speech at the State of the Union Address to Congress, in January 1941, almost one year before he declared war on the Axis Powers. Roosevelt spoke about fundamental freedoms 'humans everywhere in the world' ought to enjoy, striking on a particularly raw nerve for the Syrians who were longing for such a signal from Washington. These undeniable rights included freedom of speech and expression, freedom of religion, freedom from want and freedom from fear. FDR's advisors hoped that the speech would rip through the Arab world and halt – or at least challenge – Nazi infiltration, with an effect similar Wilson's Fourteen Points. The speech was indeed well received on the Syrian street – but taken with a grain of salt, however – because of America's tendency to emerge, then suddenly disappear, in affairs of the Middle East. America's indifference to the French occupation of 1920 despite the King–Crane Report, was still fresh in people's minds. What minimized the effect of FDR's speech was that nobody in Syria was willing to publically speak out in favour of the USA or the Allies because that sounded too pro-French at a time when the Syrian street was boiling with anti-French sentiment. Staunch US allies, like Shahbandar, were long gone, and for political reasons those that remained, such as Khoury, kept silent throughout the war. Additionally, those who had staged pro-US demonstrations in 1919–1922 were then roughly twenty years older, in their mid-forties. They had families and children and were no longer willing to stick their necks out for the USA.

Syria's strategic location in the Middle East and its occupation by the pro-Nazi Vichy regime suddenly put it on Great Britain and the USA's agendas. In June 1941 an Anglo-French Army arrived in Syria, bent on liberating Damascus from the Nazis. Resistance leader Charles de Gaulle oversaw the campaign with 6,000 troops, 12 planes, 10 tanks and 8,000 cannon. He was confronted with fierce resistance from Vichy and battles raged in Deir ez-Zour on the Euphrates, in al-Kisweh near the border with Jordan, and in the ancient city of Palmyra. By 12 June, de Gaulle's men were within ten miles of Damascus, yet a Vichy counter-attack delayed their advance for one week. On 21 June 1941, Damascus fell to the Allies and shortly after, the British and Vichy French signed an armistice in Acre, Palestine. Desperate to thwart pro-Nazi sentiment, the Free French dropped leaflets on major cities and towns throughout Syria on 28 September, promising to grant the Syrians their independence and fully abolish the mandate once the war in Europe came to an end. Shortly after the Anglo-French invasion, on 9 September 1941, Prime Minister Churchill addressed the House of Commons, stating: 'We have no ambitions in Syria. We do not seek to replace or supplant France, or substitute British for French interests in any part of Syria. We are only in Syria in order to win the war ... Syria shall be handed back to the Syrians, who will assume at the earliest possible moment their independent sovereign rights.'[21]

FDR's man in Damascus

Roosevelt then took the first step with Syria, appointing a new Consul-General in Damascus, George Wadsworth from New York, in 1942, then sending his trusted aid, General Patrick Hurley, to Damascus in April 1943.[22] What probably accelerated FDR's decision was that in 1940 the Republican presidential candidate, attorney Wendell Willkie, had landed in Damascus to drum up support for the Allies against Nazi Germany amongst the Arabs. He was the first presidential candidate to come to Syria and speak directly to community leaders saying that the USA 'did not recognise the special position of any European State in the Levant'.[23] If the Republicans won the race – which was unlikely due to FDR's thundering popularity – they seemingly already had their eyes on the Middle East.

Hurley, however, who was the most senior US official to visit Damascus since the King–Crane Commission, had arrived in Syria 23 years beforehand, in 1919. An active Republican and decorated soldier, Hurley had served as Secretary of War under President Hoover in 1929–1933. In 1941, he was promoted to brigadier general and dispatched by General George Marshall to the Far East before becoming FDR's personal envoy on a series of assignments, including Syria, aimed at drumming up support for the US war effort. Hurley arrived in Damascus in the midst of a political storm. The pro-French president Taj al-Din al-Hasani, appointed by de Gaulle shortly after the conditional independence of 1941, had died while in office in January, and the Syrians were bracing themselves for parliamentary and presidential elections later that summer. The National Bloc, the leading anti-French movement, was campaigning for office, headed by none other than Quwatli. With cowboy hat and eccentric attire, Hurley was unlike any diplomat the Syrians had ever seen in the Republic's brief history. The Syrians received Hurley with red carpets and held banquets in his honour with veteran members of the National Bloc, who only two years earlier had been branded as pro-Nazi in the USA.[24] Presidential hopefuls, such as the Damascus-based industrialist Khaled al-Azm and Quwatli, rushed to greet the US envoy, sensing a seriousness in his approach, and presented him with petitions that requested unconditional independence from the mandate. Sheikh Abdul Aziz Khani, a proxy for Quwatli, also met with the US general, delivering a confidential letter to be passed on to Roosevelt, believed to have Quwatli's fingerprints all over it. It contained lavish praise for the US President, showering him with compliments for championing freedom and justice in the international community. 'With no doubt, Your Excellency,' Khani wrote, 'the presence of the United States of America under your leadership at the forefront of the democratic world, is the greatest guarantee of success for the principles of justice and freedom.'[25] Khani added: 'All Syrians, who have proven their support for the just cause of the Allies, were pleased with the resumption of parliamentary life in their country. This restores their sovereignty under a constitutional umbrella, and they hope to get their full independence at the peace conference.' Quwatli probably believed that just as was the case in 1919, the Allies would convene a peace conference to map out the future of liberated territories, trying to force Syria onto the international agenda. Khani went as far as to praise 'struggling France' in its war against Germany, hoping that this would score points with the USA, and thank FDR for the 'hospitality of the American government' had shown to Syrian migrants 'living in America, their second home'.[26]

Hurley forwarded Khani's message, which was a clear attempt to write off Quwatli's pro-Nazi past, to FDR, describing the author as, 'a distinguished judge of Damascus'. Hurley wrote on 20 May 1943:

You should be advised, however, that Mohammad Aziz El-Khani has no national office that entitles him to address you officially as the head of government (hinting that this might have been delivered on Quwatli's behalf). The letter, I think, is intended to be rather a private letter to you.[27]

Hurley added,

The letter I am enclosing is typical expression I have received from both Muslim and Christian Arabs. The more I converse with people in the Middle East, the more I am convinced that the American and British influence should be integrated so as to leave no doubt as to the unity of purpose between Great Britain and the United States.

FDR replied on 8 June 1943 with a friendly message, stating:

My dear Mohamed Aziz El-Khani,

It has given me great pleasure to receive the message which you were good enough to entrust to General Patrick J. Hurley for delivery to me.

I can assure you that this warm expression of confidence and support from as distinguished a representative of our noble friends and allies, the Arab peoples, strengthens our hearts and our hands and spurs us with the renewed determination in the task of removing forever from the earth all trace of the Axis tyranny and restoring a world of peace, justice, and good will.

I earnestly hope and trust that the day is not far removed when, in peace, the Syrians will enjoy the blessings of full independence and, together with their Arab brothers, will offer to the world from the rich treasures of a revived Arab culture, splendid intellectual and spiritual contributions of the greatest importance to the happiness and welfare of all mankind.

Believe me, with all good wishes,

Sincerely your friend,

Franklin Delano Roosevelt[28]

Quwatli and Khani were clearly trying to shed all stereotypes about the Presidential candidate's Nazi past, seeing that the Axis Powers were no longer getting the upper hand in Europe. Suheil al-Ashi, Quwatli's military aid recalled, 'Quwatli had full faith in Franklin Roosevelt, convinced that the man was honest in his calls for democracy and wanted to see Syria and other occupied states in the Arab world, independent from European control. The two men had genuine respect for each other, and developed an excellent working relationship during the years 1943–1945.'[29] For his part, Roosevelt was also trying to endear himself to Muslims in general and Arabs in particular, seeing their value for American efforts in the Second World War. By addressing himself to a senior Islamic figure like Judge Khani, FDR was effectively speaking to a legitimate and much respected community leader in Syria who presumably, could do wonders for the USA's image in the Oriental East. Jamil Mardam Bey, a ranking member of the National Bloc, remarked in his memoirs, 'The nationalists, for their part, were pleased that the President of the United States considered them to be a leading force in the country'.[30] By meeting members of the Bloc, Hurley was granting them de facto recognition of the US government, as the legitimate representatives of the people of Syria. Mardam Bey added, 'Although they [the National Bloc leaders] had misgivings about America's Zionist policy, they were preparing the ground for any help they might need from America in event of a clash between Syria and France'.[31]

On a separate front, Quwatli asked his long-time friend Abdul Aziz al-Saud, the King of Saudi Arabia, to talk the USA into changing their perceptions of him, and did the same with Iraqi Prime Minister Nuri al-Said, who was close to the British. The two men controlled the flow of Arab oil and were certainly well received in the Roosevelt White House.[32] A British officer in Baghdad described his encounter with Quwatli, saying: 'He assured me that no Arab of reliability can possibly wish for German victory. Germans, by their treatment of Europeans, have taught the Arabs what they might expect if they came under the influence of these people who have none of the characteristics necessary for the guidance of others.'[33]

During his travels in Iraq and Saudi Arabia, the French issued a warrant for Quwatli's arrest, should he return to Syria, on the grounds of being a 'Nazi agitator'.[34] He was eventually pardoned, however, under the strong lobbying of the British, backed by the USA, returning to run for president in the summer of 1943. The elections eventually played nicely in Quwatli's favour; he filled parliament with deputies for the National Bloc and won the presidency with ease, becoming his country's fourth president on 17 August 1943. The Americans and the British, backed by the Saudis and Iraqis, reasoned that Quwatli would be a strong leader, able and willing to protect their interests in Syria, to reach his ultimate goal of independence. Quwatli, aged 50, hailed from a prominent Damascene family, and had an unblemished financial record and many war medals, having aggressively worked against both the Ottomans and the French since the First World War. America's first encounter with the man dated back to 1919, when he had met Charles Crane and asked for US support to secure the independence of Syria. When asked whether he would support an American mandate in Syria, Quwatli had flatly rejected the idea, saying that if America came to the region as an occupier, it would immediately transform itself into an enemy. Ironically, 14-years later, it was none other than Quwatli who came to a head-on collision with the USA, describing America as 'an enemy' during the presidency of Dwight Eisenhower. A fine patriot, however, he seemed to be the perfect choice for president in 1943, now that he had distanced himself from the Nazis, since other accomplished nationalists, like ex-President Hashem al-Atasi and Abdul Rahman Shahbandar, were either retired or dead.

The Quwatli era

President Shukri al-Quwatli, who ruled Syria from 1943 to 1949, invited the new US Consul Wadsworth to attend his inauguration at the Syrian parliament – refusing, however, to reserve a seat for the de Gaulle's envoy to Syria, General George Catroux. The musical band which played the French national anthem, *La Marseillaise*, was asked to refrain from playing anything non-Syrian, and one of Quwatli's first tasks was to fire the pro-French director of police, ex-Premier Bahij al-Khatib. He immediately started building bridges with the USA, receiving Wadsworth regularly at the presidential palace and affectionately calling him 'Wazwuz'.[35] The US diplomat was always eager to know more about Syria, its past, its ethnic and religious mosaic, its views vis-à-vis the First World War, and its monetary system. At one point, he asked Quwatli's foreign minister, Mardam Bey whether the Syrians intended to seek help from American banks in building their national economy, once the French mandate came to an end.[36] In 1944, Quwatli dispatched Mardam Bey to Baghdad to meet with another trusted Roosevelt aid, Loy Henderson, asking him to do more for the sake of Syrian independence, saying: 'Such an effort would realise Arab unity which in turn would serve the cause of democracy since the Arab countries, comprising around 50 million people, are opposed to Fascism.' If Arab unity were achieved, he added, 'Democracy would have a strong base in the Mediterranean both now and in the future'.[37] Quwatli then aimed higher, appealing directly to Roosevelt with an open letter, which was published in full in all major Syrian daily newspapers:

We trust that the US will not again remain isolated from the affairs of the old world order, but will rather, help to uphold justice and will aid the weak nations. Peace cannot be placed on a permanent basis if colo-nialist and expansionist ambitions are not eliminated. Support Syria's bid to become part of the freedom speaking world community that is in the making. The high principles of freedom and liberty are being put to the test. We trust that this world will not again be deceived by secret and private agreements.[38]

Copies of Quwatli's memo to the US President were sent to British Prime Minister Winston Churchill and Premier Joseph Stalin, America's ally in the Second World War. Roosevelt was late in replying, but wrote to Quwatli in December 1944, referring to an exchange of letters between Mardam Bey and Wadsworth. These exchanges, Roosevelt said, '... have constituted a response intended to define the attitude of the United States Government. I refer par-ticularly in this regard to the State Department's memorandum of October 5, 1944. I believe these documents speak for themselves and I have been glad to hear from Mr Wadsworth that you have found them reassuring.'[39] Quwatli's words, that the USA must not 'remain isolated from the affairs of the old world' seem to have struck a particularly raw nerve with the US president. He elabo-rated in his response, explaining, 'The American people have recently recorded overwhelmingly by their determination, that the United States shall assume its full share of the responsibilities, in cooperation with the nations of like mind, in creating a future of world peace, prosperity, and justice for all. I there-fore have no hesitation in assuring you that my Government will pursue these objectives with all the influence in its command.'[40]

Quwatli grabbed at FDR's good intentions, requesting that Washington upgrade the status of George Wadsworth, who was the US government's politi-cal agent in Damascus, and transform its mission into a fully fledged embassy. Such a gesture, he added, would be well received by the political community in Damascus, since it would indicate a serious US desire to treat Syria as an independent state. Wadsworth conveyed the message to Roosevelt, and the Secretary of State, Cordell Hull, immediately upgraded him to Minister (one step short of an ambassador) on 16 November 1943, much to the pleasure of the Syrians. Shortly afterwards, Quwatli appointed Syria's first Ambassador to Washington, an AUB-trained attorney, Nazem al-Qudsi, who presented his credentials to President Roosevelt in March 1945. Qudsi spoke flawless English and like Shahbandar had received a liberal US education at AUB, firmly con-vinced that Syria needed the support of the Western world to achieve domestic progress in economy, industry, military affairs and education. One of his first tasks in Washington DC was to recommend that Syria purchase property for the Syrian Embassy in the USA, rather than rely on rent, arguing that it needed a prestigious location in 'the new Rome' in order to influence US opinion about the Middle East. Domestically, an old admirer of the USA and another AUB alumnus, Fares al-Khoury, became the Speaker of Parliament under Quwatli. Saadallah Jabiri, an Ottoman-trained statesman from Aleppo, was called upon to create a cabinet, composed of seven Ministers, four of them being members of the National Bloc. Five of the seven were former Prime Ministers. Two spoke flawless English, having been educated, like Khoury and Qudsi, at AUB. They were Education Minister Abdul Rahman Kayyali of Aleppo, and Public Works Minister Tawfic Shamiyya from the Christian quarters of Damascus.

The Quwatli–Roosevelt summit

On 8 February 1945 Quwatli boarded a plane headed to Saudi Arabia, then went to Egypt with King Abdul-Aziz to meet King Farouk, who was scheduled to receive both Winston Churchill and Roosevelt as the two world leaders were heading back home from the Yalta Conference. The 'Big Three' – Churchill, Roosevelt and Stalin had met in Yalta on 4–11 February, to discuss the re-organization of Europe – similar to, yet smaller in scope than – the Paris Conference of 1919. The Third Reich was beginning to collapse, just two months before Hitler committed suicide, and all three leaders were certain that Allied victory was on the horizon. The King of Saudi Arabia, an old family friend of Quwatli, urged him to come to Egypt to meet FDR and Churchill. Quwatli eagerly accepted, as did Roosevelt. With the exception of Faisal, representing Syria although he was not a Syrian, no Syrian leader had met a US President since the collapse of the Ottoman Empire in 1918. Faisal had toyed with the idea of travelling to the USA to meet President Wilson, right after the downfall of his regime in Damascus, but that idea never got past the drawing board, probably due to Wilson's poor health.[41] Quwatli was optimistic about his scheduled meeting with Roosevelt, hopeful that if all the right buttons were pushed, the President would go one step further in applying pressure on France to evacuate from Syria. The French were insisting that before leaving Syria they needed to sign a treaty with its government, granting them military, political and economic privileges in Syria. Quwatli curtly refused such a treaty. Additionally, he was worried about the upcoming conference of the yet-to-be-formed United Nations (UN), the brainchild of FDR, which was scheduled for May 1945, in San Francisco. Syria needed to be there, at any cost, he reasoned, to present its claim to the international community. Deputies in the Syrian Parliament frantically discussed the matter, which was debated on the front pages of Syria's major political dailies.[42] Other countries, which had contributed less to the Allied war effort, had already been invited to become founding members of the UN. Quwatli felt that it was unfair for Syria, who paid the price of battles on its territories, to be absent from the international convention. Only Roosevelt, he believed, could talk the French into lifting their veto over Syria's attendance and only that would test how serious the Allies were about Syrian independence.[43]

Unfortunately for both leaders, due to Roosevelt's deteriorating health, the summit never took place. Roosevelt did manage to meet with Abdul-Aziz, but was rushed back to the USA immediately afterwards and died less than two months later, in April 1945. Quwatli instead met with Prime Minister Churchill on 17 February, at a much publicized summit on the Suez Canal, attended by Abdul Aziz, Farouk, and Haile Selassie, the Emperor of Ethiopia. As predicted, Churchill, who showed up in military uniform, tried talking the Syrian leader into signing a treaty with France, but Quwatli stubbornly refused. One of Quwatli's aids recalled, 'Quwatli went to the meeting with a positive attitude, seeing that Roosevelt and Churchill were two sides of the same coin. If he managed to convince Churchill of his argument, then it meant automatic consent of Franklin Roosevelt'.[44] The British Prime Minister started the meeting, saying: 'The interest of the Allies and the necessity of war requires you to side with France and bring peace and tranquility to this very delicate region.' Quwatli calmly replied, 'We understand what our duty is, Mr Churchill. Please do explain what you mean when you ask us to side with France? You know, more than any other person, that France is an alien within this region and a thorn in our backside. How do you expect us to side with her, and sign a treaty?' Raising his voice, Churchill responded: 'You *must* reach a compromise with France at any cost; do you understand? I am warning Syria specifically that her negative and radical policies during these difficult times will not be tolerated. Do you not understand or see what is going on around you? The entire world is threatened with destruction and entire populations are facing death and extinction. Many things have changed. What we could tolerate in the past, we will not tolerate today. We are facing a terrible world war and must do all that is possible to attain victory.'

Becoming agitated, the Syrian President responded angrily; 'I will not recognise France. I will not sign a treaty with France. I will not compromise no matter what the circumstances. Do *you* understand? What have we done to deserve all this? I swear, and God is a witness of what I am saying, that I will never commit such a crime on Syria. I will not give in to pressure and I will not yield to threats. God has destined us to live in revolt, to live in war, and to live in sacrifice. We will remain that way. We will not give up and we will not give in.' Realizing that the situation was becoming tense, King Abdul-Aziz intervened, along with King Farouk, to calm down the two leaders. Quwatli pointed a finger at the Saudi King and said: 'This man – Abdul-Aziz – is the dearest person to me on the face of this earth. I swear that if he were to force me to sign a treaty with France that contradicts with Syria's desires, I will fight him. Yes, I will fight him. If Abdul-Aziz asked for my eyes I would offer them with no hesitation, yet if he were to ask what you are asking now, I will declare war and fight him.'

Angrily, Churchill asked for a recess, and then adjourned the meeting until the following day, hoping that Quwatli would reconsider his position. The next morning the two men held another meeting, also attended by Abdul-Aziz. Churchill began by telling Quwatli that Great Britain, although an ally of Syria, wanted him to grant France some form of reward for her services in the Levant. This 'reward' he said, would come in the form of a friendship treaty. Quwatli resorted to his earlier tone, reminding the British leader, 'We have already discussed this, Mr Churchill. You know perfectly well that Syria's stance will not change. I have told you that our history with France is filled with revolts, destruction, and blood. Ever since France entered our lands and occupied us by force 24 years ago, she has not had a single day of peace and quiet. We refused her mandate and protested in every possible manner. We resorted to every form of resistance. We even tried diplomacy. We did not find one nation in this "democratic world," however, that was willing to listen. That is why we turned to armed resistance and revolted. And I am telling you, we will continue to revolt if need may come, until we attain our complete independence. We will not accept a treaty with France, and will not accept a nation chained to slavery, humiliation, and colonialism.' Pointing a finger to the sea, he added, 'We will not sign a treaty with France even if the waters of this sea turn red! We are willing to spill enough blood to turn the clear waters red, Mr Churchill.'

The British Prime Minister, steaming at Quwatli's remark, stood up and stormed towards Quwatli, coming face-to-face with the Syrian president, shouting, 'Are you threatening me? Don't you threaten me! Do you know who I am? I am commander-in-chief of the Allied Forces and I will not let anyone in this world threaten or intimidate me.' Churchill was amazed at Quwatli's stubbornness. He was the strongest man in the world at that stage of his career – having almost defeated Nazi Germany – and yet here was the leader of a small country, challenging him. Many years later, Quwatli described the situation saying: 'I swear that for a moment, I thought he was going to strangle me. He instantly turned from an angry man into a mad man.'

Quwatli tried to calm the situation; 'No, Mr Churchill, I am not threatening you. Trust me, I do know who you are, and this is why I am unable to challenge or threaten you. But if I should give what you ask of me, I would be signing my own execution warrant. We are willing to spill enough blood to turn the clear waters red Mr Churchill! My people will never forgive me. The Syrian people, Mr Churchill, have sacrificed their youth, wealth, property, and have fought France for a quarter of a century. They never gave in – not for one single day. All they are asking the Allied powers to do is add them to the list of people who are privileged to live in this new world order that you are creating. Syria deserves the respect of all the world leaders, for she preaches the doctrines that this war was launched for in the first place.' When the two men met again, Churchill was in a calmer mood and agreed to Quwatli's request – mainly no treaty with France – in exchange for 'peace and quiet' in the region, until the war was over. Churchill was a tough patriot and appreciated men of strong moral fibre. He came across with a favourable impression of the Syrian leader – and conveyed it to Roosevelt – wrapping up the meeting saying: 'The Syrians are lucky to have such a leader, Mr President.'[45]

Syria goes to war against Hitler

Injected with new confidence, Quwatli returned to Damascus and addressed the Syrian Parliament to brief them on his encounter with Churchill. Dressed in a dark suit with Ottoman fez, the Syrian leader speaking with a loud booming voice, projected power like no other predecessor, thanks to the USA and Great Britain. There were two trends in London, he noted, improvising with the audience; one being in favour of Syrian independence, headed personally by Churchill, and another more inclined to follow in the footsteps of France, taken by the Foreign Office.[46] Syria was siding with the British Prime Minister, he noted, because he fully understood that Syria would accept nothing short of full and unconditional independence. Taking everybody, including the US President and British Prime Minister, by surprise, Quwatli used the occasion to declare war on Nazi Germany and Fascist Italy.[47] He was now telling the world in no uncertain terms that Syria was now fully and publicly on the side of the Allies and the USA. Roosevelt's efforts at preventing Syria from becoming a Nazi satellite had finally worked. The declaration aroused more than a stir in London, Washington and Damascus. How could a country with no army of its own declare war on the mighty army of Hitler? The move was purely symbolic, Quwatli told his supporters, aimed at giving Syria's application to join the UN a further push. Syria was the mouse that roared, using its gesture to win the minds and hearts of statesmen in London and Washington DC. Churchill and Roosevelt, he argued, would certainly appreciate Syria's position.

He was right. Shortly after Quwatli's war speech, George Wadsworth showed up at the presidential palace in Damascus, telling Quwatli to expect an official invitation to the UN Conference in San Francisco.[48] The Syrian leader had managed to win over the President of the USA.

Before being invited, however, Syria had to sign the United Nations Declaration, which was logistically difficult since its ambassador Nazem al-Qudsi, had not yet arrived in the USA. To speed up the process, Quwatli contacted King Farouk and requested the Egyptian delegate to the USA sign on Syria's behalf. Farouk accepted, and on 12 April 1945 Khoury headed off to San Francisco. On the day of his departure, however, news of Roosevelt's death ripped through Damascus like a cyclone. Upon his return from Yalta, many were shocked to see how old, thin and frail Roosevelt looked as he addressed Congress on March 1 to brief them about his meeting with Churchill and Stalin. He spoke while seated, in an unprecedented concession to his physical incapacity, opening his speech by saying, 'I hope that you will pardon me for this unusual posture of sitting down during the presentation of what I want to say, but . . . it makes it a lot easier for me not to have to carry about ten pounds of steel around on the bottom of my legs'. Roosevelt was by then well known to have polio, but this was his only public mention of his disability. 'The Crimean Conference,' he said firmly, 'ought to spell the end of a system of unilateral action, the exclusive alliances, the spheres of influence, the balances of power, and all the other expedients that have been tried for centuries – and have always failed. We propose to substitute for all these, a universal organisation in which all peace-loving nations will finally have a chance to join.'[49] On 29 March, he went to Warm Springs to rest before heading off to the UN Conference. Two weeks later, he collapsed and died of a massive cerebral haemorrhage, at 3.45pm. Syria's mass circulation daily *al-Ayyam* carried the headline of *The New York Times*: 'Men will thank God on their knees a hundred years from now that Franklin D. Roosevelt was in the White House.' The Syrian newspapers eulogized the man as a true friend of the Arabs, a fine patriot, and a sincere advocate of democracy and human rights. No other world leader had ever received such homage in the Syrian press, not even Wilson, who had died in 1924. Fares al-Khoury, the head of Syria's mission to the UN, wrote: 'We had pinned high hopes on Roosevelt's benevolence in dealing with our affairs. It is he who has the white hand in our independence and in inviting us to the (UN) conference.' Khoury added, 'Our confidence is unwavering, however, in the American people, their sense of fairness, and love of justice'.[50]

Roosevelt goes down in the history of bilateral relations between Syria and the USA as the first US President to take the Syrians seriously, and to genuinely build a relationship based on trust, good faith and honour. Far from being a hypocrite, he believed in Shukri al-Quwatli and sincerely tried to build a friendship between the Syrians and America. That need, he reasoned early on, was to prevent Syria from falling to the Nazis. By 1943–1945, however, Syria was clearly out of the Nazi orbit, yet Roosevelt went further in advancing relations with Damascus, fulfilling his part of an unspoken pact aimed at seeing Syria independent. Syrian history textbooks were kind to the man in the years to come, mentioning him with admiration as one of the world's great leaders who helped to end the Second World War. He helped reposition Syria on the world map, attracting world attention to the plight of ordinary Syrians – and perhaps more importantly, securing Syria's seat at the UN Conference, which opened on 24 May 1945.

5

FREE AT LAST

On 19 May 1945, President Shukri al-Quwatli travelled to Shtura, a sleepy Lebanese town close to the Syrian border, to meet his Lebanese counterpart, Beshara al-Khoury. The two men were old friends and founding members in the national movements of their countries, and Khoury's Prime Minister Riyad al-Sulh was a ranking member of the Syrian National Bloc. Relations with the British, the French and the Americans were discussed at length, and the two leaders agreed neither would enter into talks with the French before a clear commitment to evacuation was given by the Great Powers. Khoury warned his Syrian counterpart not to bet too much on the British and the Americans, noting how both had failed him when the French locked up the Lebanese President, Prime Minister and entire government back in November 1943. 'If they do that in Syria,' Quwatli sneered, 'The French will have Washington and London to deal with; they will be committing political suicide in the Arab world!'[1]

Upon his return to Damascus, however, Quwatli became seriously ill, diagnosed with an ulcer perforation that led to acute internal bleeding. Foreign Minister Mardam Bey rushed to his bedside, and was asked to act as his deputy in state affairs should Quwatli's condition deteriorate. Mardam Bey, trained at the School of Political Science in Paris, was one of the most competent politicians in Syria, having previously served as Prime Minister in 1936–1939, and was a ranking member of the Damascus Office of the National Bloc. With Fares al-Khoury having just landed in the USA and Quwatli recovering, Mardam Bey became the de facto ruler of Syria in mid 1945, and presided over one of the bloodiest events in modern history, that being the French onslaught of 29 May 1945. 'Keep an eye on Wazwuz (Wadsworth)' the President had advised his minister, '... only he knows how to deal with the French and the British.'[2] By 1945, the Syrians had clearly placed all of their bets on the USA.

Mardam Bey and Wadsworth, who were the same age, had developed a strong friendship long before the US diplomat was appointed to Damascus in 1942. According to Munir al-Ajlani, a one-time associate of Mardam Bey, 'Jamil Bey trusted George Wadsworth, and would laughingly tell him: "You are more Syrian now than you are American! We should give you a Syrian passport!"'[3] During the First World War, Wadsworth had taught at AUB and befriended many Syrian notables, who all rose to become national leaders in the 1940s. He had been a good friend of Shahbandar when the latter was serving as Emir Faisal's Foreign Minister in 1920.[4] The US minister had lived and worked in the Middle East since 1914, understood Arabic perfectly yet spoke it with difficulty, knew the region well, and sympathized with its people. To make extra money while working at AUB, he had taken a clerk's job in 1917 at the US Consulate, shortly before joining the US State Department. In 1941, Wadsworth was posted to the US Embassy in Rome during negotiations between the US government and Benito Mussolini, aimed at talking the Italians into staying out of the war – or at least, not joining Hitler. When that failed, Ambassador William Phillips fled the country and Wadsworth stayed behind as Chargé d' Affaires, working with Italian authorities to evacuate embassy staff, before he returned to New York in June 1942.[5]

International affairs, Syria, cigars and golf were four topics that the US minister had in common with Mardam Bey.[6] The US minister explained the complex web of Washington politics to Mardam Bey, who had never been to the USA, and presented him with a full profile of the new US President, Harry S. Truman, who had been sworn into office to replace Roosevelt only days earlier, on 8 May 1945.

The Syrians knew very little about the new President from Missouri, apart from the fact that he had been Roosevelt's running mate in the 1944 elections.[7] When Roosevelt died in April 1945, Truman had only been Vice President for 82 days and had never really had the chance to spend quality time with FDR to hear his advice on international affairs; certainly the two men had not had the chance to discuss Syria. Both Mardam Bey and Quwatli were eager to know more about Truman the person and learn how similar – or different – he would be from his predecessor in dealing with the Middle East. One thing Quwatli and Truman had in common, Wadsworth noted, was a strong relationship with their mothers, whom they relied on for personal and political advice.[8] Everybody in Damascus knew how close Quwatli was to his own mother (popular lore in the Syrian capital said that she had advised him never to execute any person while serving as President.) The two men were avid walkers, added Wadsworth, each in the suburbs of his respective capital,

Damascus or Washington DC. Quwatli's father, however, had been a wealthy landlord from the Damascus nobility, while John Truman was a farmer and a livestock dealer. Truman had grown up playing the piano, and would wake up at 5am every morning to practise, and had worked as a music teacher during his teenage years. Quwatli had a university degree in political science from the prestigious Muluki Academy in Istanbul, while Truman was the only US president in decades without a college degree. He had served in the US Army during the First World War, married the day the Versailles Treaty was signed, and was a long-time friend and business associate of the prominent American Jewish businessman, Edward Jacobson, whom he had served with during the war. Wadsworth warned, 'I hear that Jacobson has open access to the Oval Office and is constantly asking Truman to do something for the Jews of Europe, who have received the most horrific of treatment in Germany.'[9]

Mardam Bey busily took down notes, recording every word Wadsworth said in order to present a full dossier to President Quwatli. Little did they know that just four years later, it would be none other than Truman who would approve the first overseas operation of the Central Intelligence Agency (CIA), which toppled Quwatli and replaced him with Syria's first military ruler, General Husni al-Za'im, shortly after the Palestine War of 1948. From where they saw things in 1945, however, Truman seemed to be a reasonable President, with whom they could do business. The 'other face' of Harry S. Truman was yet to be revealed – the hard way – to the people of Syria.

Armageddon in Damascus

The French, fed up with playing cat-and-mouse with the Syrians, had ordered reinforcements to Syria, determined to muscle its leaders into signing a treaty with the Free French. Demonstrations, particularly in Damascus, had become a daily routine. Young people would take to the streets demanding evacuation of the French and creation of a national army. On 20 May, a worried Mardam Bey invited Wadsworth to government headquarters in Marjeh Square, for another long talk on Syrian–US relations.[10] 'We are trying very hard, George, to keep the situation under control,' he said. 'My government is putting the most ardent effort into maintaining peace and quiet, but that is becoming very difficult, because of French provocations.' The landing of fresh French troops, he added, was 'incompatible' with Syrian independence, and asked Wadsworth to convey Syria's anger to the US State Department and to President Truman. Mardam Bey told Wadsworth that unless the French withdrew the same number of troops as those due to arrive, the Syrian government would break off negotiations with France, as agreed to by Presidents Quwatli and Khoury, and would not be responsible for any anti-French activity on the Syrian street.[11] Wadsworth said his government had already warned the French against such a move in Syria, but in case their calls were ignored by de Gaulle, they would consider taking some 'correction action' noting, however, that Syria must give the USA some time to formulate a response to the French escalation. 'Is Syria going to become another Poland?' Mardam Bey angrily asked the US diplomat, in reference to how the world powers had appeased Hitler at the start of the Second World War.[12] One week later, after violence broke out in the inland towns of Homs and Hama between Syrian youth and the French Army, the two men held another long meeting. Mardam Bey sent a letter to President Truman, via Wadsworth, and another to Prime Minister Churchill, both on behalf of President Quwatli.

Truman was too busy with the UN Conference to mind the turmoil in Damascus but Churchill cordially replied, rather swiftly, saying that he would give 'careful attention' to the crisis, noting, however, 'I cannot see that anything has happened which could possibly justify hostilities or bloodshed as the ones you refer to. Indeed, it is the duty of Syria, as well as the United Nations, to refrain from precipitating any situation which would almost certainly impede the war with Japan.'[13] Churchill failed to realize how grave the situation was in Syria. At approximately 7 pm on Tuesday, 29 May 1945, French officers stationed right across the Syrian Parliament hoisted the French flag and asked Syrian guards to salute; which they categorically refused. Dying for a pretext to strike at the Syrians, the French responded by opening fire on the Syrian troops, gunning them down in cold blood. They stormed the Syrian parliament to arrest its speaker, Saadallah al-Jabiri. The French had clearly snapped, despite all mediation by the British and the Americans, and were bent on bringing down the Quwatli regime by force. The French military commander of Damascus, Colonel Olivia-Roget, had given orders that President Quwatli, Jamil Mardam Bey and Saadallah al-Jabiri were to be arrested.[14] Jabiri had in fact walked out the back door of parliament only a few minutes earlier, so, when the French troops failed to find him, they set his office ablaze, confiscated documents, then bombarded the building with cannon fire. The second bombardment of Damascus since 1920 had begun.

Jabiri had headed back to his room at the Orient Palace Hotel, where the French could not venture due to the heavy presence of American and British guests. Instead, they rushed to government headquarters, where Mardam Bey was giving a press conference. There, they were also hindered due to the presence of reporters from VOA and BBC. French troops surrounded the building, cut off electricity, and began dropping bombs throughout its vicinity to force Mardam Bey into submission. The acting Prime Minister, in panic, attempted to telephone the US President and the ambassadors of both Great Britain and the US, but the French had already cut telephone lines throughout the capital, and sealed off Syria's borders with Jordan, Iraq and Lebanon. The entire cabinet was trapped until night fell upon the burning city. Like bandits, they escaped through the back doors of the Grand Sarail (there was no bombing on Rami Street), and desperately began knocking on doors of anyone brave enough to offer them sanctuary for the night. Mardam Bey and others found their way to the home of Khaled al-Azm, the former Prime Minister, in the Souq Saruja neighbourhood. Azm took in a total of 100 fugitives, including cabinet ministers, parliamentarians, policemen, and ordinary Syrians fleeing the French onslaught.

Mardam Bey stayed at Azm's mansion for a few hours, during which time hundreds of locals came to greet him and offer support to the government. Many had taken up arms to lead a street resistance against the French, headed by the nationalist leader Fakhri al-Barudi. Rumours gripped the capital; the people told Mardam Bey that President Quwatli had been shot by the French and that the entire government had fled to neighbouring Amman. Unable to wait for the ceasefire, Mardam Bey left Azm's house at midnight, heading to the residence of the President in the Afif neighbourhood on the slopes of Mount Qassiyun. Parked at Quwatli's gates was a British tank, commanded by a certain General Clark. Mardam Bey walked in to find a US diplomat by Quwatli's bedside, who had been escorted to the President's home by the British Army. Quwatli was in a nervous fit, shouting at the US official, 'Where is the big army that defeated Hitler?' The diplomat, trying to calm him down, was taken aback at the site of Mardam Bey, who he believed had fled to Amman, bewilderingly offering him foreign protection should he decide to stay in Syria. The offer was flatly rejected by both Quwatli and Mardam Bey, who aggressively told the US representative that they wanted Harry Truman to intervene immediately to put an end to the bloodbath in Damascus.[15] 'When King Faisal left this country twenty-five years ago, he had nothing to lose here – nothing but a throne, which we had created for him, with our own hands!' he famously told his US guest, 'I have roots in this city that go back 400 years, so go tell your government and that of France and Great Britain, that I will not leave Syria no matter what happens! Rather than preach restraint to the Syrians, the British and the Americans could use their considerable influence to pressure the French into a cease-fire!'[16]

Quwatli snapped that the USA should arrest Colonel Olivia-Roget and the commander French officer, General Beynet, and bring them to court as war criminals.[17] The era of diplomacy was over, he added, thanks to General de Gaulle's policies in Syria, noting that in future any person working for the French would be deprived of his nationality and property, and stand trial on charges of high treason before Syrian courts. The US delegate called upon General Beynet in Beirut, who they reported to be in a surprisingly cheerful mood, explaining that several French posts had been attacked, and that the French were only acting in 'self-defence'. Beynet noted, 'The situation in Damascus is not tragic. The abscess of Damascus has to be laced! Now that the barrel had been breached, wine must be drunk!'[18] Meanwhile, Quwatli and Mardam Bey spent the night writing out letters of protest to US and British officials. They addressed every American listed in the directory of the Syrian presidential palace, officials at the White House, the US State Department and congressmen from both parties. At dawn they sent out foot messengers to Riyadh, Cairo and Amman to break the news of the onslaught, since postal services had been closed and telephones had been cut off under French orders. The Egyptian consul Fathi Ridwan managed to reach Beirut, where he contacted King Farouk, who in turn contacted Churchill to complain. The Jordanian consul Abdul Monem Rifaii was shot and injured while en route to Amman via Daraa. Jabiri eventually managed to leave the Orient Palace with the Russian Orthodox Patriarch who was visiting Damascus while en route to Beirut. Jabiri accompanied him by car to the Lebanese border, then got into a Syrian car and drove to the office of Prime Minister Sulh where he held a press conference, telling the world of the 'crime' that had taken place in Damascus, before travelling to Cairo to speak to the Arab League.

By 1 June, 70 per cent of all officers and 40 per cent of all Syrian soldiers in the French-created Levant Army had deserted their posts and taken up arms with the Syrian rebels. Sultan al-Atrash, commander of the revolt of 1925, called on his followers to begin mobilizing for war in order to aid their countrymen in Damascus. In Hama, fierce resistance took place and two French warplanes were downed by Syrian youth, while the commander of a French unit was ambushed and killed.[19] In Hawran, French troops were rounded up, disarmed, and their weapons distributed to young men volunteering to march towards Damascus to help the central government. For his part, Wadsworth played a monumental role in May 1945, channelling messages back and forth between his government, the British and the Syrians. He was clearly furious at what the French had done to Syria but, unlike the case in 1925, his anger was not a result of targeted US interests in Syria. Instead, it was born out of a sincere belief that Syria had been wronged by the Free French, who should be forced, by the USA, to halt the offensive on the residents of Damascus. The

British were of the same view, and, on 30 May 1945, Winston Churchill sent a message to Truman:

> The continuance of the present situation (in Syria) will cause more grave trouble throughout the Middle East and upon our joint line of communications via Egypt and the Canal with the Far East. We should therefore be prepared to order the commander-in-chief, Middle East, to intervene to stop the fighting. Before doing so I feel I ought to know that we should have your support and approval.[20]

He added, 'In view of the continued deterioration, His Majesty's Government has no alternative but to act'.[21] The British were instructed to prevent the landing of more French troops on Syria although Benyet had done nothing to prevent the shelling of Damascus on the night of 31 May. British forces finally arrived in Damascus, fully backed by the USA – much to Quwatli's pleasure – on 1 June 1945, and immediately implemented the ceasefire. Upon arriving at the Syrian capital, the British cabled London: 'The city has been subjected to fire and much looting by Senegalese during morning. HM Minister has in no way exaggerated the damage done to the city. The scene is one of wanton destruction.'[22] They advised that the two French generals, Beynet and Olivia-Roget, be evacuated immediately from Syria, since the British could not guarantee their safety. The French troops began their long journey back home, under British pressure, after an overstayed welcome that lasted for 26 long years. The French mandate was in its final stages.

Truman's approval for British intervention came 24 hours later and the British issued a famous ultimatum to the French, asking them to enforce an immediate ceasefire in Syria. French authorities were furious at the British and American attitude, and unleashed much of their anger against Wadsworth. Loy Henderson, the US Minister to Iraq, defended his colleague against French charges by saying that he had defended the views of the US government 'with great clarity' while William Philips, special assistant to the US Secretary of State, said that Wadsworth had 'maintained exactly the right approach' in dealing with the crisis in Syria.[23] Immediately after the ceasefire came into effect, Quwatli cabled Khoury in the USA, asking him to present the matter to the UN Security Council. 'Abu Suhail, what kind of a United Nations organisation are they creating in the US, given what is happening in Damascus? Go to Truman and tell him that the French have ploughed the land in Syria, over our heads!'[24]

Khoury's stay in the USA had proven to be much longer than most Syrians expected. He served as head of the Syrian mission to the UN from 1945–1948, presiding twice, in his country's rotating capacity, over the Security Council. Using flawless English he had learned at AUB, and building on a political career that dated back to Ottoman times, the seasoned statesman passionately defended Syria's case before the General Assembly in back-to-back speeches with the Lebanese and Saudi Arabian diplomats at the UN. He also befriended congressmen left and right, both Republican and Democrat, along with representatives of the Great Powers, and Arab migrants living in the USA. He was even granted an audience with Truman at the White House (a ceremonial photo session, so unimportant, apparently, that Khoury fails to even mention it in his memoirs). Referring to Article 14 of the UN Charter, Khoury called on the Security Council take action against the French to end their 25-year presence in Syria. 'There is no justification for the continued presence of the French' Khoury boomed at the UN pulpit, 'now that hostilities in Europe have come to an end.' Their continued presence, he added, 'contradicted with the very spirit in which the United Nations had been formed'. The US representative to the UN, Edwin Pauley, backed Khoury's claim, inducing a resolution that stated:

> The Security Council takes note of the declarations made by the four parties as well as by the other members of the Council, expresses its firm hope that the foreign troops stationed in Syria and Lebanon will be withdrawn as soon as possible to do so and that negotiations to this end will be undertaken without delay by the parties concerned, asks these parties to keep it informed of the result of these negotiations.[25]

On 1 June, the representatives of the USA and Great Britain, along with a British officer, called on the Syrian president at the palace. Assembled were Mardam Bey, Lebanese Foreign Minister Henri Pharoan, Riyad al-Sulh and Jabiri. The British officer officially informed Quwatli that his army had now taken control of Syria and would restore law and order, asking for the Syrian government's cooperation. He asked Quwatli to impose a 7pm curfew on all citizens – which he promptly did – and coordinate any future actions with Truman and Churchill.[26] Quwatli sent messages of gratitude to both men, while Mardam Bey cabled his US counterpart Dean Acheson and the British, Anthony Eden. The first to reply was Eden, who wrote: 'I was glad to receive Your Excellency's message in the name of the Syrian government and should like to thank you for it. We must now work together to secure a fair solution to all the outstanding questions that will, I hope, give every satisfaction to all parties concerned.'[27] Truman and Churchill began toying with the idea of holding a tripartite meeting in London regarding Syria and Lebanon, to be attended by the British, the French and the USA. De Gaulle, furious that the two men were meddling in his own backyard, called for a wider conference, to include China and the USSR, which would discuss the future of the Middle East at large, and not just Syria and Lebanon.[28] Feeling that the two leaders were bent on forcing him to abandon France's colonies in the Levant, he was determined not to leave until he could take the British with him. If France's colonies were going to be discussed, de Gaulle implied, then so were those of the British. Churchill responded at the House of Commons on 5 June: 'The sense of General de Gaulle's speech was to suggest that the whole trouble in the Levant was due to British interference. So far from stirring up agitation our whole influence has been used to precisely the other direction.'[29] Quwatli snapped that Syria would refuse the outcomes of any conference, be it three or six great powers, if the Syrians were not invited to attend. Instead of such a conference, he suggested a tripartite summit, between himself, Harry Truman and Winston Churchill, which would take place at some neutral territory, either Cairo or Geneva.[30] The logistics of such a meeting, the two leaders noted, were difficult, due to everybody's preoccupation with the final stages of the Second World War.

Churchill's brief interlude with Quwatli in February 1945, and the fact that the USA had helped the British end the onslaught in Damascus, did not mean that London or Washington were willing to befriend the Syrians – or treat them as political equals. The polite rebuff was intended to bring Quwatli back to earth by telling him not to get his hopes up with regard to a Syrian–American or Syrian–British honeymoon. Back home, the transfer of the administrative powers, from the French to Syria, began on 1 August 1945. On 4 August, the French transferred the entire cavalry brigade to Syrian authorities. On 12 August, the Military Club became Syrian property, and a few days later the Military Hospital was given to Syria. By the end of August, the Syrians had taken over military headquarters, all government buildings, military bases all over the country, the air force building, the Arwad Island, the Citadel of Damascus and the Citadel of Aleppo. President Quwatli declared 1 August the official day of the creation of the Syrian Army, registering it as an official holiday.[31] On 20 August, it was announced that the Troupes Spéciales, who had just been transferred to Syrian control, would be renamed the Syrian National Army and placed under the direct authority of the President of the Republic, who would also serve as Commander-in-Chief of the Syrian Army.

Khoury returned briefly to Syria to take part in the national celebrations, and due to his excellent relations with world leaders – especially the USA – he was called upon to form a new cabinet for Syria. The cabinet was created on 24 August and included prominent friends of the USA, such as Muhsen al-Barazi, the Minister of Interior, and Ahmad Sharabati, an MIT-trained engineer who was the local agent for General Motors in Syria. This cabinet presided over the final stage of evacuation of French troops, which ended on 15 April 1946. Two days later, on 17 April, the Syrians celebrated their first Independence Day. At 9.30am, a 21-cannon salute was fired from all the castles around Damascus, indicating that the French had finally left. The celebrations started with church bells and calls of 'Allahu Akbar' (God is Great) from mosques. The President of the Republic paraded through the capital in a convertible, waving to cheering crowds as the band played the new national anthem. A spectacular military parade was held on Beirut Street, which was led by seven soldiers, holding seven Arab flags (Egypt, Jordan, Saudi Arabia, Lebanon, Iraq and Palestine). Then came Syrian knights on white horses, while the Iraqi Air Force hovered above, on behalf of the Syrian Army, writing 'SYRIA' in steam across the skies of Damascus. Then came Syrian Police, followed by the Syrian Boy Scouts and veteran warriors from the Revolt of 1925, dressed in traditional garb. Schoolgirls in white came up to the podium and presented the guests with Damascene flowers, followed by representatives of each Syrian province, giving the President a small silk sack, filled with soil of each Syrian city. Collectively the guests raised the Syrian flag while Wadsworth applauded nearby, seated with foreign dignitaries celebrating what the Syrians have since called, 'Eid al-Jala'a' (The holiday of emancipation).

The other face of Harry Truman

In November 1945, Loy Henderson arranged for a meeting between all US diplomats in the Middle East and President Truman. By then Hitler had killed himself and the USA had dropped atomic bombs over Hiroshima and Nagasaki in Japan, forcing the Japanese Emperor to surrender, effectively ending the Second World War. Relations had begun to sour between the US government and its wartime ally, the Soviet Union. Wadsworth flew back to Washington, and after briefing Truman on the situation in Syria, warned that unless the USA take the lead in Syria, they ran the high risk of losing their influence with the Soviet Union.[32] This was to be Wadsworth's last mission as Minister to Syria. He was recalled back to the USA on 8 February 1947, and subsequently made his country's ambassador to Turkey. In Damascus, he was replaced by the skilled and eloquent Paul H. Alling, in April 1945.[33]

Alling, a veteran soldier from the First World War, had served as his country's vice consul in Beirut in 1924–1928 and held office briefly in Damascus during the Great Revolt, from 1926–1927. Like Wadsworth, he knew Syria well, was well-versed in Arabic, and sympathized with the country's nationalist aspirations. For Mardam Bey and Quwatli, no choice could have been better for Harry Truman. In 1945, Alling became a diplomatic agent to Morocco, before being appointed to replace Wadsworth in Syria. Although appointed and sworn into office, Alling never came to Damascus. A last-minute decision at the State Department reasoned that he would better serve his country's interest at the US Embassy in Karachi, which was established in the summer of 1947. Alling headed off to Pakistan and instead, another diplomat, James Hugh Keeley from California, was sent to Syria.

Keeley's tenure in Syria was to be the stormiest yet for a US diplomat in Damascus, witnessing the start of a series of coups and counter-coups that rocked the Syrian capital, starting in March 1949. Now that the USA had helped Syria declare independence, the nature of the relationship had shifted, seemingly overnight. Gone were the days of clear US sympathy for Syria, mirrored by the policies of men like Crane, Wadsworth and Roosevelt. As an independent state – and a founding member of the UN – Syria was now expected to deliver on a series of issues that were vital to US interests in the Middle East; mainly oil and the creation of the State of Israel in 1948. There was no third party such as France or Great Britain overshadowing bilateral relations after 1946, making the relationship more transparent – and difficult – for both parties. Apart from his deep interest in Zionist aspirations in Palestine, Truman effectively knew and cared very little about the Arab world and its long history. The Syrian President, trained in politics under the Ottoman Empire, was trying hard to understand what this new world power was all about. Great powers, Quwatli believed, had imperial ambitions, like the Ottomans, the British, and the French. Could it be that this one – the USA – was really any different from all mighty nations that had preceded it? Would an alliance between Syria and the USA come with strings attached for the politicians in Damascus? Quwatli spoke almost no English, had never been to the USA, and relied mainly on advice of those more seasoned than him in international affairs, such as Mardam Bey and Khoury. They knew the USA, and always told him nothing but good things about it, as a land of freedom of opportunity, good faith and good deeds, which had saved the world from Hitler and freed Syria from the French. For that, Quwatli was willing to give America the benefit of the doubt, treating it with admiration and respect – until it proved him wrong, orchestrating the *coup d'état* of 1949 in Damascus – sending him to jail and bringing down his entire government. Harry Truman, who like Quwatli cherished his mother and always sought her good advice, proved to be anything but the saviour for the political elite in Damascus that they had believed in 1945.

6

THE SYRIAN MUSSOLINI

James Keeley was appointed 'Envoy Extraordinary and Minister Plenipotentiary' to Syria on 8 October 1947 – 16 months after the country achieved its independence from France. He was the second US Minister to Syria since bilateral relations were established in 1944, and the first in the post-French era. Prior to his appointment, Keeley had been a junior diplomat in Beirut in the 1920s. During the Great Revolt of 1925, the young Keeley had hired a car and travelled alone to the troubled Druze Mountain to meet with tribal chiefs working with the revolt commander, Sultan al-Atrash. On returning to Beirut, he reported on what he had witnessed among the Druze, and the boiling anti-French sentiment in Syria, to the US State Department. The French, who came across Keeley's report, were furious, declaring him *persona non grata* and promptly expelling him from both Syria and Lebanon. His superiors at the State Department eventually negotiated a settlement with the French, allowing him to return to the region, provided that his duties were restricted to consular affairs.[1] Like many American officials who came to Syria before him, Keeley was also highly sympathetic to the Syrian case and wanted to help the country rebuild after 26 years of French occupation. He had no clue that his tenure, which lasted until 1950, would be filled with covert and highly undiplomatic conduct; toppling the democratically elected President of the Republic and replacing him with a military officer who looked, sounded and acted like Benito Mussolini.

Upon his arrival in Damascus in the autumn of 1947, Keeley supervised the design and construction of a new US ambassador's residence in the Syrian capital, in the elite residential district of al-Rawda, which continues to serve as the residence until the time of writing in 2010. Speaking to Imad Moustapha, the Syrian Ambassador to Washington in 2006, Keeley's son Robert recalled, 'When my father came back to Syria in October 1947 as the first US representative to the newly found republic, he was hailed as a hero because of the past incident between him and the French. Those were the happiest days in the life of my parents who dearly loved Syria and enjoyed their post in Damascus. But a tragic incident happened that had a very negative impact on my father and caused him deep sorrow that lasted for decades after he had left Syria and retired from the Foreign Service.'[2] Keeley was referring to his father's encounter with General Husni al-Za'im, the Chief of Staff of the Syrian Army during the first Arab–Israeli War of 1948.

Breakdown of the Quwatli regime

The post-independence years were difficult for Syria. After 400 years of Ottoman rule, followed by 26 years of French occupation, the Syrians suddenly found themselves free at last, with very little knowledge of how to run state affairs on their own. The country had been patriotically yet superficially held together in the long fight against colonial rule, but once the French had left Syria in 1946, most decision makers had no clue on where to take things. The entire political class was drawn from the urban notability that had survived the upheavals of the past 30 years; big landowning families from the urban interior; Damascus, Aleppo, Homs and Hama. Minorities were almost completely absent from political posts, although strongly represented in the newly formed Syrian Army. Government investment poured into the big urban cities, mainly Damascus and Aleppo, while rural districts and the Syrian coast received very little government attention or subsidies. The country suddenly found itself torn apart by internal rivalries, between civilians and officers on one front, and between urban dwellers and peasants on the other.

Most Syrians were young – below the age of 25 – while the politicians in power, Shukri al-Quwatli and his generation, were all in their mid-fifties. The National Bloc, which commanded the Syrian street in the 1930s, was dissolved after independence and renamed the National Party. The new party was founded by one-time members of the Damascus Office of the National Bloc, and pledged its loyalty to President Quwatli. Its leadership included the attorney Sabri al-Asali, a Quwatli protégé who was close to the Saudis, Lutfi al-Haffar, a former Prime Minister and Deputy President of the Damascus Chamber of Commerce, and Fares al-Khoury. A notable exception from Aleppo was Saadallah al-Jabiri, Quwatli's long time comrade who had served as parliament Speaker and Prime Minister during the years 1943–1946. These ageing politicians, who had drawn their popular base from university students and urban dwellers during the mandate, were suddenly too old and unattractive for a rising generation of young Syrians, who wanted younger leaders who better mirrored their own political aspirations. Immediately after independence, young men in their thirties and early forties began to challenge Quwatli's generation, those such as Nazem al-Qudsi and Rushdi al-Kikhiya from Aleppo, and Akram al-Hawrani, head of the Arab Socialist Party, from Hama. Jabiri, an enigmatic nationalist with unwavering loyalty to the President, died shortly after independence, in 1947, transforming the National Party into a political machine for the Damascus political and business elite. On the whole, the party was close to Saudi Arabia and Egypt – just like Quwatli – and therefore, automatically hostile to the Hashemite dynasties in Iraq and Jordan. On a larger scale, the National Party was close to the USA, which had helped it achieve independence in 1946. The Hashemites, after all, still harboured the dream of ruling a kingdom from Damascus and worked relentlessly on regaining King Faisal's lost throne in Syria. Faisal had died in 1933 but his elder brother, King Abdullah of Jordan, and only grandson, King Faisal II of Iraq, were adamant in uniting Iraq, Syria and Jordan under the Hashemite crown. They found strong allies in a rising political class in Aleppo, which was geographically close to Iraq, and longed for a union with Baghdad. A powerful opposition to Quwatli soon emerged in Aleppo following Jabiri's death, revolving around Qudsi and Kikhiya, and manifested itself in a political machine that preached Aleppine interests, called the People's Party. Quwatli, a long time opponent of the Hashemite family, insisted that if any union was to be made, it would be built on republican values rather than monarchial ones, and claimed that Jordan and Iraq should be incorporated into Syria under his leadership, and not the other way around. Other parties that emerged in the post-French era, with agendas very different from that of Quwatli, were the Muslim Brotherhood, the Syrian Social Nationalist Party (SSNP), the Arab Socialist Party, the Baath Party and the Syrian Communist Party (SCP).

In 1947, Quwatli committed the monumental mistake of amending the Syrian Constitution to allow for his re-election as President. The move infuriated the opposition, and a nation-wide campaign was launched to bring down the Quwatli regime through the ballots. In the parliamentary elections of 1947, the National Party won only 24 of the 127 seats in parliament, testimony to how unpopular its leaders had become, while 50 seats went to independents, and 53 were taken by the opposition based in Aleppo and rural Syria. Several candidates on Quwatli's list, such as the doctor Sabri Qabbani and the merchant Anwar al-Shallah, were strongly defeated at the polls while veterans such as Asali and Haffar were only just re-elected.[3] Former friends such as Munir al-Ajlani now shifted to the opposition, while veterans such as ex-president Hashem al-Atasi retired from political life, disgusted with the manner in which the President was handling Syrian domestics. The opposition was strengthened with powerful politicians such as Sami Kabbara, publisher of the anti-Quwatli daily *al-Nidal*, Baath Party founders Michel Aflaq and Salah al-Bitar, the Aleppo attorney Rashad Barmada, and Shahbandar's long time ally, former Prime Minister, Hasan al-Hakim. Akram al-Hawrani, the godfather of modern socialism in Syria, won with 10,856 of the 18,502 votes in the conservative city of Hama, overshadowing the large landowning families who had been firmly in power for more than 500 years.

Quwatli banked on his nationalist credentials, however, and the political cunning of men such as Mardam Bey and Khoury, and eventually managed to amend Article 68 of the Constitution, securing a second term at the presidential palace. Khoury was re-elected speaker on 27 September 1947 and Mardam Bey was asked to form a new cabinet. It included seasoned statesmen who were coloured pro-West, such as the lawyer Said al-Ghazzi, who became Minister of Economy, Muhsen al-Barazi, a pro-American attorney who became Minister of Interior, and Ahmad Sharabati, an MIT trained engineer who worked as the business agent for General Motors in Syria, as Minister of Defence. Mardam Bey himself held on to the Ministry of Foreign Affairs.

Syrian–US relations, however, began to deteriorate in the immediate post-independence era, fuelled by growing fear and mistrust of the increasing influence of the SCP, which was on good terms with Quwatli. The party had been originally founded as the Communist Party of Syria and Lebanon in 1924, recruiting an enigmatic ideologue, Khaled Bakdash, in 1930. Bakdash, a Damascene Kurd educated at the Communist University of the Toilers of the East in Moscow, became Secretary General of the party in 1936, the same year that he joined a National Bloc delegation in Paris, negotiating an independence treaty with the French government. Under his leadership, the party opposed the Vichy French in Syria, and in reward, was licensed by mandate authorities during the era of the Free French. It presented itself as part of the Syrian political fabric, a nationalist party committed to expelling the French from Syria, attracting an army of followers among university students and professors, high school teachers, and women from the middle class of Damascus who sought to emancipate themselves from male-dominated society. Bakdash's role in Syrian society, tolerated by the USA during their war-time alliance with Moscow in 1943–1945, became suddenly dangerous and unwelcome in 1947. Several of Quwatli's aids whispered that Bakdash's influence spelled trouble, especially for the USA. Quwatli refused, however, to take any action against the SCP, claiming that they had committed no wrong and were abiding by the laws that regulated political life in Syria. When Quwatli approached the USA in 1947, requesting arms for his newly created army, the US Congress refused, probably fearing that Syria was in the early stages of becoming a Soviet satellite.

The Truman administration viewed Syria in terms of its strategic location in the heart of the Middle East, 'athwart oil pipelines and air routes, its possible role in a crisis as an area of ingress from the Eastern Mediterranean, and the vigorous activity of its government and people in the politics and cultural life of the Arab World'.[4] Five years later, in April 1952, the National Security Council (NSC) outlined its policies towards the region through resolution 129/1 titled, 'United States objectives and policies with respect to the Arab states and Israel'. The NSC targets were listed as:

1. To overcome or prevent instability that threatens the West's interests in the region.
2. To prevent the extension of Soviet influence and to enhance the West's influence.
3. To ensure that the resources of the area (oil) are available to the United States and its allies for use in strengthening the free world.
4. To strengthen the will and ability of these countries to resist possible future aggression by the USSR.

To do all of the above, the USA needed stability and an ultimate peace treaty in the region, two elements that could not be achieved with the increasingly uncooperative regime of Shukri al-Quwatli.[5]

The Tapline Crisis

The second reason for US concern at the state of affairs in Syria was Quwatli's refusal to license the Trans-Arabian Pipeline (Tapline), an oil pipeline running from Qaisumah in Saudi Arabia to Sidon in Lebanon, through Syria. Construction of Tapline, reportedly the world's largest oil pipeline supply, had begun in 1947, months after Syria had won independence. It was mainly managed by the US company, Bechtel, and originally scheduled to terminate in Haifa, which was still under control of the British mandate in Palestine. Due to hostilities on the Palestinian front as a result of repeated clashes between Arabs and Jews, an alternate route was sought through Syria, via the Golan Heights. The Tapline affair created a storm of controversy in the Syrian press and parliament. Politicians were sharply divided on whether Syria should accept or obstruct the oil company's transit request. The company, after all, was a direct threat to the powerful Iraqi Petroleum Company (IPC), operating in the region for decades and jointly owned by some of the world's largest oil companies – none of them being US. The largest single shareholder was the British government-controlled Anglo-Persian Oil Company, which by 1914 held 50 per cent of the shares, followed by Royal Dutch/Shell. After the First World War, US oil companies were allowed to buy into the oil giant and in 1925, IPC got its first concession in Iraq, next to the oil-rich city of Kirkuk. Quwatli feared that if Tapline was empowered through Syrian territory, this would upset IPC and the British – who had helped Syria achieve its independence, more so than the USA. He also feared that Syrian public opinion would reject Tapline on its territory, seeing it as a new form of indirect foreign economic control. The USA was furious, repeatedly trying to talk Quwatli into changing course, with little success. He felt Syria should simply not get involved in any business disputes between the USA and the UK.

Syria and the Palestine War

The USA's support for Israel in May 1948 was the third source of agitation between Syria and the USA – and exploded during the Truman years. Quwatli was angered with the UN Partition Plan for Palestine, issued in November 1947, and the USA's support for carving Palestine into Arab and Jewish states. The Partition Plan, or UN General Assembly Resolution 181, was approved by a vote of 33 to 13, with 10 abstentions, on 29 November 1947. Syria naturally voted against the plan, while the USA strongly supported it. The USA had recommended a temporary UN trusteeship for Palestine, once the British Mandate ended in May 1948. On 15 May 1947, the UN appointed a committee, UNSCOP, with 11 states – none of them being Great Powers – to survey the situation in Palestine. UNSCOP released its findings in August, recommending that Great Britain terminate its mandate and grant independence as soon as possible. A majority of nations, Australia, Canada, Czechoslovakia, Guatemala, Netherlands, Peru, Sweden and Uruguay, recommended the creation of independent Arab and Jewish states, with Jerusalem to be placed under international administration. A minority including India, Iran and Yugoslavia, called for a federal union, based on the US model, for Palestine.

According to the Partition Plan, the land allocated to the Arab state was approximately 43 per cent of Mandatory Palestine, consisting of all the highlands, except for Jerusalem, plus one third of the coastline. The Jewish state was to receive 56 per cent of Mandatory Palestine, a larger area to accommodate the increasing number of Jewish immigrants arriving from Europe. The bulk of the proposed Jewish State's territory, however, consisted of the Negev Desert, and sole access to the Red Sea. Syria flatly rejected the plan, arguing it violated the rights of the Arabs in Palestine. Sixty-seven per cent of the inhabitants, around 1.2 million people, were not Jewish after all, and the Jews constituted only 608,000 people. President Truman noted in his memoirs: 'The facts were that not only were there pressure movements around the United Nations unlike anything that had been seen there before, but that the White House, too, was subjected to a constant barrage. I do not think I ever had as much pressure and propaganda aimed at the White House as I had in this instance. The persistence of a few of the extreme Zionist leaders – actuated by a political motive and engaging in political threats – disturbed and annoyed me.'[6]

The Syrians began to prepare for war 24 hours after the Partition Plan was passed at the UN. In November 1947, they co-sponsored the Arab Liberation Army (ALA), a volunteer force of Arab recruits sent for guerilla war in Palestine. The Syrians provided the ALA with money, arms and recruits, including two parliamentarians, Abdulsalam Ujayli, a physician and novelist, and Akram Hawrani. The ALA was commanded by a Syrian officer named Fawzi al-Qawikji, and counted among its prominent members Adib al-Shishakli, who was to become the President of Syria in the 1950s. On 15 May, the Syrian Army went to war in Palestine, right after David Ben Gurion announced the creation of Israel. Eleven minutes after Ben Gurion's declaration, Truman offered recognition to the State of Israel, shattering any goodwill that had existed earlier between Damascus and Washington DC. Official US recognition did not come until 31 January 1949 but by then the Syrians were officially at war in Palestine and anti-American sentiment was soaring on the Syrian street.

Demonstrators took to the streets of every major Syrian city, chanting anti-American slogans. Synagogues were attacked in Damascus and Aleppo, while American flags were burned in Damascus, along with posters of President Truman.[7] The Syrians, government and public alike, felt betrayed by the USA. Nothing mirrored their feelings better than the slogan used in popular demonstrations: 'Ya Truman ya wadi' shu zanb al-tifl al-radi?' (Truman O Low Grade Man, what is the crime of the infant child?) The offices of General Motors were set ablaze by angry rioters, and 24-hour security was deployed at the residence of Minister Keeley, who now feared for his life. What made matters worse for the troubled US administration was that the Quwatli government did not lift a finger to stop the demonstrators. On 24 February 1949, the Egyptians signed an armistice agreement with Israel, followed by the Lebanese on 23 March, and the Jordanians on 3 April. Syria curtly refused to sign off on an end to battle with Israel, and categorically refused to attend the peace talks in Rhodes, only adding to American disappointment with the Syrian president.

The US and Husni al-Za'im

Historians have argued on whether the first *coup d'état* in Syria was a brainchild of the USA, or whether the USA simply supported al-Za'im when he approached them with the idea in early 1949. We do know that rising communist influence in Syria, Tapline, and the armistice talks with Israel were the three factors that accelerated the coup and made it perfectly reasonable for US decision-makers to back it. According to Minister Keeley's son, 'In 1948, the Commander of the Syrian Army, General Husni al-Za'im, approached the US embassy in Damascus, telling them in secret that he was planning a *coup d'état* against President Shukri al-Quwatli. The Americans were very supportive of this idea given the fact that Husni al-Za'im had promised to sign a peace treaty with Israel. Contrary to all allegations, we were not behind al-Za'im's coup. We did not plan for it, and did not offer it any material support. But when he approached us about it, we encouraged him, and told him we will support his military take-over.'[8] Miles Copeland, the CIA officer at the US Embassy in Damascus, recounted a very different story in his landmark book, *The Game of Nations,* which was published 20 years after the al-Za'im coup, in 1969. According to Copeland when dialogue between the USA and Quwatli became impossible in 1948, a 'political action task force' was created to bring down Quwatli, headed by Major Stephan Meade, an assistant military attaché at the US Embassy in Damascus. Copeland claims that he wrote to the CIA and US State Department, saying, 'If you cannot change the board, then change the players'.[9] He confessed to having 'searched for a man, preferably an officer, who would have more power in his hands than any other Arab leader ever had before'. This was needed, he added, in order for this officer to make what he described as 'an unpopular decision' such as peace with Israel, adding, 'The only kind of leader who can acquire such power is one who deeply desires power for the mere sake of it. Husni al-Za'im was power crazy.'[10]

Husni al-Za'im was born into a Kurdish family in 1888 and began his career as a junior officer in the Ottoman Army, shifting into the French-created Troupes Spéciales after the mandate was imposed in 1920. He rose to the rank of colonel under the French, siding with Vichy France against the Free French in 1940–1941. When de Gaulle took Damascus during the Second World War, al-Za'im was discharged from the army, for receiving illegal funds from Vichy, and briefly jailed at an infamous prison in the ancient city of Palmyra. He roamed the streets of Damascus penniless and unemployed in the mid-1940s, begging friends in high places to talk Quwatli into enlisting him in the Syrian Army. Under the urging of Muhsen al-Barazi, one of the President's top ministers, al-Za'im was eventually brought back into uniform, despite his blemished financial past and repeated rumours of homosexuality. Al-Za'im showed unwavering loyalty to his new boss and rapidly rose in rank to become Director of Military Police, and eventually, army commander during the war of 1948. Skilled in military affairs, popular with the officers and ostensibly loyal to the regime, Quwatli felt that he would come into handy if Mardam Bey's authority crumbled during the Palestine War. Only al-Za'im, Quwatli reasoned, would keep the army and the street under control if the country hovered on the edge of rebellion.

We do not know how many times the USA met with al-Za'im, or when the secret talks began between him and Stephan Meade. The US Mission in Damascus was essentially divided on whether to encourage a coup or not in Syria, many claiming that it was professionally wrong and unethical to involve themselves with Syrian domestics. The CIA had only just been established in 1947 and never before had it carried out an overseas operation; certainly nothing of this magnitude. Keeley and the US State Department began to accept the idea with 'mild enthusiasm' while Deane Hilton, a young diplomat, remained vehemently opposed to it, claiming that the USA should never support a military regime, not even a temporary one, in Damascus. Keeley hoped that after a brief military interlude, where all of the USA's concerns would be properly addressed, Syria would restore its parliamentary regime, and rid itself of military rule. Husni al-Za'im made it clear to the USA, from day one, that he did not plan to do that soon 'if' he came to power. He promised to put corrupt politicians in jail, to reorganize government, bring social and economic reforms, and 'do something constructive about the Arab–Israel problem'.[11]

During the weeks preceding the coup, al-Za'im had at least six meetings with Meade, briefing him in 'great detail' on his plans to seize power in Syria.[12] He also strangely conveyed the same message to the French and the British missions in Damascus.[13] Abdullah al-Khani, a young employee at the presidential palace, recalled having dinner with French embassy staff on the eve of the coup, and having been advised by one lady 'to go to bed early' because 'something major' was going to happen in Damascus.[14] Mardam Bey and Khaled al-Azm, Quwatli's new Prime Minister, both warned him that al-Za'im was planning a coup, but strangely, the President refused to believe all rumours, insisting that Husni al-Za'im was 'our son'.

According to one account, Meade and his superior officer, Colonel Lawrence Mitchell, knew in advance of al-Za'im's plans to bring down the Quwatli regime. In his seminal work *The Road Not Taken*, Itamar Rabinovich claims that al-Za'im continued to meet with Meade even after the coup was launched, where they would have 'discussions in an atmosphere of intimacy and familiarity not typical of talks between a country's ruler and head of state and an assistant military attaché, albeit of a superpower'.[15] Keeley had less frequent meetings with al-Za'im, preferring to channel messages to him through Stephan Meade. According to official US documents, al-Za'im met Meade on 3–7 March 1949, and showed he was willing to go to great lengths to obtain direct or indirect US assistance for the coup he was planning to launch in Syria. He claimed he wanted 'to see his country military allied with the United States,' adding that a strong and stable government – in his own words – 'a dictatorship', would give the USA 'a reliable and permanent authority with whom to deal in Syria'.[16]

During numerous meetings with US officials, al-Za'im outlined a four-phase plan to topple the Quwatli regime. In the first phase, he would seize power and install a political figure as head of state, while exercising real power from behind the curtains of the Ministry of Defence. Coinciding with the first phase, he noted, 'would be a general communist round-up', promising to send anti-US politicians 'to desert concentration camps'.[17] Al-Za'im gladly gave Meade a long list of communist officers in the Syrian Army and Meade, impressed at al-Za'im's collaboration, gave instructions to ensure the latter's personal safety 'at all times'.[18] Once rid of Quwatli, al-Za'im hoped for US military aid as part of his second phase. That aid, he stressed, must arrive after he came to power, not before, to empower himself before the Syrian public and legitimize his regime in the Arab neighbourhood. American technical and training missions would follow in phase three, particularly in the fields of aviation and armour, while phase four would be dedicated to mobilization of the entire country, under his military supervision, including expansion of the army and enforcement of social reforms. He cited Kemal Atatürk as his model, promising to strike at traditional feudal landlords who had been in power since the late Ottoman era, breaking their hold over land, and introduce agrarian reforms. He also pledged to modernize the medical system in Syria, and implement sweeping changes in Syrian schools, universities and courts. Al-Za'im claimed 'there is only one way to start the Syrian people along the road to progress and democracy and that is with the whip', adding emphasis to this statement by striking his desk with his riding crop. Al-Za'im felt that 'three to five years will be required to obtain satisfactory results from his program, and following this he plans a gradual lessening of the regimentation of the population over a ten-year period'. He speculated that he 'would be able to develop, with the aforementioned aid and missions, an effective fighting force of 40,000 within one to one and a half years' time'.[19]

When they talked about Israel, al-Za'im said that Quwatli would demand Galilee in any peace talks, whereas if he came to power, he would permit the Israelis to keep Galilee in exchange for amending the current frontier to give Syria all territory on the east bank of Lake Tiberais from El-Kursi to Samakh. He would also ask that Tiberais be internationalized, the eastern half to Syria and the western half to Israel. In reporting to the State Department, Meade wrote: 'Although unscrupulous, bombastic and a complete egoist, it must be admitted that he [al-Za'im] has a strong personality, unlimited ambition and the backing of the Syrian Army. If the ever present element of fate happens to be in his favour, al-Za'im may realise his desire to be dictator of Syria.'[20]

The two men met again on 14 March, two weeks before the coup took place, and this time, al-Za'im specifically asked that the US 'provoke and abet' internal disturbances in Damascus 'essential for a *coup d'état*' or, that the US give him funds specifically for the purpose.[21] Meade noted that al-Za'im risked becoming a 'Banana republic dictator' while Deane Hilton said that al-Za'im 'did not have the competence of a French corporal'.[22] He radiated power and leadership, they added, 'but apparently was not very clever'.[23] Other descriptions of the man included lack of persistence, corrupted; 'oozing with self confidence yet apparently very insecure'.

The coup

Backed by heavyweight officers in the Syrian Army, al-Za'im ordered his troops to march on Damascus shortly after midnight on 29 May 1949. One unit headed through the sleeping capital to the President's residence and another was ordered to arrest Prime Minister Khaled al-Azem. A third was dispatched to the headquarters of Damascus Radio and a fourth to pick up officials from the Quwatli government. Not a single shot was fired on the night of 29 March. When the soldiers invaded Quwatli's home, easily disarming the one guard on duty, the President apparently confronted them in pyjamas, stunned by armed men breaking into his residence. One of the officers, Ibrahim al-Husseini, read out the arrest warrant, allowing Quwatli to change his clothes before being taken away to the infamous Mezzeh Prison. The troops escorted him to his bedroom, along with his wife, the First Lady Bahira al-Dalati. When handing him every item of clothing she would whisper to the president, 'Is it the Jews, Abu Hassan?' He would shake his head with a silent 'no' and she would ask again, 'Then is it King Abdullah?' Not for a moment did she think that ordinary Syrians would stage a coup against their own President, who only three years earlier had been hailed by the entire population as founder of Syrian independence. It was either the Jordanians or the Israelis, she believed, certainly not a Syrian – certainly not the USA.

The Truman administration was among the first in the world to recognize and legitimize the regime of Husni al-Za'im in Syria. They sent him an official letter of recognition on 27 April 1949 prompting strong nations such as France and Great Britain to follow suit. Initially only Jordan and Iraq recognized al-Za'im in the Arab world, due to their poor relations with ex-President Quwatli. The Saudis and Egyptians were stunned by the coup at first, demanding that al-Za'im preserve Quwatli's life in order to be accepted by Arab heavyweights. He complied, releasing Quwatli from jail by mid April, after securing his resignation from the presidency, and banishing him into exile in Alexandria, in exchange for Egyptian and Saudi support. Recalling the mood in Damascus on 29 March 1949, Ambassador Keeley's son Robert commented in 2006, 'The US was thrilled by the fact that very close allies and friends were now in power in Damascus. The Tapline agreement was signed, and al-Za'im started secret talks with Israel. We were so happy with al-Za'im that when he requested military assistance from the US and the purchase of some American weapons we were ready to oblige. However, when we informed David Ben Gurion, the Israeli Prime Minister, of al-Za'im's request, he strongly objected, telling us that it will worry Israel a lot to see the US starting to provide its enemies with arms. So, the whole idea was sent to the backburner.'[24] Al-Za'im, however, was no democrat; immediately after coming to power he abolished the Constitution, shut down parliament, closed newspapers, and outlawed all political parties, enforcing martial law and arresting anyone who uttered the slightest opposition to his regime. Throughout the 137 days that he remained in power, the USA did not even once voice its displeasure at his human-rights record, or criticize the lack of political freedoms in Syria.

Armistice talks with Israel

Immediately after coming to power, al-Za'im fulfilled his promises to Meade and launched armistice talks with the Israelis, under the auspices of the UN. Three of his trusted top lieutenants were handpicked for the job; Afif Bizreh, Mohammad Nasser and Fawzi Selu. Salah al-Din al-Tarazi, a brilliant legal mind, was attached to the delegation as advisor to the Ministry of Foreign Affairs.[25] The talks took place in no-man's-land along the border, next to the village of Mishmar Hayarden, which the Syrians had taken during the war of 1948. The talks, al-Za'im knew well, were not going to be easy since the Israelis insisted that Syria, which had ended the war in control of territory west of the international border, withdraw its forces to the same international border. President Quwatli, who had curtly refused such a demand, reasoned that from its strategic current position, Syria could get access to the region's important water sources along the River Jordan and Lake Tiberias.[26] Al-Za'im, however, did not want to be distracted by short-term gains, not knowing how long the US umbrella was going to last, preferring to discuss a complete peace treaty with the Israelis, which he hoped would forever ally his regime to the USA.

'He wanted peace with the Israelis for the sake of a new relationship with the United States', recalled his military aid, Haitham Kaylani. 'He wanted to make himself indispensible to the Americans and saw no better way to achieve that than to go full board and sign peace with Israel.'[27] On 16 April, less than two weeks after the talks had started, Ben Gurion noted in his diary: 'Mordechai (Makleff) and Josh (Palmon) spoke with al-Za'im's representative without the UN participation. The Syrians proposed a separate peace with Israel, cooperation, and a common army. But they want a border change ... half of Lake Tiberias ... I told them to inform the Syrians in clear language that first of all there would the signing of an armistice, on the basis of the previous international border, and then [there would be] a discussion of peace and alliance. We will be ready for maximal cooperation.'[28] The US and the Israelis were taken completely aback by al-Za'im's offer – certainly too good to be true – and feared that the Syrian general was bluffing, at first unable to digest the fact that an Arab leader was willing to sign a peace with the newly created State of Israel.

To prove his good intentions, al-Za'im gave clear orders in early April that he wanted an armistice signed by the summer of 1949.[29] He dared not express his real intentions to the Syrian public, however, promising a new round of battle and telling them that the armistice was just temporary, imposed on Syria by the USA, which Syria would soon be working around.[30] 'If they [the Americans] continue to pressure me,' he warned, 'then I will turn to the Soviets, and let World War Three start from right over here – from Damascus!'[31] This was al-Za'im's way of clearing his own name before the people of Syria, projecting himself as an independent leader whose future was completely independent from the USA. As requested, however, the armistice was in fact signed on 20 July, less than three months after he came to power, and immediately afterwards, al-Za'im told US diplomats in Damascus that he wanted to meet with Ben Gurion and was willing to settle 300,000 Palestinians in northern Syria, in exchange for US military aid.[32] According to Ambassador James Keeley, al-Za'im had 'intimated willingness as part of a general settlement including realistic frontier adjustments, accept quarter million refugees if given substantial development aid in addition to compensation for refugee losses'. He added that al-Za'im was willing to solve the Palestine problem through 'a policy of give and take', advising his government to take the Syrian leader's offer very seriously.[33]

Once through with the armistice talks, al-Za'im neatly propped himself as President of the Republic, conducting a plebiscite that won him nearly 99 per cent of the popular vote. Dressed in full military uniform with white gloves, a monocle, and a Marshal's cane custom-made exclusively for him, al-Za'im chomped on cigars and paraded through the streets of Damascus, promising the Syrians that he was here to stay for good. Less than two months later, however, on 14 August 1949, Husni al-Za'im was toppled and killed by a military *coup d'état*. Ambassador Keeley happened to be out of the country, vacationing with his family in Italy. Robert Keeley notes that news of the executions on that very date was 'devastating to my father on a personal level. He could not overcome the feeling of guilt.'[34] He describes it as a 'crazy adventure' that cost the life of the Syrian President and his Prime Minister, Muhsen al-Barazi, also a close friend of the USA. Copeland, who helped bring him to power 137 days earlier, confessed to Stephan Meade: 'This is the stupidest, most irresponsible action a diplomatic mission like ours could get itself involved in.'[35] Strangely enough, al-Za'im was captured and killed neither because of his contacts with the Americans, nor for signing an armistice with Israel, but rather, for the betrayal of Lebanese philosopher Antune Saadeh, head of the SSNP.[36] Most Syrians only heard of his unorthodox relations with the USA and Israel after Copeland published his book in 1969.

Meade and Copeland were clearly frustrated however that al-Za'im had not been able to blend in with Syrian society, as Quwatli had done before him, and was still regarded by most people as an instrument of Western influence in Syria. Despite all the efforts put forth at bringing him to power and bolstering his rule, al-Za'im had wasted everything they had done for him with one foolish move – betrayal of Antune Saadeh – which cost him support of the officers in the Syrian Army. At one point in mid-1949, al-Za'im probably believed that he would rule for another 50 years because everybody who mattered in the neighbourhood – the Americans, the French, the Turks, the Israelis, the Egyptians and the Saudis – were all supportive of his new administration. He would famously spend hours before the mirrors admiring himself from head to toe and once told his wife, 'You will be queen of Syria one day'. Most Syrians today tend to view al-Za'im through the narrow prism of US interests in the Middle East. There is nothing to prove, however, that al-Za'im was brought to power by the USA, only various accounts that confirm how pleased the USA was with his coup, and how distressed it had been with Shukri al-Quwatli.

If al-Za'im was so powerful, most Syrians ask, and so loyal to the USA and his own personal agenda, why then did the USA not lift a finger to protect him in the summer of 1949? One reason is that the USA had no clue that the coup was being hatched against Husni al-Za'im. Had it known – especially given Sami al-Hinnawi's, the coup mastermind's strong connection to the British and the Iraqis – then the least it could have done was warn its Syrian ally. Most ordinary Syrians and Arabs in general do not accept that, tending to give too much credit to the USA – citing the Mossadeq interlude in Iran – but forget that Syria was still relatively new and unknown to US officials. The margin of trial and error was therefore still pretty high. It is very probable that the USA helped or encouraged him come to power but unlikely it had the intention or the ability of help him maintain his job as President of Syria. Another reason, strongly defended as popular lore on the streets of Syria, is that al-Za'im had outlived his usefulness and no longer mattered to the USA. His erratic behaviour and diminishing popularity in Syria had made the Syrian presidency an international embarrassment. Rather than bear with his madness for what remained of his term (his constitutional term ended in 1953) the USA decided to let his opponents take a grab at him – refusing to get immersed once again in Syrian domestics. From where they saw things, al-Za'im had carried out all that had been expected from him: an armistice, a crackdown of the SCP, and signed off the Tapline agreement.

Copeland expresses frustration at al-Za'im's downfall – perhaps because his friend was so careless that he made himself an easy target for Colonel Sami al-Hinnawi, who arrested and shot him in August 1949. Arrogance got in the way, and so did too much reliance on the USA, which did not have the means to protect him. Had al-Za'im lived and managed to push the right buttons with the USA and Ben Gurion, then it is probable that we might have had an Arab–Israeli peace deal long before Camp David in 1978. Albion Ross, the Damascus correspondent for *The New York Times*, filed a story on 18 August 1949, headlined 'End of Zayim Rule Perils Peace Plan'. All information gathered in the article had been fed to him by the US Legation in Syria. Ross notes, 'The deaths of President Husni Zayim and Premier Mohsen el-Barazi and the apparent restoration of Republic government in Syria have, ironically, wrecked the basis of existing plans for a solution of the Palestine problem and the restoration of peace in the Middle East'.[37]

7

THE RISE OF COLONEL SHISHAKLI

Veteran British journalist Patrick Seale famously spoke of the 'struggle for Syria' in the post-French era, (he eventually used the phrase as a title for one of his books, published in the early 1960s). On one level, this was a struggle between the Hashemite dynasties in Iraq and Jordan, and the royal families of Saudi Arabia and Egypt. But it was also a struggle between the USA (which backed the Saudis) and Great Britain, the traditional patron of both Jordan and Iraq. Although staunch Second World War allies, by 1949, the Americans and the British were beginning to disagree on their share of the Middle East in terms of political influence, access to oil, and trade routes. After the forced exodus of France from the region, Great Britain realized it could not rule the region alone and needed the political and economic might of the USA for support. It did not want US influence to become too strong, however, fearing that this would minimize Great Britain's legacy and standing in the Arab world, eventually driving them out of the region for good. At a micro level, the grinding competition between both great powers climaxed in Syria during the years 1949–1951, carried out by proxy, through Saudi Arabia and Iraq.

The King of Saudi Arabia had toppled Sharif Hussein, father of both King Faisal and his brother King Abdullah I, from the throne of Mecca in the early 1920s. Since then there had been an ongoing feud between the Hashemite royals and King Abdul-Aziz, who for years had been supported in his claims to the Hijaz by ex-President Shukri al-Quwatli and a number of Syrian notables. The Syrian leader had his own reasons to dislike the Hashemites. One was personal disgust at how they had handled the fiasco at Maysaloun in 1920. Rather than stand firm to defend the nation against French aggression, Faisal had simply packed up and left, heading to London to plead for a throne – any throne – as a replacement to the one lost in Damascus. As the national identity of most Syrians began to take form in the 1920s, the idea of an 'imported' king became increasingly less attractive, especially when compared to homegrown republican rule. The Saudis, unlike Faisal and Abdullah, had no territorial ambitions in Syria. They supported Syrian claims from a distance, with no strings attached, never meddling in Syrian domestics. During the 1930s, for example, the Hashemites had bankrolled Shahbandar, Quwatli's main rival in Syrian politics, a man who was strongly pro-British and pro-Hashemite, wanting to re-establish the Hashemite crown in Damascus. When Quwatli became President in August 1943 he quickly discovered the extent to which the King of Jordan had infiltrated the Syrian political class. Abdullah would hold secret meetings with several ranking officers in the Syrian Army (al-Za'im included) encouraging them to launch a coup and call upon him to assume his 'legitimate duties' as King of Syria. Abdullah considered Syria a natural right for him and his family – granted by the British during the famous Hussein–McMahon correspondence of 1915.

Hence, the Hashemites rejoiced when Quwatli was overthrown in 1943, believing that Husni al-Za'im would right all the wrongs inflicted on them since the overthrow of Faisal in 1920. The first to visit Syria in the early hours of the coup were two Iraqi officials, dispatched by Prime Minister Nuri al-Said to meet with al-Za'im and see whether he was ready to ally Syria with Baghdad and Amman, or follow the same path as his predecessor. Al-Za'im cautiously refused to commit until seeing what the Saudis had to offer his new government. When Saudi endorsement – and financial support – began to arrive in mid-April, al-Za'im immediately distanced himself from the Hashemites. At one point he famously said, 'I will personally shoot anybody who mentions Iraq in this country!'[1] This was the price King Abdul-Aziz was willing to pay to keep Syria out of the Hashemite orbit. As a result, al-Za'im immediately closed his country's borders with Jordan, and stories began surfacing in the Syrian press accusing Abdullah of conspiring against the republican regime in Syria. Naturally, when al-Za'im was overthrown four months later, the Hashemites rejoiced, again seeing a natural ally in the coup mastermind Sami al-Hinnawi. This time, however, their optimism was not based only on wishful thinking, because al-Hinnawi was a declared friend and supporter of Hashemite Iraq. The Saudis sulked while Egypt declared a three-day mourning period over al-Za'im's death.[2]

Colonel Hinnawi surprised observers by declaring that he had no intention of becoming President or ruling from behind the scenes through the army. He had launched the coup, he said, to 'save the country from al-Za'im's dictatorship', claiming that it was now up to the civilians to decide who they wanted as President and what kind of government they wanted for Syria.[3] By most accounts, Hinnawi was a simple man who had no political ambitions. Had he wanted to make himself President in the summer of 1949, he could have easily done so, given the tremendous influence that officers had over civilian life in Syria. In the minds of most Syrians, however, if al-Za'im was an American stooge then Hinnawi had Great Britain's fingerprints all over him. A conference was indeed called for in Damascus, chaired by Hinnawi and attended by many veterans: Nazem al-Qudsi, Khaled al-Azm, Fares al-Khoury and the veteran ex-president Hashem al-Atasi. Quwatli was unable to attend due to his extended exile in Alexandria. Nationwide elections for a constitutional assembly took place, to draft a new legal document for Syria. This assembly was soon transformed into a fully fledged parliament in December 1949, electing Atasi at the age of 75 as 6th President of the Republic.

Atasi, a former Prime Minister under Faisal and President under the French in 1936–1939, made Hinnawi Chief of Staff of the Syrian Army and appointed Nazem al-Qudsi Prime Minister. Qudsi was head of the People's Party, a political machine that strove for unification with Iraq and had been the prime opposition movement to Quwatli in 1947–1949. Most of its members, heavyweights from the business community in the northern city of Aleppo, had commercial and political interests in Hashemite Iraq. One notable non-Aleppine in the People's Party, who nevertheless worked relentlessly for union with Iraq, was Adnan al-Atasi, the President's son. The new Prime Minister's colleague Rushdi al-Kikhiya, a co-founder of the People's Party, was elected as the Speaker of Parliament.

The Atasi–Qudsi–Kikhiya troika, supported militarily by Sami al-Hinnawi, seemed to be a godsend to the Hashemite family in Baghdad. These four men were among Iraq's strongest supporters in the Syrian political scene and all of them were both eager and willing to create a Syrian–Iraqi union. For the first time since Faisal's humiliating exodus from Damascus 30 years ago, the Hashemites felt that a return to Syria was now within reach. Faisal's grandson, King Faisal II, came to Damascus to meet the new Syrian leadership and discuss a federal Syrian–Iraqi union. It was decided that the crown of Syria would go to the Hashemites, while the premiership would be held by a Syrian figure. The two countries would coordinate monetary policy, foreign affairs and mutual defence, maintaining individual systems of administration in Damascus and Baghdad. The Syrian–Iraqi union never got past the drawing board, however, because in late December 1949, yet another *coup d'état* rocked the young Syrian nation – the third in one year – topping Sami al-Hinnawi and bringing a young officer, believed to be close to the USA, to power. His name was Adib al-Shishakli.

America's new man in Damascus

The new coup was a surgical operation within the Syrian Army – aimed only at removing Hinnawi – while keeping Atasi, Qudsi and Kikhiya in power. Hinnawi was jailed, charged with selling out to Iraq and endangering Syria's republican government. He spent a few months at the infamous Mezzeh Prison, but was soon banished to Lebanon where, in a classic case of revenge killing, he was gunned down while boarding the Beirut tram in 1950 by a relative of former Prime Minister Muhsen al-Barazi. Deprived of their military arm, advocates of a union with Iraq were left literarily crippled, unable to advance the union project any further. Shishakli was a 39-year-old officer from the conservative city of Hama. He had absolutely no sympathy for the Hashemite royals in Iraq, insisting 'I will never let Syria be ruled from Baghdad!'[4] Unlike al-Za'im, who had a troubled political, financial and sexual past, Shishakli's financial, moral and political history were unblemished. He had served in the French-created Troupe Spéciales but deserted during the infamous bombing of Damascus in May 1945, earning widespread respect among fellow officers. Like many Syrians of his generation he bitterly remembered the events of 1920, when the Hashemite royals had accepted General Gouraud's ultimatum, and fled Syria after the battle of Maysaloun. Shishakli considered Faisal, his brother Abdullah, and grandson Faisal II 'imported' royals from the Arabian Desert, who were both unfit and unable to rule a cultured, urban and refined country like Syria. In 1948 he had volunteered to fight in Palestine, befriending both al-Za'im and Hinnawi and earning the respect of both men for his courage at the battlefront. He helped al-Za'im topple Quwatli in March and then helped Hinnawi topple al-Za'im in August. Having mastered the art of military coups, he then got rid of Hinnawi in December. People on the streets of Damascus whispered in secret that this new strongman was friends with the USA, because 'only America can topple England's man in Damascus!'[5] There is no evidence, however, to prove that Shishakli had any contacts with US officials prior to the coup of 1949; however all available US, British and Syrian archives show that the USA was pleased at seeing Adib al-Shishakli rise to power in Damascus.

US reactions to the Shishakli coup

During these troubled months, US foreign policy was very distant from the internal affairs of Syria. President Truman had just been elected for a second term earlier that same year – his first full term as US President – and had little time for Syrian domestics. He was more interested in preserving access to petroleum resources in the Arab world and preventing the Soviet Union from getting the upper hand among the Arabs. He had only served as Vice President for 83 days under Roosevelt, meeting FDR only twice in private. He knew very little about FDR's vision for the Arab world but understood that upsetting King Abdul-Aziz was a red line, fearing the Saudi King would cancel US air bases in Dhahran. Apart from that limited objective, Truman had too much on his plate in Washington DC, adjusting to a new world order and catering to the war-torn home front, to pay much attention to the game of musical chairs between Syrian officers. According to one of al-Za'im's aids, the Syrian leader had been approached by embassy officials and advised to establish direct contact with Truman, weeks before his execution in August. Al-Za'im eagerly complied, sending him a giant photograph of himself, personally inscribed, dressed in full military uniform, decorated with flowery Arabic text. When the parcel reached the White House, Truman reportedly remarked, 'Who is this notorious character who looks like Mussolini?'[6] It is impossible to verify how authentic the story is, although al-Za'im's right-hand man Haitham Kaylani swore on his military honour that it was true and that he had heard it personally from al-Za'im himself. If it is true, then seemingly, Truman was completely uninvolved with the Syrian debacle of 1949, hinting that it must have been handled strictly by the CIA and the US Embassy in Damascus.

Something changed in US policy, however, in the immediate aftermath of December 1949. The USA suddenly reasoned that Shishakli was a man with whom they could do business. The communist scare in the USA was snowballing and several officials at the State Department warned of increased Soviet influence in the Middle East. As far as the USA was concerned, neutrality – a popular phrase in Syrian politics – was impossible and communism was a crime that must be combated at any cost. Maarouf al-Dawalibi, a prominent member of the People's Party and leading parliamentarian from Aleppo, gave a speech in the Syrian Chamber stating: 'Should the American pressure on Arab countries, which is intended eventually to Judaise them, continue, I hope that a referendum will be held in the Arab world so that all and sundry will know that the Arabs would prefer a 1000 times to be a Soviet republic rather than a palatable Jewish morsel.'[7] Dawalibi, an ally of President Atasi and Prime Minister Qudsi, noted that Syria would never normalize its relationship with the USA until the issue of Palestine was resolved and Palestinians were returned to their original homes. His words prompted another parliamentarian, Ahmad Hajj Younes, to publicly call for an official military alliance between Syria and the Soviet Union, causing the US military attaché in Damascus to describe them as agents of 'black Soviet propaganda'.[8]

With promises to emancipate Syrian women and free them from the chains of male-dominated society, the SCP had plenty of followers in Damascus, much to the displeasure of the US government. Ambassador Keeley, perplexed by the red scare of the cold war, accused two active Syrian women of being agents of Soviet propaganda. One was Falak Tarazi, sister of Salah al-Din al-Tarazi, the Secretary-General of the Syrian Foreign Ministry, who headed an NGO called Partisans of Peace Society.[9] Falak, 38, a well-known Syrian journalist, had made a name for herself writing in the Egyptian paper *al-Risala* and the Lebanese periodical, *al-Adib*.[10] Fluent in French, she was a declared communist who had international connections with prominent literary figures such as Jean Paul Sartre, having written her first book in 1939, shocking Damascus out of its stuffy puritanism.[11] She referred to women in her writings as 'social engineers' and pillars of post-war society, arguing that their kingdom was no longer inside the home and that they should integrate into the work force, in large numbers, to obtain their natural rights as fully fledged Syrian citizens. In 1943, she had given an explosive speech to a gathering of Syrian politicians in Damascus, including Jamil Mardam Bey and Fares al-Khoury, calling for an immediate ban on polygamy and instantaneous divorce – two practices that marginalized Syrian women, she said.[12] Rather than support an open-minded and liberal woman who heralded change into Syrian society, the USA kept her under 24-hour surveillance, slandering her publicly due to her communist affiliations.

Maqbula Shalak, 30, was another controversial woman being closely watched by the US Embassy because of her communist background. She had studied law at Damascus University unveiled, graduating in 1944, and established herself as a leading short-story writer and columnist in the periodical *al-Tariq*. During the Second World War she had lobbied heavily against Nazism, calling on women to leave their homes to stand up to Hitler, accusing him of being 'an enemy of women, freedom, and culture'.[13] Shalak and Tarazi had circulated the communist-backed Stockholm Peace Petition, calling for a ban on atomic weapons, gathering more than 60,000 signatures, and prompting the US Embassy to remark that they had, 'an abnormal craving for publicity'.[14] The Embassy even went as far as to request that the Syrian Foreign Ministry fire Salah al-Din al-Tarazi if he could not control his 'spinster sister'.[15] The two women stood behind the League of Syrian Women for the Protection of Maternity and Childhood, also labelled as a vehicle for communist influence among Syrian women. When the two women petitioned the US

Embassy asking the US to stop threatening the world with nuclear weapons, Ambassador Keeley wrote them off as 'gullible and half-educated dupes of Soviet propaganda'.[16]

Coinciding with Dawalibi's thundering statement in Parliament and the US Embassy's tension with Tarazi and Shalaq, Syrian ambassador to the USA, Farid Zayn al-Din, gave a speech at a conference organized by American Friends of the Middle East, sending shockwaves throughout the upper echelons of power in Washington. Although an alumnus of AUB and one of the founding fathers of the UN, Ambassador Zayn al-Din said that Soviet propaganda was 'extremely persuasive' and the Soviet attitude to Palestine and Algeria had been 'at least ten times more effective in swaying opinion (in Syria)' than everything done by the USA over the past decade.[17] In response to these outbursts, a State Department memorandum warned in 1950 that Syria would 'impulsively rush so far down this dangerous path [towards the USSR] that it will be impossible to return'.[18] The USA must therefore press Syria to understand 'the dangers of such infiltration' and hand over 'Syria's most irresponsible political elements, who are in complete devotion to the interests of the Soviet Union and Marxist dogma'.[19]

The USA was distressed that amidst all this communist fervour, very few credible Syrians were willing to come out and express public support for the USA. Some, like the independent ex-Prime Minister Khaled al-Azem, did voice opposition to Dawalibi's remarks in private, telling Ambassador Keeley that so long as the USA's policy remained biased towards Israel, there was very little that moderate voices in Syria could do to help defend the USA before Syrian and Arab public. For his part, Keeley constantly wrote to his superiors at the State Department, asking them to tone down their public support for Israel or face the risk of losing the entire Arab world to the Soviet Union. Based on all of his alarms, the USA announced in early 1950 that Syria was eligible for technical and economic assistance, as part of the Point Four Program (the fourth point in President Truman's inauguration address). It also announced that Syria was eligible for possible military aid under the Mutual Security Program, created to help 'less developed countries' fight off communist infiltration. Although Shishakli was ruling Syria from behind the scenes, through a puppet Defence Minister named Fawzi Selu, everybody in the international community knew that he was the real strongman of Damascus.[20] US assistance, therefore, was testimony of trust and good faith towards Syria and its new leader. The USA reasoned that Shishakli – an advanced version of Husni al-Za'im – was planning to eventually assume open control of Syria. He was seemingly more interested in conciliating his power, and building a strong economy, than launching a war of liberation for Palestine. If they succeeded in luring him into the US orbit through generous grants and political support, they reasoned that he could, given his unrivalled position in the Syrian Army, advance their interests in Syria and the Middle East and curb the rising communist influence in Syrian society.

Ambassador Keeley left his job in Syria on 22 July 1950, six months after Shishakli's coup, and was replaced by Cavendish W. Cannon, a 55-year-old diplomat from Utah. Unlike both his predecessors Wadsworth and Keeley, Cannon had not been to the Middle East prior to his posting in Damascus and knew very little about the Arabs and their way of life. After serving in the US Marine Corps during the Second World War, he entered the Foreign Service and drifted through posts in Zurich, Sofia, Athens and Yugoslavia before arriving in Damascus and presenting his credentials to President Atasi on 30 October 1950. Tellingly, after ceremonially meeting Atasi at the Presidential Palace on a hill overlooking Damascus, Cannon drove down to Army Headquarters to 'present his credentials' to Adib al-Shishakli – head of the shadow cabinet in Syria.[21] According to a press release distributed by the Army, Shishakli promised that Syria was willing to work for a stable Middle East, provided that the US stops 'taking sides with Israel'.[22]

Cannon had mixed impressions of Colonel Shishakli. The man was everything diplomatic dispatches described him to be; tough, sober, reliable, but he was by no means a stooge for the USA as Husni al-Za'im had been, or as the State Department wanted him to be. Additionally he was clearly more interested in combating Israel than in limiting communist influence in the Middle East. Shishakli was also a worldly officer who took great interest in Zionist influence within the political community in Washington DC, wanting to digest the US–Zionist relationship to better understand why the Arabs were defeated during the war of 1948. Much of the data on Zionism in the USA was gathered for Shishakli by his media advisors, Nazih al-Hakim and Ahmad Isseh, two skilled journalists who were well connected to the outside world and who understood the dynamics of US politics.[23] Contrary to what the Americans believed, he was never too excited about a relationship with the USA. One typical statement in 1950, by Vice President Alben Barkely described Israel as 'an oasis of liberty in the desert of oppression'.[24] That single statement was enough to whip up massive anti-American demonstrations on the streets of Damascus, to which Shishakli turned a blind eye, chaired by the Baath Party, the Communist Party, and the Muslim Brotherhood. At one point in April 1950, a bomb went off at the garden of the US Embassy in Syria, signalling how strong anti-Americanism was rising on the Syrian streets.[25]

Truman himself was close to the Zionists, Hakim and Isseh wrote to Shishakli, unlike his State Department, which was more even-handed in dealing with the Arab–Israeli conflict. When serving as a senator, he had established a strong relationship with leading American Zionists, endorsed applications of Zionist emigrants to the USA, and strongly condemned the Nazi genocide. Among the lasting friendships formed during his career as senator and joining him in the White House in 1945 were Eddie Jacobson (a former business partner), Max Lowenthal and Rabbi Stephan Wise.[26] General John Hilldring, a high-ranking Zionist, became member of the US delegation at the UN, and James McDonald, another Zionist, was named first US Ambassador to Israel. David K. Niles, the son of a Jew, was another advisor on military affairs. Truman remarked to the Israeli Ambassador to the US Abba Eban, 'The striped-pants boys on the State Department are against my policy of supporting Israel. They will soon find out who is the President of the United States!'[27] Shishakli read these reports with great interest, and was unimpressed by the character of Harry Truman, seeing that he was no match for two predecessors who the Syrians admired, Woodrow Wilson and Franklin Roosevelt.

Even if he wished, Adib al-Shishakli could not accept US assistance in 1950. Hashem al-Atasi was still the President of the Republic and any decision of that magnitude needed to be signed off by the head of state, not by the Deputy Chief of Staff of the Army. Atasi for that matter, a worldly statesmen trained during the Ottoman era, was clearly uninterested in allying himself with the USA, given Truman's Zionist connections and his backing for the creation of Israel in 1948. Additionally, there were strings attached to any US assistance to Syria: a pledge not to use these arms to fight Israel, to which Shishakli could not commit. Negotiations eventually collapsed over what the Americans described as 'considerable growth of anti-American sentiment (in Syria)'.[28] One US official based in Damascus noted that Syria was more interested in complaining about US loans to Israel, than in 'preparing an application for a loan for itself'.[29] To take Syrian–US relations any further, Shishakli had to assume full power himself and get rid of the civilians he had propped up in 1949. The chance to do so came in November 1951, when President Atasi called on none other than Maarouf al-Dawalibi to create a cabinet. In addition to being a declared admirer of the USSR, Dawalibi was also a bitter opponent of the officers, blaming them for all the ills Syria had gone through since the Palestine War. Dawalibi had nothing but disdain for Shishakli – and the bad blood was mutual. Since staging his first coup in 1949, Shishakli had conditioned that any civilian cabinet appoint a military officer – that being his right-hand-man Fawzi Selu – as Minister of Defence. This was intended to secure veto power for the officers within the cabinet and ensure the union project with Iraq drowned if ever raised in the Syrian government. All prime ministers during the years 1949–1951 had strictly abided by this rule, fearing that if they refused Shishakli, he would stage another coup and bring down the Atasi administration altogether. Dawalibi, a stubborn man with strong backing among religious establishments in Aleppo, was one that did say 'no' to Adib Shishakli, granting the portfolio of defence to a civilian. After Shishakli encouraged him to change course or suffer the consequences, Dawalibi stuck to his guns, refusing to reshuffle his cabinet. Shishakli struck again – arresting the new Prime Minister, his entire cabinet, and leaders of the People's Party. An infuriated President Atasi summoned him to his office at the presidential palace to scold him for his political gambling but was unable to stand up to the military strongman of Syria; he presented his resignation in early December 1951. With the ageing President out of the way, Shishakli issued a military decree naming Fawzi Selu as head of state, Prime Minister, and Minister of Defence. Although still not officially President, Shishakli could now sign presidential decrees through Selu, a colourless man who, like Hinnawi, had no political ambitions. Shishakli continued to rule from behind the scenes, one step closer, however, to the Syrian presidency.

During this time, a popular saying emerged on the streets of Damascus; 'Kul shi shakly, illa al-Shishakli', meaning 'everything is fake, except for Shishakli'. The illusions of state created by Sami al-Hinnawi had indeed crumbled by November 1951. So had the fragile Syrian–Iraqi union, brainchild of the weak civilian government of Syria. All of it had indeed proven to be false and all that continued to matter was military might of the Syrian Army. Shishakli proved to be the smartest of all the Presidents who came to power in Damascus since the Republic was created in 1932. He understood the balance of power in the cold war and knew why all of his predecessors – Shukri al-Quwatli, Husni al-Za'im, and Hashem al-Atasi – had fallen. They had failed to realize how powerful the US giant had become after the Second World War and, rather than ride with the prevailing current coming from Washington, chose to ignore, abuse or obstruct it, leading to their respective downfalls. Shishakli promised the people of Syria – and the USA – that he would be a different kind of leader in the Middle East.

1   King Faisal I (centre) with French Prime Minister Georges Clemenceau attending the
Paris Peace Conference in 1919. This is when Faisal met US President Wilson for the first
time, thereby launching Syrian–US relations.

2   The draft letter authored by the residents of Damascus and presented to the
US fact-finding team, known as the King–Crane Commission, when it came
to Syria shortly after World War I, in 1919.

3   The nationalist leader Abdul Rahman Shahbandar, who worked on establishing
Syrian–US ties during the Wilson and Harding Administrations.

4   Prime Minister Jamil Mardam Bey, who co-led the anti-French struggle in the mid-1940s
and worked hard at cementing Syrian–US ties during the Quwatli–Roosevelt era.

HEADQUARTERS
UNITED STATES ARMY FORCES
IN THE MIDDLE EAST.

CAIRO, EGYPT.

May 20, 1943.

Honorable Franklin D. Roosevelt,
President of the United States,
The White House,
Washington, D. C.

My dear Mr. President:

I am inclosing herewith a letter addressed to you from Mohammad Aziz el Khani, distinguished judge of Damascus. The letter, date equivalent to April 8, 1943, is written in Arabic and is accompanied by a translation in English.

Mohammad Aziz el Khani is not only a distinguished judge of Damascus, he is also the head of the Moslem Religious Judiciary in that area. He is a man of fine reputation and outstanding ability.

You should be advised, however, that Mohammad Aziz el Khani has no national office that entitles him to address you officially as the head of a Government. The letter I think is intended to be rather a private letter to you.

Almost invariably the members of the Moslem faith with whom I have conversed have shown an understanding of the principles by which you are actuated and have expressed complete confidence in your leadership. The letter which I am inclosing is typical of the expressions I have received from both Moslem and Christian Arabs.

The more I converse with the people in the Middle East area the more I am convinced that the American and British influence should be integrated so as to leave no doubt as to the unity of purpose between Great Britain and the United States.

I am, yours respectfully,

P. HURLEY
Brigadier General, U. S. A.

Incl.

5   A letter from General Patrick Hurley to President Roosevelt,
dated May 1943, regarding the situation in Syria.

6   US President Harry Truman receiving Syrian Prime Minister Fares al-Khoury at the
White House in 1945.

7 President Shukri al-Quwatli and Prime Minister Jamil Mardam Bey in 1948.

8 Prime Minister Fares al-Khoury (left) at the White House with Syria's first Ambassador to the USA, Nazem al-Qudsi in 1945.

9　President Husni al-Za'im, the first military ruler of Syria, who was brought to power in
what is generally believed to be a CIA-backed coup, in March 1949.

10　Prime Minister Fares al-Khoury at the founding conference of the
UN in 1945.

11   President Hashem al-Atasi, who came to power after the pro-US President Husni
al-Za'im, pictured in Damascus in 1951.

12   President Adib al-Shishakli, being sworn in as the 7th President of Syria in 1953.

13 US First Lady Eleanor Roosevelt at the Presidential Palace in Damascus during the era of
President Shishakli in the early 1950s.

14 US Secretary of State John Foster Dulles at the Presidential Palace in Damascus during
the Shishakli era. He was the first senior official ever to visit Syria.

15   President Shukri al-Quwatli in 1957, during the height of his tension with US President
Dwight Eisenhower.

16   Prime Minister Sabri al-Asali, at the height of Syrian–US tension, in 1957.

8

IKE COMES TO DAMASCUS

In 1951, Humphrey Bogart's black and white thriller *Sirocco*, premiered in Syrian cinemas. The film struck a raw nerve in the Syrian capital because it told of an American Harry Smith selling arms to rebels in Damascus during the rebellion of 1925. Bogart, thanks to his memorable performance in *Casablanca* ten-years earlier, was a household name in Syria, popular among a rising generation of young girls, frequent movie-goers, all from the Damascus elite. These girls used to promenade unveiled in public, visit ice-cream parlours with friends, and dance at private parties to the music of Frank Sinatra. The conservative among them used to wear a headscarf, tilted neatly backward, in Audrey Hepburn fashion. At home, their rooms were decorated with pin-up posters of American icons such as Clark Gable, Gregory Peck and Humphrey Bogart. Young men from the same social strata also had plenty of admiration for Bogart, and would often wear a long raincoat like him, with collar raised, cigarette dangling from their lips, imitating Rick, his tough character in *Casablanca*. Once in 1950, a rumour spread among students at the Damascus University Faculty of Law, that Bogart was filming *Sirocco* in the old alleys of Damascus. Young men and women flocked to the Old City, followed by an army of newspaper photographers, carrying notebooks for autographs, only to realize that 'Bogie' was nowhere to be found.[1]

When *Sirocco* came to Damascus, Syrians rushed to movie cinemas to watch the first Hollywood production that depicted them on screen – and were not pleased with the result. The people of Syria were depicted in a condescending fashion, as an underclass, sometimes as fools. Cinema columns in major Syrian dailies were highly critical of the film, claiming that it did them a great injustice – adding insult to injury in light of boiling anger with the Truman Administration's approach. Bogart's film coincided with other visits by prominent Americans to Syria, which tried, with various degrees of success, at breaking the bilateral mistrust and shattering stereotypes between both peoples. In 1952, Adlai Stevenson, the presidential candidate, came to Syria for a tour of the Middle East and met with both President Hashem al-Atasi and Colonel Adib al-Shishakli at the presidential palace.[2] Then came the world-famous deaf-blind author and activist Helen Keller in April 1952 – arguably the most famous American to visit Syria since Charles Crane's 1922 trip.

Helen Keller's trip to Syria was officially sponsored by the US State Department. Syrian newspapers were filled with stories of the 'miracle girl' who had overcame congenital illness causing her to become blind and deaf while still an infant, obtaining a university degree in 1904 – before any Syrian woman had obtained a college education. Syrian women were inspired by her visit to Damascus, regarding her as a role model who would help them shatter the chains of male-dominated society. By the First World War, Keller had become world famous as a speaker and author, mainly as an advocate of the working classes and people with disability, as well as a friend of famous figures such as Alexander Graham Bell, Charlie Chaplin and Mark Twain. Her autobiography *The Story of My Life*, written during her college years, had been translated into Arabic and reprinted several times in Damascus.[3] While in Syria, she planned to visit associations and schools for the blind – strange considering there were none in Syria. The trip was part of a three-month expedition in the Middle East, which covered Jordan, Lebanon, Israel and Syria. The State Department advised that she visit Israel last, and Adib al-Shishakli made it clear that regardless of who she was and what kind of publicity she would bring for Syria, Helen Keller would not be allowed to enter Syria if she had an Israeli stamp on her passport.[4] Secretary of State Dean Acheson wrote to the US Embassy in Damascus saying that the visit, 'should be publicised as an example of American interest and friendship with the Near East'.[5] Photographs of Helen and material written in Arabic were distributed throughout public venues in Syria.[6] Upon arriving in Damascus, she was given an audience with Shishakli, and met with women's rights-driven NGOs, then addressed the press saying that Syrian women were, 'moving rapidly towards social maturity and independence'. She told her Syrian hosts she hoped for a school of the blind to open soon in Syria, which Shishakli promised to arrange in the near future.[7] She also visited a milk distribution centre and spoke to the 500 women who worked there, urging them to stand up for their unalienable rights in society. A total of 23 dailies, 5 weeklies and one monthly covered the Keller visit at length, describing her as 'a living miracle' who was an 'outstanding envoy for the United States'. Munir al-Ajlani, the former Minister of Education in 1950, recalled 'Helen Keller, this respectable old woman, helped remind us that there was another side to the United States – a human one. The US was not only Harry Truman – the atomic bomb on Japan or the support of Israel. She was an excellent ambassador for her country; an honourable and hard-working woman with character. Actually, Helen helped shatter all the stereotypes created by Harry Truman and reminded us of our own shortcomings for having failed to create proper institutions to help children with disabilities.'[8]

Eisenhower comes to the White House

The world changed for Syrian–US relations when Dwight 'Ike' Eisenhower, the five-star general of the Second World War came to the White House in January 1953, along with his young Vice-President, Richard Nixon. Arabs welcomed the new Administration, believing that the new US President would be more even-handed in dealing with the Middle East than Truman had been. Shishakli also had something in common with Eisenhower; both were military men and decorated war heroes who spent a long career in the army before devoting themselves to politics. Eisenhower's 1948 memoirs, *Crusade in Europe*, could be found in Shishakli's library, on his favourite reading list.[9] His new Secretary of State, John Foster Dulles, was a 'respectable man', or *rajul muhtaram* in Arabic, who knew how to walk the tightrope between Arabs and Jews, reported the popular Damascus daily *al-Ayyam*.[10] In May 1952, Ambassador Cavendish Cannon had been withdrawn from Damascus, having served in office for less than two years, and was replaced by James S. Moose, who was to prove the strongest and most controversial of US Ambassadors to serve in Damascus since the mid 1940s. With a new Ambassador in Damascus, a new figure at the State Department, and a new President in the White House, Syrian politicians inhaled a breath of fresh air, relieved that the difficult years of the Truman White House had finally come to an end. Shishakli's man, President Fawzi Selu, sent a congratulatory cable to President Eisenhower on 25 January 1953, less than one week after the new president had been sworn in to office.

The Syrian press had followed the presidential race in 1952 between Eisenhower and Democrat Adlai Stevenson, the Governor of Illinois with great interest. During earlier elections, news from the USA only made it to the third and fourth pages of big Syrian dailies, while smaller ones and evening periodicals barely paid attention to Washington politics. This time things were clearly different, as major dailies such as *al-Ayyam*, *al-Qabas* and *al-Nidal* ran front page of the presidential race – publically rooting for Eisenhower. Abdul Ghani al-Otari, publisher of the general interest magazine *al-Dunia*, explained saying: 'We published what people wanted to read. Previously the only news that mattered for ordinary Syrians was whether Clark Gable was going to do a sequel to *Gone with the Wind*, or whether Marlon Brando was going to get an Oscar for *A Streetcar Named Desire*. That film premiered in Syria, by the way, while the presidential race was underway in the US. With Eisenhower, things were different. Everybody wanted to know how this decorated general, a war hero, who Syrians had first heard of during the War, was going to become President of the United States.'[11] Unlike the case with Wilson, Roosevelt or Truman, who were completely unheard of in Damascus prior to their election, 'Eisenhower was both a public name and public face, very familiar to the political elite in Damascus'. Additionally, Eisenhower was the first Republican to enter the White House in 20 years, and the oldest President in living memory for most Americans, at the age of 62.

After the Japanese attack on Pearl Harbor, Dwight Eisenhower had been assigned to the General Staff in Washington, where he served until 1942, drafting war planes to defeat Japan and Nazi Germany. He rose to become Chief of the War Plans Division, then Assistant Chief of Staff under George Marshall, who developed an immediate admiration for Eisenhower and appointed him Commanding General of the London-based European Theatre of Operations (ETOUSA). In November 1942, he became Supreme Commander of the North African Theater of Operations (NATOUSA), earning the confidence of President Roosevelt. Following Germany's 1945 surrender, Eisenhower became Military Governor of the US Occupation Zone based in Frankfurt, Germany. When the Arabs went to war in 1948, Eisenhower was away from the public eye, busy with a new job, being President of Columbia University, which lasted until he became Supreme Commander of NATO forces in Europe in 1950.[12] He remained in that post until 1952, returning briefly to Columbia, until becoming US President in 1953.

Eisenhower's running mate Richard Nixon, who in 1974 was to be the first US President to visit Syria, was younger, aged 40 than the President. The Syrian press took a particular interest in him, frequently citing his conservative upbringing as a Quaker, as the son of a grocery store owner, noting that he did not drink, dance or swear.[13] As for John Foster Dulles, the new State Secretary, he too was a subject of close observation among the political elite, since his policies would have a direct effect on bilateral relations with the USA. The George Washington University-trained attorney had been raised to a political family in Washington, both his grandfather John W. Foster and his uncle, Robert Lansing having served as Secretary of State before him. In 1919, the young Dulles had worked as legal consul to President Wilson at the Paris Peace Conference and had conversed with King Faisal and his Syrian aid, Jamil Mardam Bey. By 1953, however, Mardam Bey was in self-imposed exile in Egypt and Faisal had been dead for 20 years. Dulles made an early impression on both men as a junior diplomat by forcefully arguing against imposing crushing reparations on Germany and calling for an honourable solution to all territories liberated from the Ottoman Empire. Afterwards, he served as a member of the War Reparations Committee at the request of President Wilson. In 1945 he had met and been visibly impressed by Syria's representative to the UN Conference in San Francisco, Prime Minister Fares al-Khoury. Reportedly, when hearing Khoury defend his country at the General Assembly, the young Dulles commented, 'It is impossible for a nation with men like these, to be occupied!'[14] The relationship between Khoury and Dulles remained relatively strong as they represented their countries at the UN General Assembly throughout the late 1940s. Many in the upper echelons of Damascus had read Dulles' 1950 classic *War or Peace*, a critical analysis of US policy of containment, basically targeting President Truman. Dulles argued that 'containment of communist influence' should be replaced by 'liberating' Soviet-influenced countries from communist doctrine.[15]

The agent of that liberation was Ambassador James Moose. A diplomat with the Department of State since 1928, he had served briefly in Greece before enrolling at the National School of Living Oriental Languages in Paris, where he studied French, Turkish and Arabic. In 1933 he was posted to Baghdad, followed by Tehran in 1937, before becoming head of the first American Legation in Saudi Arabia.[16] He remained in Saudi Arabia during the Second World War, after which he was assigned to Iraq again, then to Damascus, Syria as a chargé d'affaires under President Quwatli. In the late 1940s and early 1950s Moose spent several years travelling around Africa, South Asia and Europe as a Foreign Service inspector of US Embassies overseas, before landing as Ambassador to Damascus in 1952. Moose knew the Middle East, and Syria in particular, inside out. Shortly after his appointment, the young Ambassador sent a forceful letter to the State Department, warning that if Syrians were not given immediate military aid by the USA, the Syrians would look elsewhere, mainly towards the Soviet Union. As early as 27 January 1953 Dulles warned the White House that the USSR was trying to 'inspire the Arabs with a fanatical hatred for the US'.[17] He even told Eisenhower, 'Stalin, when he was negotiating with Hitler in 1940, said that area [the Middle East] must be looked upon as the center of Soviet aspiration.'[18] Therefore, Dulles argued, the USA must answer immediate worries of the Arabs in general, rather than lecture them on how to shelter themselves from the communist scare. Israel for its part was worried by the ascent of the new US administration, claiming that he would 'be tempted to win Arab military cooperation with deliveries on arms'.[19]

Shishakli put on a bulldog face ahead of facing the new US administration. Enthusiastic though he may have been to engage with the USA, he needed to come across as a tough negotiator and ardent Arab nationalist in order to appease the Syrian street, which was still boiling with anti-Americanism due to the creation of Israel five years earlier. One of Shishakli's early manoeuvers was raising a slogan to protect Arab oil from giant companies in the USA and Europe, demanding that Syria get no less than 49 per cent of savings from transport rights through Syrian territory of the IPC and Tapline.[20] He then concluded a Treaty of Friendship with Iran's nationalist Prime Minister Mosaddeq on 24 May 1953.[21] Mosaddeq was immensely popular in Syria – a symbol of anti-imperialism – who in May 1951 had nationalized the Anglo-Iranian Oil Company (AIOC), which was controlled by the British government, and cancelled its oil concession, which was due to expire in 1993. If the doors to Washington did not open to Syria, Shishakli seemed to be saying in 1952–1953, then he would become another Mosaddeq.

Dulles in Damascus

Days before Shishakli signed his alliance with Mosaddeq on 15 May, John Foster Dulles became the first US Secretary of State ever to visit Syria when he arrived in Damascus. His visit was part of a regional tour, aimed at marketing the new Eisenhower Administration within Arab capitals and curbing communist influence in the Arab world. His visit signalled that a new era had dawned; for the first time ever, a constant stream of VIP Americans were landing in Damascus, bringing the world's attention to the old capital of the Umayyads. Previously, Syria had only appeared in the US press during times of crisis – the downfall of the Ottoman Empire in 1918, the Great Revolt of 1925, or the al-Za'im coup of 1949. In less than 11 months, however, Syria had been visited by former First Lady Eleanor Roosevelt, a former presidential candidate, an iconic American author, and now, by the US Secretary of State. By that time, Hashem al-Atasi had long resigned from office, leading the opposition from his hometown in Homs, and Shishakli was firmly in control of the state, through Colonel Selu. Although the Syrian leader had turned down the Point Four Program, the USA reasoned that if the right strings were pulled with Shishakli they could get him to commit to an alliance with Washington against the Soviet Union. He had no communist background after all, and had earned Western respect by muzzling the pro-Soviet opposition leader, Maarouf al-Dawalibi, back in 1951. During his meeting with Dulles, Shishakli began by expressing 'great hope that the new administration's foreign policy will not be poisoned' by Zionism.[22] Shishakli spoke good English yet insisted that an interpreter be present, making a point by addressing his US guest in Arabic.

Shishakli told Dulles that unlike most Arabs, he was a pragmatist who knew that annihilating Israel, or 'pushing the Jews into the sea' was not possible. 'What is possible' he noted, 'was getting Israel to abide by UN resolutions', mainly in regard to Palestinian refugees.[23] Shishakli said that he deplored spending over 50 per cent of Syria's budget on defence, claiming that this money could go to education, science, services and research, but noted that this was impossible, given the permanent state of war created in the Middle East by the 1948 creation of Israel.[24] After marketing himself as a hardcore Arab nationalist, Shishakli then uttered the magic words. First, he requested that an American school be opened in Damascus, similar to the one found in other countries in the Middle East, then made a polite appeal for US arms, noting he needed them 'to fight off communism, in order to keep Syria independent'.[25] The school, he said, would serve the families of diplomatic missions based in Syria, and educating Syrians wanting a liberal education for their children, 'right here in their own country'. Dulles, clearly impressed by both remarks, welcomed the school suggestion, and gave the 'strongest and most categorical assurance' that the USA was opposed to the expansion of the frontiers of Israel but noted that in order for the Syrian–US relationship to blossom, 'it must be confident that Syria will not attack Israel'.[26] He also made sure to remind Shishakli that the USA 'does not favour Israel at the expense of Syria'.[27]

Dulles also welcomed the request for arms, proposing to send survey missions to Damascus to study the exact character of the equipment needed, and to train and establish joint military planning with the Syrians – on the condition, however, that these arms not be used at any point to fight a new war with Israel.[28] Shishakli refused to commit, realizing such a restraint would be too difficult to sell on the Syrian street, although he was dying to walk that extra mile with the USA. The Muslim Brotherhood, the Baath Party, and the SCP were already furious with the early signs of a Syrian–US honeymoon, pointing their guns towards Shishakli while describing him as a US stooge. If such a commitment was ever leaked to the press, Shishakli knew that he would be committing political suicide. As the two men spoke, these leftist parties staged massive demonstrations on the streets of Damascus, calling on Dulles to leave Syria. Heading one of the demonstrations was Shishakli's eldest son Ihsan, a young Baathist. Dulles asked his Syrian host to explain how his son was chanting anti-American slogans, sarcastically noting, 'How can you control the Syrian street, Your Excellency when even in your own house there are leftist tendencies that preach anti-Americanism?' Shishakli smiled, 'They accuse me of being a dictator. I might be a dicta-tor in politics, Mr Dulles, but I am a democrat at home. I cannot impose my political views on my son.' The meeting ended with a warm handshake, according to the Damascus press, and a statement from Dulles to reporters saying that Shishakli was a 'wise leader, with whom we can do business'. Immediately after Dulles' departure, the Syrian Foreign Ministry approved the opening of an American school in Damascus – yet for logistic reasons, such as finding a suitable plot of land, the project did not materialize until after Shishakli's downfall, in February 1954.[29]

After returning to the USA, Dulles briefed his colleagues at the State Department and President Eisenhower at the White House that Syria had 'some promise' since, due to its proximity with the USSR, it was more aware of the Soviet danger than other Arab countries.[30] Shishakli was an 'impressive figure' with a 'much broader vision and deeper understanding of the relations of his country to world problems' than most of his Arab colleagues.[31] Syria had high economic potential, he added, at low cost, meaning that it could absorb a larger number of Palestinian refugees, if the right strings were pulled with Shishakli, being 'a good start for liquidation of the problem which poisons Arab relations' with the USA.[32] One of the conclusions reached by Dulles after his meeting with Shishakli was that if the USA wanted to polish its image in the Arab world, it should 'seek to allay the deep resentment against it that has resulted from the creation of Israel'. It was now a fact, Dulles noted, that the Arabs were 'more fearful of Zionism than communism' and that, 'many of the Arab countries are so engrossed with their quarrels with Israel or Great Britain or France that they pay little heed to the menace of Soviet communism'. In cases, however, where 'the Soviet Union is near' (such as Syria) there was, he noted, 'an appropriate appreciation and awareness of the danger'. Dulles also reasoned that the 'political stability required for internal progress and building of defensive strength of the area is lacking and the position of the Western powers has dete-riorated to the point where they are not at present serving as factors of stability'. If the USA wanted to score any points in the region, Dulles advised, it had to change course with regard to the Arab–Israeli Conflict. A heated debate ensued during the summer months of 1953 in Washington DC, on whether American foreign policy could balance between meeting Arab demands and not abandon-ing their commitment to Israel. According to prominent American historian David W. Lesch, 'The short and long term answer was "no"; the Eisenhower administration was not able to juggle the interests and demands of the countries concerned and integrate them neatly into American plans.'[33] US aid to Israel, after all, during the years 1948–1953 had amounted to an impressive $250 million, while similar aid to all the Arab and African countries combined, was no more than $108 million – showing just how difficult impartiality really was for the Eisenhower administration.[34]

Shishakli had indeed worked hard at marketing himself as a friend of the West, while making sure not to tarnish his Arab credentials. The Syrian press had often described him, at his own request, as 'Israel's Number One Enemy'.[35] In as much as he wanted US arms to secure a firm relationship with the West, he could not commit to Dulles' conditions. US support, he reasoned however, would shelter him from Husni al-Za'im's fate. He knew that the officer class could not be trusted and that ambitious men in uniform were lurking in secret, waiting for an opportune moment to bring him down. A commitment not to combat the Zionist state would have spelled political disaster for Shishakli among the same men who had helped him come to power in 1949 and 1951. In order to cement his position, Shishakli asked Fawzi Selu to step down in the summer of 1953 and called for nationwide presidential elections in July, followed by parliamentary elections in October. All traditional parties, outlawed since 1951, were excluded from parliamentary elections, with the exception of his own creation, the Arab Liberation Movement (ALM). Shishakli was the only candidate for the presidency, and won with 99 per cent of the popular vote, becoming the 8th President of the Syrian Republic, on 10 July 1953. He reduced the number of seats in the Syrian Parliament to 83 (60 of them went to the ALM) and called on a respected French-trained academic, Maamoun al-Kuzbari, to become Speaker. Now constitutionally placed as the leader of Damascus, Shishakli was in a position to take bolder decisions related to foreign policy. In a long-observed traditional gesture, the new President issued a pardon for all political dissidents, bringing prominent critics like Michel Aflaq, Salah al-Bitar and Akram al-Hawrani, back to Syria from their exile in Lebanon.

What made things more difficult for Shishakli – perhaps intentionally – was Israel. The Israelis were concerned with the de-militarized zone (DMZ) on the Syrian–Israeli border, treating it as Israeli territory, although according to the armistice agreement signed with al-Za'im, it enjoyed 'sovereignty in abeyance pending a final peace settlement'. Israel was trying to divert the waters of the River Jordan, through construction of the Banat Ya'qub Canal, which would leave eight canals in Syrian territory virtually empty.[36] Shishakli brought the matter to the UN Security Council on 12 October 1953 claiming Israel had failed to comply with the orders of General Vagn Bennike to the Chief-of-Staff of the UN Truce Supervision Organization (UNTSO) to cease construction on Banat Ya'cub. Two days later, on 14 October, Israeli troops, dressed as irregulars attacked the Jordanian village of Qibya, killing 53 people in response to repeated attacks by Palestinian guerillas from the Jordan-controlled Palestinian West Bank. Shishakli, fearful that another regional confrontation might break out, called his troops into high alert and sent 24,000 men to the front (about two-thirds of the Syrian Army's total strength). On 20 October, Dulles announced that all economic aid to Israel had been suspended, in response to the Qibya attack, after the USA, Great Britain, and France jointly criticized Israel's behaviour at the Security Council.[37] Dulles was furious with the soft-spoken Israeli Prime Minister Moshe Sharett, who had failed to prevent the Qibya massacre, claiming that Jordan was doing its best to combat Palestinian militancy, while Tel Aviv was 'belittling its efforts' with a response that was completely 'out-of-line'.[38] Zionist pressure caused him to quickly change course on 28 October, resuming economic aid worth $26 million, much to Shishakli's dismay.[39] The embassy in Damascus lamented the 'manner and magnitude' of the grant that was announced, claiming that it had affected Syrian confidence in the USA and returned all parties to the same conditions of mistrust that had existed under Truman.[40] Another attempt was made at getting Shishakli to swallow the bait in September 1953, when the USA allocated $10 million in military assistance to Syria, part of a congressional grant to the Middle East. The State Department said that it expected 'political dividends' from this deal and expected Syria not to employ these arms against Israel and enter into official talks to defend the Middle East against a possible Soviet attack. The Defence Department responded, however, that there were no funds for such a project in 1954, claiming that Dulles had to have a 'very strong case' to justify prioritizing arms to Syria, given its un-impressive record to date in combating communism.

Israel rocks the boat

Coinciding with the Qibya massacre was the visit of President Eisenhower's envoy, Ambassador Eric Johnston, to the Middle East. Johnston had put forth a project to irrigate the Jordan Valley through redistribution of the Jordan River waters, which was strongly backed by Secretary Dulles. Johnson tried to formulate a formula to regulate water usage between Syria, Jordan and Israel, proposing, for example, the creation of a dam on the Hasbani and Banias rivers to provide power and irrigate the Galilee area along with a water quota of 394 million cubic metres for Israel, 775 million cubic metres for Jordan and

45 million cubic metres for Syria.[41] The Syrians were furious with Johnston's visit. The man was no stranger to the politicized elite in Damascus, who by now were well-versed in US politics. He had been President of the Motion Picture Association of America (MPAA) which had produced the infamous 'Hollywood blacklist' banning dealings with prominent people in the motion picture industry accused of communist affiliations. Whenever the Syrians were criticized for refusing the slightest form of contact with the Israelis, they would point to the MPAA case, arguing that if Johnston banned Charlie Chaplin from the USA, then anything was possible in the Middle East. Nevertheless, the unpopular Johnston was welcomed in Damascus on 30 October, two weeks after Qibya, while popular anti-Americanism in Syria was at its highest level in years. The Syrian press gave brief, yet front-page coverage to his visit, claiming that President Shishakli had met with a special envoy of President Eisenhower – but with no details.[42] Johnston marketed his plan to Shishakli, who said that it ought to be studied by the Syrian government, but reminded his US guest that it would be very difficult to implement so long as Israel was not abiding by UN Resolutions. The fact that Shishakli actually received Johnston, and did not flatly reject his water plan, is revealing of how conciliatory the Syrian leader's approach was becoming towards the USA – at the expense of his popularity on the Syrian street, which was deteriorating by the day since the July presidential elections. A group of politicians had already assembled in Homs, headed by veteran ex-President Atasi, publicly promising to bring down 'the dictator' who was accused, by students at Damascus University, of 'dealing with the Zionist state and creators of the Zionist State'. In December 1953, Shishakli attended a graduation ceremony at Damascus University and was confronted by one of the students at the Faculty of Law. Speaking to the packed auditorium the student stated, 'I refuse to take a degree from a person who has no respect for the law and rules a country in which law is lacking!' Shishakli and his security services were furious. They stormed the university in search of the rebel student and when confronted by the university President, Constantine Zureik, struck him on the face, before marching on the campus, prompting students to chant: 'Even France did not do this.'[43]

Many have argued that Shishakli's readiness to deal with the USA after becoming President, was a sign of growing strength and lack of concern for gaining popular Syrian support. Others argue, however, that Shishakli, feeling increasingly vulnerable and afraid, felt more in need of Western allies to back him against his local enemies than ever before since 1949. The State Department, after all, noted in late 1953, 'There is no evidence of intrigue or disloyalty to the present government within the Army'.[44] The British had a similar assessment of the situation; 'As in the past, there were dark clouds on the horizon, although there was no reason to suppose that the president could not deal adequately with the situation.'[45] Shishakli was becoming increasingly concerned that a regional defence system was being crafted by the USA, in which Syria would be left out unless it jumped on board with the Eisenhower Administration's Middle East agenda. Vice President Richard Nixon had visited Karachi in December 1953, discussing a military-aid agreement with the Pakistani government, which in turn was negotiating a military-defence agreement with Turkey. Rumours were spinning in the region that Iraq was also about to walk into the American-sponsored Pakistani–Turkish alliance (which eventually became known as the Baghdad Pact), much to Shishakli's horror. In February 1954, the USA announced that Pakistan was eligible for US military aid, and by April Turkey and Pakistan had indeed signed the agreement, coinciding with official talks over military cooperation, between Iraq and the USA. Shishakli feared his international prestige would be damaged if he was left out of such a regional deal. Moreover, the standing of Syria, which, neither affiliated seriously with the USA nor with the USSR, threatened to make his regime vulnerable both in the neighbourhood and at home. Once empowered by the USA, Turkey and Iraq might, Shishakli reasoned, jump-start territorial ambitions in Syria. What made this all the more concerning for the Syrian President was a proposal in January 1954, from Iraqi Prime Minister Fadil al-Jamali, for an Arab Federation, a long-time ambition sponsored by the Hashemite family in Baghdad. Although Shishakli could not refuse the idea of Arab unity, newspapers in Syria published numerous articles critical of the Jamali plan, claiming that it was 'inspired by foreigners'.

Conclusion

Probably frantic and frightened that his time was up, in January 1954 Shishakli made the dire mistake of turning to the Soviet Union, when Moscow used its veto power at the UN to bring down a resolution that mildly criticized Israel for the DMZ affair. The move destroyed whatever confidence Eisenhower and Dulles still had in Shishakli, proving that his country's support for the USA in the Cold War was purely pragmatic, rather than ideological, and thus unreliable. Why support, or engage, they reasoned with a regime that was unpopular at home, had come to power via tanks rather than ballots, and was unable to take a firm position with regard to the Soviet Union and the rise of communism? All impressions of the man gathered during the years 1949–1951 vanished, and Shishakli suddenly appeared as a weak and confused leader, unable to take firm decisions on the direction he wanted to lead his country, with or against the USA. The fate of both Shukri al-Quwatli and Husni al-Za'im continued to haunt him – one had fallen because he had obstructed US plans in the region while the other collapsed because he had relied heavily on the USA. Shishakli's fate was sealed when, in February 1954, a rebellion broke out in Homs, Aleppo, the Syrian coast and the Druze Mountain. Rebellious elements in the Army, backed by the Baath Party and ex-President Atasi, coalesced to bring down the Syrian leader. Shishakli at first answered with brute force, sending his army to crush the insurgency in the Druze Mountain, killing an approximated 600 people – mostly civilians. As was the case with al-Za'im in 1949, those rioting against the President had no unified reason for wanting his downfall. Some were furious of his autocratic attitude within the Army, accusing him of harbouring sectarian tendencies and sheer favouritism for Sunni Muslim troops, at the expense of Druze, Alawites and Christians. The political classes were angry with Shishakli for outlawing parties and pre-siding over a uni-polar government headed by his own ALM. Islamists accused him of being too secular, while Arabists accused him of being a stooge of the USA. Ultimately, Shishakli's iron fist collapsed on 25 February 1954. The 44-year old President – by far the strongest in Syria since the 1932 creation of the Republic – resigned from office, ostensibly to prevent the continued Syrian bloodshed.

The gambler in Adib al-Shishakli had been finally defeated. None of those of whom he had bet upon – not officers or Americans – had stood by his side at curtain fall. Shishakli was given asylum by the pro-West government of Lebanese President Camille Chamoun then went briefly to Saudi Arabia before heading to his final exile in South America. He resurfaced briefly in Syria with an attempted coup in 1956, but the aftershocks of the Shishakli regime were drastic. Politically, the civilian class, disgusted with officer politics under both al-Za'im and Shishakli, decided to restore President Atasi to power, to continue what was left of the presidential term he had started in December 1949. Atasi and his team acted as if the Shishakli era had never passed. The constitution of 1950 was restored, along with the 1949 Parliament, which was packed with members of the People's Party. The controversial Prime Minister Maarouf al-Dawalibi who was coloured pro-Soviet by the Americans, was sym-bolically restored to power for a few hours, given that his cabinet was dis-solved by Shishakli, rather than constitutional procedures, during the coup of 1951. Psychologically, the Shishakli interlude had done a great disservice to the USA at a grassroots level in Syria. What use was Shishakli's honeymoon with the USA, ordinary Syrians were asking, if the USA was unable to bolster his regime when ordinary Syrians rebelled against it? A public resentment of both the USA and the officers, believed to be Shishakli's strongest backers, surfaced on the streets of Damascus, and this was especially true of the political class. Pro-Americanism suddenly became difficult and in many cases, domestically synonymous with political suicide.

9

TURNING BACK THE CLOCK

Shortly after returning to power in March 1954, President Hashem al-Atasi summoned Ambassador James Moose to the presidential palace and told him that all agreements negotiated between Syria and the USA under Adib al-Shishakli were now on indefinite hold. This was a particular reference to military aid and the Johnston Plan, he explained, adding that Syria had no desire to take sides with either the USA or the USSR in the cold war.[1] The USA initially had little interest in Atasi, who at the age of 80, was due to retire from political life in September 1955. Talking him into any deal in what remained of his presidential term was useless, given that there had been minimal contact between him and the USA during his presidential term in the mid-1930s and late 1940s. Atasi had the reputation of being a hard-line nationalist who had headed the anti-French movement in the first half of the twentieth century, and since then developed an intense dislike for any Western ambitions in Syria. The Eisenhower Administration, therefore, decided to wait and see what the upcoming parliamentary and presidential elections would bring for bilateral relations between Syria and the USA, watching from a distance nevertheless, to see how the 'struggle for Syria' developed between Egypt, Saudi Arabia and Iraq.

The rise of Colonel Nasser

During the first half of the 1950s, two important players in the struggle parted the scene, further complicating the complex web of Syrian–US relations. One was King Abdul Aziz of Saudi Arabia, who died in 1953 after over 30 years in power, bequeathing the throne to his son, King Saud. The late monarch had played the go-between in Syrian–US relations during the 1940s, especially during the Quwatli era, and was known within political circles in Damascus as constantly having the ear of any occupant of the White House. His son, the new monarch, remained committed to his country's US alliance, inheriting as well the historic animosity between the House of Saud and the House of Hashem that ruled in Amman and Baghdad. That was one reason why he had been a close friend of ex-President Shishakli in the last year of his tenure in power; he had hoped that by embracing Syria he could keep it out of the Hashemite clutches. According to US Ambassador Moose, Saudi Arabia had paid up to SP 300,000 to pro-Shishakli elements in the Syrian Army, in a desperate attempt to keep the former President in power, to no avail.[2]

The other major change was in Egypt, when, on 23 July 1952, a group of officers in the Egyptian Army toppled the young flamboyant monarch, King Farouk I, another old friend of both the Syrians and the USA. A group of young men, known as the Free Officers, toppled Farouk and sent him onboard his royal yacht *el-Mahrousa* into exile in Europe, along with his entire family, with orders never to return. Shishakli had known the Egyptian officers well, having served with them at the warfront in Palestine in 1948. All of them were in their mid-to-late thirties, five generations younger than Atasi, making communication between Damascus and Cairo increasingly difficult in the immediate post-Shishakli era.

Atasi was unimpressed by Colonel Gamal Abdul Nasser and the rebellious officers who surrounded him. They looked, spoke and acted like the officer class in Syria, which Atasi and his generation had so detested. With the exception of their General Mohammad Naguib, who headed the newly created Revolutionary Command Council (RCC) because of the seniority of his rank and advancement of his age, the Egyptian officers were all younger than President Atasi's youngest son, speaking a rough and aggressive political language unfamiliar to the Ottoman-trained Syrian leader. Atasi, therefore, found familiar and safe territory for Syria in Iraq, which was still ruled by the dynasty of King Faisal I, under whom Atasi had served as Prime Minister in 1920. Fadil al-Jamali, the Iraqi premier who had formulated the plan for Arab unity shortly before Shishakli's ouster in 1953, was an old friend of the Syrian president, and so was his immediate successor, the six-time Iraqi Prime Minister, Nuri Pasha al-Said. Nasser, trying to market himself as a pan-Arab leader, naturally detested the Jamali Plan, considering it a product of British imperial scheming since it hoped to revive the ancient Hashemite ambition in Syria – a view shared by many Hashemite critics in the Syrian capital. The fact that Shishakli was a sworn enemy of Iraq, launching his original 1951 coup to thwart Iraqi influence in Syria, made the Iraqis all the more happier to see the end of him.

They embraced the coup of 1954 and were among the first to welcome the return of Atasi to power and his immediate restoration of a parliament packed with members of the Iraq-backed People's Party. Quite unintentionally, Atasi was forced to take sides in the cold war, rallying behind Iraq and the USA, against the Soviet-backed Gamal Abdul Nasser.

Nasser began to spread anti-Iraq propaganda from Cairo, shortly after the Syrian coup of 1954. His famous 'Voice of the Arabs' radio station, which launched daily attacks on the Hashemite family and its allies, had been set up in January 1954 and reached every home inside Syria with a one-hour daily broadcast. By July 1954, the broadcast had been expanded to four hours, launching a loud war of words against Baghdad, much to the displeasure of President Atasi and his People's Party allies who were suddenly being scrutinized for their relationship with Iraq.[3] Supporting the Baghdad government shortly after it had ventured into an alliance with Pakistan and Turkey, began to sound like a capital offence, similar to pro-Americanism. Atasi's new Prime Minister Sabri al-Asali (another old friend of Iraq), added insult to injury when he gave an interview to *The New York Times* journalist Kenneth Love in Damascus, saying that Syria offered 'open endorsement' of the Turkish–Pakistani–Iraqi alliance – words echoed by his pro-Western Foreign Minister, Faydi al-Atasi.[4] Rather than waiting for Atasi to leave office, the Eisenhower Administration rapidly began to make use of his presence while it lasted, sending General Arthur Trudeau, the Deputy Chief-of-Staff of the US Army, to Damascus for talks with the ageing Syrian President.[5] Trudeau hinted that Syria might be eligible for US aid if it continued to side with Iraq against the rising and troubling influence of Gamal Abdul Nasser. While the US General was in Syria, Prime Minister Asali went to the Lebanese summer resort of Brummanah for unofficial talks with ex-Iraqi Prime Minister Jamali.[6] Realizing how important it was to avoid being labelled pro-American, the Asali cabinet tried to avoid speaking about Iraq in public.[7]

The first to take note of the Syrian government's new attitude was the SCP, which staged large demonstrations in Damascus on 29 May, criticizing the pro-Iraq policy of Prime Minister Asali.[8] The Baath Party, also fearful of Iraqi ambitions in Syria, teamed up with the communists in stirring up street-wide demonstrations against Asali, finally succeeding in bringing him down in early June 1954, only four months after he came to power. Atasi attempted to calm the situation, calling on the independent attorney Said al-Ghazzi to form a cabinet, which declared complete neutrality in foreign policy, and claiming its only job was to administer the upcoming parliamentary elections, scheduled for late August 1954.

The Eisenhower Administration did not give up, however, resorting to the United States Information Agency (USIA) to help win the minds and hearts of ordinary Syrians. Although USIA had limited funding, only $100,000 annually, it hired native Arab speakers in 1954 to translate and broadcast the speeches of President Eisenhower and Secretary Dulles into Arabic, where they tried to shatter earlier stereotypes on the Syrian street by publicly declaring that they had never favoured Israel at the expense of the Arabs.[9] In the summer of 1954, the USIA got the chance to flex its muscles, when the Syrian government announced that it was going to sponsor an annual fair in September (the fair has since become a much anticipated annual event, known as the Damascus International Fair). Slated as the largest in the Middle East, the Damascus Fair was held under the patronage of President Atasi, with stands for 26 countries including Egypt, Turkey, France, Germany, Russia, China and the USA.

The Cinerama in Damascus

Harris Peel, the director of the US Information Office in Syria, came up with the brilliant idea of sending the Cinerama, which had never been shown outside the USA, to the Damascus Fair. The Cinerama gave a three-panel ultra-wide screen projection of motion pictures in panoramic view and had premiered with a thundering success in New York in 1952. 'People did not watch it; they experienced it,' wrote mainstream Syrian dailies, thrilled to report that Cinerama was premiering in Damascus ahead of any other world capital.[10] If this was not going to enchant the Syrians, Embassy officials reasoned, nothing would. The Damascenes, after all, were always hungry for American films, preferring action-filled Western thrillers of Hollywood to the sentimental romantic flicks of French cinema. A large outdoor theatre was built at the fairgrounds, and Cinerama opened on 2 September 1954, attended by 1,500 notables from Damascus, including President Atasi. Those who could not get tickets to the show climbed trees and nearby rooftops to get a glimpse of the amazing American large-screen spectacle. Injuries were a nightly event as un-ticketed fans fell from snapped branches to break arms and legs. The Russians in their own right had spent $500,000 building the biggest pavilion at the Damascus Fair, pouring men, material, and hiring 1,200 Syrians to build a 40,000 square-metre pavilion, decorated with the Red Star, but were certainly not prepared for the American cinematic invention. The four projectors and 72-speakers for the American Cinerama were sent to Syria by Warner Bros, and shipped by the US Air Force, along with a 62,000-watt generator (Cinerama alone could use all of the electricity of Damascus).[11]

The first VIP screening took the Damascenes on a roller coaster, without them having to leave the ground, then had them tour the USA by plane, visiting the Grand Canyon and Niagara Falls. The whole experience was set to a sound track of 'America: the Beautiful'. A free two-day show ensued, attended by rural residents and shepherds who had come from faraway districts to see what the USA had brought to the East. The US Information Agency distributed 150,000 tickets for free during the show's month-long run, and informal estimates had a total of nearly 250,000 attendees, out of a total Damascus population of 360,000. The Russians were furious with the success of Cinerama, while other countries presented at the Fair complained of 'unfair competition'.[12]

The elections of 1954

Syrians may have been swept away by the Cinerama, but nevertheless did not take their emotions with them to the polls two weeks later, on 24 September 1954. The elections were carried out in an orderly manner, revealing results, however, that were horrific – to say the least – for the Eisenhower White House. Out of a total of 142 seats, the hard-line anti-American Baath Party got 17 seats, along with 4 sympathizers, giving them a total command of 21 seats.[13] That raised their lot from 5 per cent in the Parliament of 1949 to 15 per cent in the Parliament of 1954. The pro-Western People's Party, which saw union with Iraq as part of a patriotic Arab nationalism approach, lost 50 per cent of their seats – mainly due to their unwavering commitment to Baghdad, more-or-less sealing the fate of Iraqi ambitions in Syria. Thirty independents with close ties to leftist elements in the Syrian Army, marched into Parliament under command of the independent presidential-hopeful, Khaled al-Azm. What struck a particular raw nerve in Washington DC was the victory of Khaled Bakdash, the President of the SCP, who became the first communist parliamentarian in the entire Middle East, campaigning of course on an anti-USA platform.

Pro-Western politicians such as Sabri al-Asali and Munir al-Ajlani tried to allay US fears by saying there was very little Bakdash could do within the chamber, since he was only one out of 142 parliamentarians, claiming that it was Syrian Kurds rather than Syrian communists who had won Bakdash a parliamentary seat.[14] The communist scare, however, had hit Damascus at full speed, leading to a collision between Syria and the USA that lasted more-or-less until 1961, and affected bilateral relations between Damascus and Washington like nothing before. President Atasi, realizing how worried the USA was with Bakdash's victory, called on a trusted friend of the USA, the 77-year old Fares al-Khoury, to form a cabinet in November 1954. Khoury's cabinet, hailed as a return of the traditional class of urban notables to power, was immediately coloured pro-West. The Ministry of Foreign Affairs went to the pro-Western statesman from Homs, Faydi al-Atasi, while veterans of the People's Party such as Rashad Barmada became Minister of Defence, and Ali Buzzo became Minister of Justice. A close friend of Iraq, Munir al-Ajlani, was appointed Minister of Education, while Ahmad Qanbar, a loud critic of the officer class, became Minister of Interior.

Prime Minister Khoury and President Atasi had led parallel careers, dating back to the Ottoman era. Both had been born in the 1870s and had grown up in Ottoman Syria. They had supported Faisal's short lived Arab kingdom in 1918–1920, with Khoury serving as Finance Minister in a cabinet chaired by Atasi himself. Under the mandate, they had worked together to co-found the National Bloc, the leading anti-French movement, and had co-authored the Syrian Republican Constitution of 1928. They had also both taken part in the Franco–Syrian independence talks of 1936 and, when Atasi became President shortly after the treaty was signed, Khoury served as his Speaker of Parliament until 1939. Although never too fond of the West, both were civilized, refined and worldly statesmen who looked down upon dictatorial rule and viewed Gamal Abdul Nasser as no different from Adib al-Shishakli or Husni al-Za'im. The militarization of Cairo politics, they believed, would have a drastic effect on the Arab neighbourhood, giving birth to leftist parties and politicians in Syria who would want to wrestle power from the civilians – power that had been reclaimed with blood, sweat and tears from Colonel Shishakli back in February. Five years of military rule (1949–1954) were more than enough for the civilian class in Syria to make them think twice before steering their country in the direction of Egypt. While Atasi had never travelled beyond Europe, Khoury knew the USA well, having served as his country's representative to the UN during the second half of the 1940s. If forced to choose between Nasserism and Iraq, then they both opted for an alliance with Baghdad. The Iraqi leaders, after all, were old trusted friends who had served with them since the days of the Faisal era. Nasser was young – too young – and came from a country that, back in the mid-1950s, was still seen as distant from the Middle East. Nasser and his RCC were seen as 'too emotional' and lacking real political experience, while both Khoury and Atasi were grey with age, having spent more than 50 years in the complex world of Arab politics.[15] In future years Atasi was to famously grumble before one of his pro-Egyptian ministers: 'Do you realise what you are doing? You are giving this country away on a silver platter, to the young Pharaoh!'[16] Additionally, much to Nasser's displeasure, both Atasi and Khoury were good friends of the former King of Egypt, Farouk I, who was now spending his exile in royalty on the seaside in Italy. They spoke, acted and belonged to a generation of politicians who had admired and collaborated with the Mohammad Ali dynasty – which Nasser had dismantled – either with Farouk himself or his father, King Fouad I. Friends of Farouk, Nasser reasoned, were no less pro-Western than Farouk himself. Sending a new Syrian ambassador to Baghdad made matters worse, signalling that a new era had dawned, and a meeting between Khoury and King Faisal II took place in Beirut in November 1954, hailed by the Syrian press as a sign of strength of the Syrian–Iraqi relations.

The return of Fares al-Khoury

On 9 December 1954, Prime Minister Khoury gave an interview to the Egyptian weekly *al-Musawwar*, sending shockwaves throughout the upper echelons of power in Cairo. 'Let us accept American arms and defend ourselves against Israel. Accept American weapons and attack Israel when we can. I assure you I can explain our position before the United Nations and the International Court of Justice. What is important is having means to attack,' he said.[17] An odd remark for someone of Khoury's calibre, given that he knew – as everyone in Syria knew – that when it comes to the Middle East, one cannot dislocate Israel from the USA. Rather than appeal to the anti-Israeli nationalists among the Syrian public, Khoury only made things worse with such a poorly prepared statement which enraged the Baath Party, the Communists and the Muslim Brotherhood. It resounded badly with politicians in the US Congress, appalled that someone whom they considered a friend would speak with such thundering logic against the State of Israel.

The short-lived Khoury cabinet was able to concentrate very little on Syrian domestics, since its agenda was dominated by the controversial Turkish–Pakistani pact, which had been signed in February 1954 and was about to expand to include a similar pact between Iraq and Turkey. The Baghdad Pact, as it came to be known, was modelled after the North Atlantic Treaty Organization (NATO) and committed its members to mutual cooperation and protection, in addition to non-intervention in each other's affairs. It had a clear objective of creating a strong belt of nations along the south-western front of the Soviet Union to help combat and curb rising communist influence among the Arabs. From day one, Nasser and the new regime in Cairo had rejected the Baghdad Pact, claiming that it was an imperialist tool aimed at invading the region – an attitude shared by Saudi Arabia for totally different reasons – since the new King Saud deplored any rise in the position of Iraq at the expense of his own kingdom and its relations both with the Arabs and the USA. The Syrian political class was divided on the pact. Leftist parties and students at the Syrian University were indoctrinated against it, while an older generation of politicians favoured a less aggressive approach, believing that only through an alliance with the West – and the USA – could they build a strong nation immune to officer ambitions and strength of the IDF. By joining the West in a military alliance, they hoped to professionalize the Syrian Army and ward off the ambitions of young officers who were closely allied to the Baath or Communist parties.[18]

President Nasser called for a conference of Arab Prime Ministers in Cairo from 22–29 January 1955, mainly to lecture Iraq on the wrongs of the Baghdad Pact as a Western scheme. Earlier, in the summer of 1954, Nasser had met Nuri Pasha in Cairo to discuss the proposed pact, advising him to wait until the British evacuated the Suez Canal to see if they deserved an alliance with the Arabs or not. Far from taking the Egyptian leader's advice, Nuri al-Said carried on with his foreign policy, refusing to attend the Cairo conference in January 1955, claiming that he was confined to his bed by illness, instead sending his predecessor, Fadil al-Jamali, along with the Iraqi Deputy Prime Minister, Ahmad Mukhtar Baban and Deputy Foreign Minister, Burhan al-Din Bashayan. Nine days before the conference, however, the Iraqi Prime Minister announced that he would be concluding a pact with Turkey on 13 January, infuriating the Egyptian President, whose official radio declared in January that, 'Any alliance with Turkey, the friend of Israel, necessarily means an indirect alliance with Israel itself'.[19] Nasser himself clearly declared, 'No Arab country should join the alliance. It is a defence pact which ignores the interests of the Middle East.'[20]

Leftist parties in Syria were criticizing the Baghdad Pact as a creation of the USA around the clock. Turning a deaf ear to the loud cries, however, Prime Minister Khoury went to Cairo with his Foreign Minister Faydi al-Atasi, but not before summoning Ambassador Moose to government headquarters on 13 January, to make clear the USA should not raise its hopes too high with regard to Syria agreeing to sign the Baghdad Pact. While both agreed Damascus could not continue living in isolation as a result of the polarization that was gripping people by the throat, they nevertheless could not afford to be too vocal about the problem given the rising popular resentment towards Iraq in the Syrian capital. It was, after all, the Hashemites who had signed off an agreement with Chaim Weizmann in 1919 and then had fled Syria hours after the invading French Army had marched into Damascus in 1920. Hashemite influence was a bad brand name in Syria, given the boundless ambition of the likes of King Abdullah of Jordan and King Faisal of Iraq, both of whom spent a lifetime trying to replace the locally elected politicians in Syria with the Hashemite crown. Nothing was off limits to the Hashemite royals, from buying off politicians to political assassinations, helping stage coups, and playing one party against the other, as had been the case since 1949.

It was no secret that President Atasi and Prime Minister Khoury wanted to join the Baghdad Pact to ward off Nasserist and Soviet influence in Syria. A brief yet high-profile visit by Turkish Prime Minister Adnan Menderes to Damascus on 13 January 1955 only helped complicate the situation for pro-Western Syrian statesmen since he reportedly landed in the Syrian capital to talk the Syrian leadership into joining the Baghdad Pact. Prior to the Prime Minister's take-off to Cairo, the Parliament's Foreign Affairs Committee, chaired by the Baathist Salah al-Din al-Bitar, reminded Khoury of his cabinet policy statement from the November before, in which he promised to remain 'absolutely neutral,' refusing to join either the US or the Soviet blocs. In addition to Bitar, the Committee contained two of the loudest anti-Khoury and anti-US politicians in Syria, Khaled Bakdash and Akram al-Hawrani of the Arab Socialist Party, whose political machine had merged with the Baath during the Shishakli era. Meanwhile, Cairo timed an onslaught on the pact and anybody who even thought of joining it – a clear message directed at Atasi and Khoury. Pro-Nasser politicians stirred up massive anti-Khoury demonstrations in Damascus, forcing the Prime Minister to push a bill through parliament preventing school students and teachers from taking part in political demonstrations.

Regional dynamics meant the Baath had moved closer than ever before to both the Communist Party and Egypt, identifying a common enemy in the Hashemite royalty in Iraq. And, due to their rising influence on the Syrian streets, Khoury could not continue defying them for too long. In Cairo, he refused to adhere to Nasser's argument with regard to Iraq, eventually preventing the Conference from issuing a strongly worded condemnation of Baghdad. He went ahead with a provocative scheme against Nasser, warmly embracing the Egyptian Muslim Brotherhood, which had set up base in Syria after having tried and failed to assassinate Nasser in Alexandria in 1954. Nasser was furious at the Syrians for offering sanctuary to the Brotherhood, which he labelled a terrorist organization, and repeatedly called on Khoury to do something about the loud anti-Egypt campaign they had launched from Syria. When that failed, he temporarily withdrew his ambassador from Syria on 13 November, putting the differences between the Syrians and the new leaders in Cairo into sharp relief. Not stopping there, the Syrians further provoked Nasser by giving asylum

to Egyptian journalist Mahmud Abu al-Fath, publisher of al-Misri, the official mouthpiece of the Wafd Party, who came to Syria after the Nasser government sentenced him to 15 years in jail and confiscated all of his property. He
was treated as a guest of honour by both President Atasi and Prime Minister
Khoury, who held a banquet in his honour. Abu al-Fath eventually travelled
to Iraq, under the sponsorship of the Syrians, and was given both asylum and
Iraqi citizenship by Nuri Pasha.[21] On 4 December 1954, Nasser had hanged
six Muslim Brotherhood members in Egypt, arousing massive anti-Egypt demonstrations across Syria, which held up traffic, and nearly brought schools and
university to a grinding halt. To Nasser's horror, the Syrian government refused
to lift a finger to suppress the brotherhood's activities and did nothing to stop
the brotherhood's Syrian leader, Moustapha al-Sibaii (a native of Homs like
President Atasi) who spoke from the pulpits of Damascus mosques, accusing
Nasser of being a US agent.

Khoury's cabinet began to fall apart when, on 31 January 1955, it faced
a Baath-dominated Syrian chamber, shortly after the Prime Minister's return
from Cairo. The budget committee, chaired by Akram Hawrani, rejected
Khoury's budget, prompting Economy Minister Fakhir al-Kayyali to resign
from office on 5 February, rendering the government unconstitutional. Making
life more difficult for the Prime Minister was the walk-out by Lutfi al-Haffar,
another veteran politician, from the National Party co-chaired by Khoury, on
the basis that he objected to the polarity dividing the Syrian political classes
between pro-Egypt and pro-Iraq.[22]

Conclusion

The demise of Fares al-Khoury, who eventually retired from political life
in 1955, spoke volumes about where things had reached in Syria. Here was
a man, hailed as co-founder of the Syrian Republic only nine years earlier,
now being ejected from power with little ceremony or appreciation, by a dis-
gruntled Syrian population that had wanted something new for Syria. All of
his personal attributes, and a long list of war medals earned combating the
Ottomans and French, were not enough to save Khoury from the fate of many
who boarded the US boat in the 1950s, trying to ride the high waves of Arab
nationalism coming from Cairo. In retrospect, Khoury could by no means be
written-off as simply 'pro-American' since he never spoke a language similar
to pro-US figures of future generations, like Shah Reza Pahlavi of Iran, or
President Hamid Karzai of Afghanistan. Additionally, he owed the USA neither his political existence nor his legacy, although they were not glad to see

the end of him, yet in the complex world of the 1950s the audacity of defying Nasser or cuddling up to the USA spelt out political destruction for even the most respected and seasoned of statesmen.[23] Just three years after his resignation, Khoury grumbled as he watched Syria and Egypt merge to form the United Arab Republic in 1958, telling British journalist Patrick Seale, 'It was done in a minute, in a foolish minute'. His granddaughter, Colette Khoury, a ranking novelist and parliamentarian in the 1990s, recalled visiting his home in 1958, on the day union was signed, 'Fares Bey was bent in two, clearly very frustrated by what was happening'. She was a young woman, passionate about union with Nasser's Egypt, but the former Premier shouted that 'Union cannot be scrambled like this! These people scrambled it! Wait and see, Gamal Abdul Nasser will take this country 200 years back into darkness!' Not surprisingly, when Khoury resigned in February, the mouthpiece of the Egyptian government, al-Jumhuriyya, wrote a inflammatory article, accusing him of having wanted to sabotage the Cairo-based Arab League, and falling just short of branding him an agent for the USA.[24]

Nasser, from where Khoury saw things, was a manifestation of what the Eastern Bloc and communism would do to Syria, as opposed to the possibilities of an alliance with the USA. What makes his words all the more intriguing is that pro-Americanism came to a grinding halt in Syria after Khoury's resignation in February 1955, closely followed Atasi's retirement in September. Those who had faith in what the USA had to offer had from here on to shut up or face the fate of all those who preceded them in moving towards the USA.

10

ROPES OF SAND

Replacing Fares al-Khoury as Prime Minister of Syria, for what remained of Hashem al-Atasi's tenure, was none other than Sabri al-Asali, another friend of Iraq, who had held the premiership for 100 days in the immediate post-Shishakli era. Asali, known by his *nom de guerre*, 'Abu Shujaa' (Father of the Brave) was relatively younger than both men, aged only 52 in 1955. A lawyer by education and practice, the plump politician began his career in the National Bloc of Damascus under the French, serving briefly as political consultant to King Abdul-Aziz of Saudi Arabia in the 1930s. He was never a front man in the struggle against the French although he flirted with an ultra-nationalist organ in the 1930s called the League of National Action, only to resign and join the Bloc under the urging of Shukri al-Quwatli in 1936. During the Quwatli presidency of 1943–1949, he served as a member of parliament and Interior Minister, barely surviving an assassination attempt during the Palestine War. He was retired by General al-Za'im in March 1949 but re-emerged in 1949–1951 as a loud supporter of his former patron Quwatli, and Saudi Arabia, and a silent patron of Iraq.

Asali was a skilled politician with little ideological background, willing to support whatever regional or international power seemed to be getting the upper hand in Syrian politics, be it American, British, Iraqi or Egyptian. Patrick Seale described him as 'At the bottom ... an old-style politician, without program, principle, or ideology, whose frequent subsequent appearances as Prime Minister were less an indicator of his political weight than of the fact that was acceptable as a pliant compromise candidate, to both right and left wings in the Chamber'.[1] Over the next three years, Asali was like a political chameleon, siding with the Iraqis, the Egyptians, the Americans and the Saudis in turn, with the single purpose of keeping his coalition cabinet alive. When Asali came to power, the US Embassy in Damascus reported, 'Pro-West elements in Syria still have considerable strength but need courage to use their strength at a critical moment because they fear that the army will intervene to install an even-more radical government.'[2] At that stage Asali was considered pro-West, in need of US endorsement, just like his predecessor, Fares al-Khoury. Within a short period of time, the USA realized how deceived it had been with the Syrian Premier, who rather than knocking on doors of the White House, had steered his country down the long road towards the Soviet Union.

During his first tenure as Prime Minister, Asali had excluded both the Baath party and Akram al-Hawrani from any cabinet posts, although they had played a leading role in bringing down the Shishakli regime. Asali had tried to stage a comeback in 1949 by cuddling up to the Iraqis – reversing views that had coloured his career for years and earning him little respect among the indoctrinated elite of young Baathists, Communists and Islamists. The fact that he was partner in a prestigious law firm that worked for leading American companies, including Tapline, made him even more suspicious.[3] He formed his cabinet on 13 February 1955 and tried to appease all tastes across the political spectrum. Wahib al-Ghanim, a young physician and Baath founder, was named Minister of State and Acting Minister of Health, while the French-trained attorney, Maamoun al-Kuzbari, a former protégé of President Shishakli, was made Minister of Justice. The enigmatic Khaled al-Azm, an independent, became Minister of Foreign Affairs, while Leon Zamariyya, a pro-Western notable from Aleppo, became Minister of Finance. His cabinet received a 66–54 vote of confidence within the Syrian Parliament on 24 February – the same day the Baghdad Pact was signed. In his cabinet policy statement, Prime Minister Asali promised 'complete neutrality', declared that Zionism was Syria's number one enemy, and rejected adhering to any Western pact – all the magic words needed to keep the officers, the leftists and the Egyptians at bay.

A few days after Asali came to power, Nasser dispatched his National Guidance Minister, Salah Salim, to Damascus to assess where Asali really stood with regard to the political football underway over the fate of Syria. Coinciding with the Egyptian Minister's visit was a clear remark from the Egyptian leader: 'No Arab country should join the [Baghdad Pact] alliance. It is a defence pact which ignores the interests of the Middle East, and at the same time, aims at frustrating the work of the Arab League.'[4] Seeing the fate of his predecessor, and the rising discontent with Iraq on the Syrian street, Asali decided to place his full weight behind Egypt, sending his Foreign Minister Khaled al-Azm to sign a mutual defence agreement with Cairo and Saudi Arabia, in March 1955.[5] Although the Saudis were pro-USA, they were also vehemently anti-Iraqi, wanting to curb and eventually eliminate the influence of Hashemite Iraq in the Arab world, which had historically run through Syria. He tried a last minute attempt at mending broken fences between Cairo and Baghdad, dispatching Azm to Iraq in mid-March, but Nuri al-Said was uninterested in any rapprochement with the young Nasser.[6] What made things easier for the Syrian Prime Minister to turn his back on the Iraqis was an Israeli raid on the Egyptian-controlled Gaza Strip on 28 February 1955, which led to the killing of 40 Egyptians, sending emotions soaring on the Syrian street in favour of Nasser. After Ariel Sharon, then a young officer in the Israeli Defence Force (IDF), raided Gaza, Nasser realized how weak his army actually was, telling his aides, 'We need arms at any cost, even from the devil himself!'[7] The Gaza raid was a turning point in the history of the Middle East; the result of an internal power struggle between the moderate Prime Minister Moshe Sharett (who had tried to talk to Husni al-Za'im back in 1949) and the hard-line ex-Premier, David Ben Gurion. Upon hearing of secret talks in Paris between an Egyptian envoy and an Israeli diplomat, Ben Gurion saw to it that sabotage attacks were carried out within Egypt, against American and British targets, to damage Nasser's relationship with the West. When the secret cell was uncovered, Nasser lifted a muzzle he had placed on Egyptian newspapers, allowing them to criticize Israel at will, and turned a blind eye to the military activities of Palestinian commandos, known as 'fedayeen,' through the Gaza Strip. Despite a personal appeal from Sharett, Nasser could not but execute the Israeli spies, triggering a response from the IDF on 28 February.[8]

Speaking to British journalist Patrick Seale, Salim recalled the situation right after the Gaza raid saying, 'I will be frank with you; we were desperately weak. Our armed forces were short of everything.'[9] So began an ongoing Egyptian hunt for arms, which took Nasser to Czechoslovakia in September 1955, and to other countries in the Eastern bloc, with Syria closely following behind. The *Jerusalem Post* commented on Asali's apparent backflip, saying: 'We hope that the Israeli raid has convinced many Syrians that the military pact with Egypt has increased the danger to Syria instead of guaranteeing Syria's defences.'[10] Syria claimed, shortly after signing the agreement with Egypt, that it formally rejected the Baghdad Pact. After what happened in Gaza, one Syrian cabinet minister recalled, 'It would have been absolute madness for any politician with the right mind to opt for any alliance with the West, in particular, the United States, which was seen as Israel's principle backer in Gaza'.[11]

The downfall of Husni al-Barazi

One of the few who remained loudly pro-USA in Syria, even after the Gaza raid, was former Prime Minister Husni al-Barazi. Scion to a wealthy landowning family from Hama, Barazi was an Ottoman-trained politician who had started his political career as a member of the National Bloc, working with respected nationalists like Fares al-Khoury and Hashem al-Atasi. He backed out on the Bloc in 1939 and briefly served as Prime Minister under the pro-French regime of President Taj al-Din al-Hasani in 1941. After leaving office, Barazi held on to his parliamentary seat and was famously the only deputy in the Syrian Chamber to speak in favour of the UN Partition Plan for Palestine in 1947. His bold views and highly pro-USA positions made him a polarizing figure, shunned by the politically ambitious who feared any association with him would spell political suicide. Barazi disappeared from public life after the Palestine War only to re-emerge when his cousin, Adib al-Shishakli came to power in 1951. During the Shishakli years, Husni al-Barazi established a newspaper in Syria, *al-Nass* (The People). Unlike most mainstream media, it did not claim objectivity in the cold war but was loudly in favour of the USA, calling for Syria to pursue the same path as Jordan, Turkey and Iran. In all of his editorials, Barazi would warn that Syria had nothing in common with the Soviet Union, claiming the communists wanted to rob ordinary Syrians of their wealth and commitment to religion, be it Islam or Christianity. For obvious reasons, the newspaper had very low readership and would sell no more than a handful of copies throughout Syria. Viewed as a tool for US propaganda, it attracted few advertisers and was often bankrolled from Barazi's own pocket.

Barazi strongly denied receiving funding or instructions from the USA, claiming that *al-Nass* was an independent Syrian publication, free to express its admiration for the USA without necessarily having to have a US connection. He would write about pro-Russian officials in Syria, describing them as 'vandals who aim at ruining this country's economic and agriculture potential'. The officers who backed them, according to Barazi, 'were bent on looting and stealing, and were the filthiest of men, both educationally and morally'. At one point he boldly editorialized, 'We need a surgical operation to remove the cancerous military from the political life of Syria'. He would mock Gamal Abdul Nasser, referring to him as 'Nasserov' and would later reflect: 'I was convinced early on of his Soviet tendencies. He will eventually bring not only Egypt but the entire Arab world, to complete collapse. Nasser is a harmful and destructive element in the region'.[12]

It came as no surprise for the pro-US publisher when his office was ransacked by Syrian intelligence in late 1954, while he was on a trip to Turkey. All property was confiscated, the editors were all arrested, and the newspaper's licence was suspended. When Barazi angrily telephoned what remained of his staff from Ankara, he learned that they were closed down on charges of 'spreading destructive venom that strikes at the social and ethnic fabric of society'. Al-Nass was not only accused of being a propaganda tool for the USA, but Barazi of being an agent for the CIA, although the man had lost any real political influence since leaving the premiership back in 1941. A warrant for his arrest quickly followed, despite his background and high profile contacts. A military court sentenced him to death in absentia, forcing him to spend the remainder of his years in Lebanon, where he died 21 years later, in 1975. His story speaks volumes about the state of affairs in Syria and how difficult – and costly – it had become for anyone to look, sound or act pro-USA.

False alarm of an Iraqi invasion

Barazi's story did not arouse more than a stir in diplomatic circles in the Syrian capital; it was overshadowed by rumours that Iraq was planning for a military offensive on Syria, to come to the aid of what remained of its allies in Damascus. According to Waldemar Gallman, the US Ambassador to Baghdad, Iraqi officials approached him in March 1955, less than one month after the Gaza raid, saying that they had received a note from President Atasi, who claimed to be under tremendous pressure from leftists within Syria to sign the military pact with Egypt.[13] They tried to paint a picture of a rift between the Syrian President and his Prime Minister, one being pro-Iraq and the other suddenly emerging as pro-Egyptian. Reportedly, Asali had told the President that unless the pact was immediately signed, a coup was imminent in Syria. Asali had been approached by two Syrian officers, Chief-of-Staff Shawkat Shuqayr and his protégé Abdul Hamid Sarraj, who claimed to be speaking on behalf of 300 junior officers who wanted to distance Syria from Iraq and terminate the Syrian–Iraqi honeymoon, seeing it as an extension of US influence in the Middle East. Shuqayr reportedly reminded the Syrian leader of how Syria and Egypt had collaborated centuries ago, to fight off the Crusades, claiming that a similar pact should go into effect in the twentieth century.[14] Both Shuqayr and Sarraj were former disciples of Shishakli, known for harbouring pro-Egyptian loyalties within the Syrian Army. According to Ambassador Gallman, Atasi had asked the Iraqis to intervene in Syria – militarily if need be – to prevent Asali from signing the pact with Egypt. The Iraqis had told Gallman that they were ready for military intervention, which would be temporary, aimed only at 'saving Syria from communist infiltration'. John Foster Dulles was deeply alarmed by the Iraqi warning, sending a note to his ambassador in Syria, asking him to beg Hashem al-Atasi to reconsider his invitation to the Iraqis.

Dulles wrote to the embassy in Syria:

> Inform Iraqi Foreign Minister immediately. US Government would be deeply concerned over Iraqi military intervention in Syria, even at request of the Syrian President. Gaza situation very tense. Intervention would heighten Israeli apprehensions and might tip the balance of decision within Israel in favor of activist program which could launch Israeli military action against one or several Arab states. Furthermore, Department fears mere intervention by Syrian President under whatever presumed authority of Syrian Constitution, might not be considered sufficient expression of Syrian popular will and might be vigorously opposed by much of the Syrian Army.[15]

The ageing Syrian president was warned that the USA would not necessarily recognize a government brought to power by military might of the Iraqi Army. Ambassador Moose did meet with both President Atasi and Prime Minister Asali on 16 April, where Atasi and Asali both denied having received such a threat and having asked the Iraqis to intervene militarily in Syria.[16] It eventually emerged that no such idea was in fact on the table of the Syrian president, but the Iraqis inflated the entire deal, to test the pulse of the US administration if they were to venture into Syria in a last-minute attempt at thwarting the rising influence of Nasserism among the residents of Damascus.

Watching all these developments was the US Government, which was receiving repeated cables from Ambassador Moose, warning of the rising communist trend in Syria.[17] The writing had been on the wall for months, warned Moose, referring to China's participation at the Damascus International Fair, the victory of Khaled Bakdash, and now, the Syrian–Egyptian alliance, which had explicit backing of the Soviet Union, given Moscow's strong relations with Nasser. Dulles wrote back: 'It does not appear in the Department's present view that there is anything we can usefully do in Syria to affect the situation.'[18] Soviet Foreign Minister Molotov met with the Syrian Ambassador in Moscow, Farid al-Khani, saying that his country was 'prepared to help Syria maintain its independence and freedom' in the face of American, Iraqi and Turkish pressure. The Soviet Ambassador to Damascus showed up at Asali's office in the Grand Sarrail, to deliver the same message.[19] Alarmed, the Turks amassed their troops on the Syrian border in March 1955, prompting Nasser to snap, on Cairo Radio, 'If Turkey believes that force will settle the situation in Syria, then Turkey must remember that she too has a neighbour which is stronger than she is (in reference to the USSR)'.[20] The US Embassy remarked, 'Continuation of the Asali cabinet endangers US interests by giving opportunity to the Communists to gain control of essentials of power within a few months'.[21]

The Syrian–Soviet Honeymoon

From 1955 until 1958, Sabri al-Asali took Syria down the road to a firm political and economic alliance with the Soviet Union, reasoning that such a foreign policy was required in order to maintain strong ties with Nasser's Egypt. The Egyptians, after all, had received an offer for an unlimited amount of arms, including tanks and planes 'of the latest design', from the Soviet Union. This was in exchange for deferred payment in Egyptian cotton and rice, said the Soviet Ambassador to Moscow, who added that Moscow was willing to help finance the Aswan High Dam.[22] The RCC met to discuss the Russian offer in May 1955, and before accepting, decided to try their luck with the West, one last time. President Nasser met with the British and American Ambassadors to Egypt and bluntly threatened to head East, if arms were not given to Egypt. According to those surrounding Nasser, Washington and London 'thought he was bluffing'.[23] The Syrians watched, taking the cue from Nasser, as Cairo embraced Dmitri Shepilov, Editor-in-Chief of the mass circulation Russian daily *Pravada*, who landed in Cairo on 22 July and wrote in favour of closer ties between his country and both Egypt and Syria. Shepilov, earmarked to become the next Soviet Foreign Minister, was one of the strongest voices in the USSR, with undeniable power to influence his country's foreign policy.

Watching the scene in Egypt, Chief-of-Staff Shuqayr began toying with the idea of buying arms from the Soviet Union to empower the Syrian Army. In the immediate post-Shishakli era, he had managed to secure 11 Mark IV tanks from France, but purchasing arms from the French was no longer acceptable on the Syrian street, given the outbreak of the Algerian Revolution, prompting General Shuqayr to turn to Prague during the tenure of Prime Minister Asali. Syria needed an additional 39 Mark IVs, and Czechoslovakia had received a large shipment of them from the Soviet Union. They were bought by the Syrian Army and delivered in giant crates to the port of Beirut. Lebanese officials, suspicious of the shipment had 'accidently' dropped one of them on the quay side, revealing the great shoulder of a tank. Learning the lesson well, Shuqayr had all future arms from the USSR, mainly Russian T54s, shipped directly to the newly opened port of Lattakia on the Syrian coast.[24] Recalling the event, Shuqayr described, 'the armour rolled down through Syrian villages, to the cheers of the peasants'.[25] Eventually the Czechs sold more arms and equipment to Syria, totalling $23 million, in trucks and anti-aircraft guns outfitted with radar.[26] Additionally, 18 Syrian pilots, including the young officer Hafez al-Assad, were sent to Egypt to learn to fly Soviet-built MIGs. Between 1954–1956, Syrian exports to the USSR and Eastern Europe grew from $700,000 (0.5 per cent of total Syrian exports) to more than $11 million (8 per cent). These exports were mainly textiles and agricultural products. Imports from the USSR and the Eastern bloc (machinery and vehicles) nearly doubled in value from $5 million (2 per cent of all imports) to nearly $8 million.[27] Syria sent shockwaves throughout the USA by accepting proposals from Czechoslovakia and East Germany to build several cement manufacturing factories, worth $6 million, a textile factory for $500,000, and a sugar processing plant for $2 million. Talks commenced with Poland to construct a railway in Syria, worth $65 million, while Bulgaria offered electrical equipment worth $1 million, and Hungary made an offer for an electricity generating plant for $670,000. Realizing that the Soviets and their allies were getting the upper-hand, US oilmen advised the US government to catch up before it was too late, prompting Tapline to reduce the cost of the 20,000 barrels it sold to Syria, per day, in November 1955, and to increase the transit fees it gave to Syria through the 1949 agreement with Husni al-Za'im.[28]

Adding to US fears was a Syrian plan to begin construction of an oil refinery in Homs. Several international companies bid for the project, including Standard Oil of New Jersey (partial owners of Tapline) and Procon Ltd. of London, in addition to a company from Czechoslovakia. When the deal went to Czechoslovakia, despite its expensive office, the USA sensed disaster since the 'whole Western European economy is absolutely dependent on the availability of Middle East oil'.[29] The Foreign Office in London warned the State Department not to reveal 'too bluntly' the extent to which Middle East oil-producing and transit states 'have all Western Europe by the throat'.[30] Not only did the deal go to the Czech company, but in the summer of 1957, Syrian Parliament pushed for a bill exempting the Czech company from paying taxes to the Syrian government.[31]

In July 1956, Assistant Secretary of State for Near Eastern Affairs George V. Allen asked Undersecretary of State Herbert Hoover, to call Howard Page of Standard California Oil and urge him to 'improve the existing offer' he had made to the Syrians. Hoover agreed and in turn, called on the US Ambassador to Baghdad, who was asked to talk to Prime Minister Nuri al-Said. The ageing Iraqi leader tried to talk the Syrians into accepting Procon's offer, which was effectively, $200,000 less than the Czech one, and tried to push similar buttons with King Saud, who had the ear of the Syrian Prime Minister. The Iraqis were even asked to provide Procon with money to help them seal the deal with the Syrians. Procon's offer of $15.7 million came close to the Czech company's offer of $15.5 million. Henry Cabot Lodge, the US Ambassador to the UN, wrote about Syria's policy being 'in-line' with that of the USSR, claiming that Syria had abstained from voting on whether to accept China into the UN. It even backed up giving the pulpit of the UN to North Korea so that it could spread anti-American propaganda.[32]

   The war on Gaza, outbreak of the Algerian Revolution against France, and American indifference to the grievances of the Arabs, made it all the more reasonable for Syria to look to the Eastern bloc throughout the second half of the 1950s. On 18 April 1955 Foreign Minister Khaled al-Azm went to the famous Bandung Conference in Indonesia, where Afro-Asian economic, political and cultural cooperation were put on the table. The event brought Gamal Abdul Nasser to the world's attention as a regional heavyweight, more so than just a president of Egypt. Although scion of a leading aristocratic family, which was anything but socialist, Azm had already allied himself with certain heavyweight Nasser supporters in the Syrian Army. He hoped that they would back him in the presidential elections scheduled for August 1955. At Bandung, he could not but nod to everything said by Nasser, upsetting the US envoy, Adam Clayton Powell, a Republican senator from New York. All countries present, including Syria and Egypt, agreed to oppose colonization and stand at arm's length from the tension of the cold war between the USA and USSR, giving birth to what in 1961 became known as the Non-Aligned Movement.

Khaled al-Azm in New York

On 22 June 1955, two months after Bandung, Azm was invited to attend the 10th anniversary of the UN in New York. It was a hallmark visit to the US for one of the top politicians in Syria. Azm was the first Syrian official to visit the USA since bilateral relations were established during the Second World War. Although not educated at an American university, he respected the American way of life, along with the country's capitalist system, its banking sector, infrastructure, educational advancement and the liberalism of American society. In that sense, he resembled men like Nazem al-Qudsi, Syria's first Ambassador to the US, and former Prime Minister Fares al-Khoury, Syria's representative to the founding conference of the UN. From his grand mansion in the old Suq Saruja neighbourhood, Azm had lived an aristocratic and cosmopolitan life, touring the world capitals taking photos with a sophisticated camera, while most Syrians had never travelled beyond their native cities. His unveiled wife, Layla, was a daily gambler at a prime night club in Damascus, something frowned upon by conservative society, and so was the fact that he had an adopted daughter carrying his family name, which was taboo in Islam. These traits created a natural barrier between Azm and ordinary Syrians, who saw him as a distant aristocrat with a life very different from that of their own. The business community, however, adored Khaled al-Azm for his economic programmes, seeing him as a visionary, as did a rising generation of independents, mainly university graduates who wanted a non-partisan to represent them in Syrian politics. His mastery of languages, rich understanding of international culture and respect for capitalist economies, made him an early admirer of Western Europe. With him at the helm of the Foreign Ministry, it was believed that he would bring Syria closer to the USA and its allies. The reality was to prove very different.

While travelling to the USA, Azm made a stopover in Paris for talks with senior French officials. The French Foreign Minister was already in New York, meaning that Azm had to settle for his Deputy, who received him at the Quai D'Orsay, a venue that Azm knew well, having served as his country's Ambassador to France in 1947. Azm asked for French arms, defending his argument by reminding his French host at every interval that if these weapons did not come from Paris, the Syrians would have to look 'elsewhere', in a direct and provocative reference to the Soviet Union. Azm was then taken on a tour of a tank factory in the suburbs of the French capital, and granted an audience with French President Rene Coty. In his memoirs, Azm recalls hearing the 'myth' of France's affection for its former colony, when the French President expressed a desire to visit Syria. 'I avoided inviting him,' he noted, 'knowing that the people of Syria would not be forthcoming.'[33] Both the French President and officials at the Quai D'Orsay complained to Azm of the rising anti-Western tone of Syrian media, asking him to tone down the rhetoric against France, Great Britain and the USA. The Syrian Minister was eventually informed, however, that no deal would be made between Syria and France, due to US pressure on the French government, as long as Syria remained allied to Egypt, the Eastern Bloc and the Soviet Union. It was the final straw. In his memoirs, Azm recalls claiming that the USA and Western Europe had left Syria with no choice but to come knocking on the doors of the Kremlin, which was more than ready to sell arms to the Arabs at what he described as 'scrap prices'.

With this encounter in mind, Azm landed in Boston, USA on 17 June, before heading to New York, where he was greeted by Syria's Ambassador to the US, Farid Zayn al-Din, and Ambassador to the UN, Rafiq al-Asha, two AUB alumni. He was taken on a tour of the Empire State Building, and lodged at the prestigious Waldorf Astoria Hotel. He met with World Bank President John McCloy, then headed to Chicago where he called on Aldai Stevenson, the former Democratic presidential candidate of 1952, who was planning to run against Eisenhower again in 1956. Stevenson, who was staying at his 70-acre ranch near the wealthy Chicago suburb of Libertyville, was known to the Arabs for his intellectual demeanour, eloquence and even-handedness when dealing with international affairs. Azm's choice of Stevenson is puzzling, however, given that due to his country's stand-off with the Eisenhower administration, there were plenty of people to call on, in attempts to mend Syrian–US relations, who were more influential in Washington circles. Azm had probably met the man during his 1953 visit to Syria, and affiliated with Stevenson who, like him, came from an influential political family.[34] The Syrian team kept its fingers crossed, hoping that this man might be the new President of the USA, given his absolute dislike for anything related to the Eisenhower White House. They seemed optimistic that Stevenson knew Syria well ever since serving as his country's deputy delegate to the founding conference of the UN in 1945.[35] It was a long three hour meeting, which Azm recalls, 'was my first encounter with American cooking'. Although Azm and Zayn al-Din went to great lengths to defend their country's friendship with the USSR, their host disappointed them by showing 'absolutely no interest in what we were saying'.[36] The man had seemingly parted ways with the Syrians, due to their Soviet connection, making them lose yet another influential voice in the US political elite.[37]

In New York, Azm had the chance to meet both Eisenhower and Dulles, along with his two counterparts, Harold Macmillan of Great Britain, and Vyacheslav Molotov of the USSR. During a banquet held in honour of the international delegates, Azm finally came face-to-face with Dwight Eisenhower, an encounter that made the Syrian minister very uneasy. 'He (Eisenhower) paced around his guests, shaking hands and conversing either at length or briefly, depending on the weight attached to any particular country. Naturally, my share was a slight bow, followed by a cordial "How do you do?" The situation was different with Fadil al-Jamali (from Iraq) and Charles Malik (from Lebanon) who were given special care and hospitality (because of their icy relations with the Soviet Union)', he later wrote. Azm clearly expected a cold handshake, given the recent surge in Syrian–Soviet relations but tried to build bridges with the Eisenhower White House by requesting a one-on-one with John Foster Dulles. Reaching out to the USA and trying to purchase arms from France were the final loud cry from the Syrians, who were trying their luck with the West before taking a deep and seemingly irrevocable dive into the Soviet orbit.[38] His request was turned down by the State Department, which replied that Dulles was too busy at the UN to meet the Syrian Minister.[39]

As the days passed, Azm increasingly lost hope in reaching any compromise with the USA. When preparing his UN speech, which was riddled with criticism for the USA, he decided to deliver it in English, although his knowledge of the language was mediocre. Azm nevertheless wanted the words to reach the US diplomats present at the General Assembly, with no translation. He memorized the speech, word-for-word, and with a calm and articulate voice, rose to the podium to speak before the General Assembly, looking the American representative straight in the face, with a mixed French and Arabic accent. Halfway through, he was interrupted by the chairman of the session, being a representative of the Netherlands, who reminded Azm that this gathering was aimed at finding common ground within the UN and not building on differences between member states, a polite way of asking him to refrain. Azm tried to respond in English, but his language skills failed him and he instead replied in both French and Arabic. Khaled Bey was furious, pointing to the Soviet Minister Molotov, who had delivered a thundering speech the day before, filled with blatant criticism for the USA. He asked why the UN tolerated such rhetoric by a powerful country like the USSR and deprived it to smaller states like Syria.[40] Throughout the lengthy chapter in his memoirs in which he describes his visit to the UN, Azm makes no attempt to hide his gloating at the Mayor of New York refusing to meet the pro-US King of Saudi Arabia. He mentions how King Saud stumbled at the General Assembly, due to bad eyesight, while rising to deliver his country's speech. 'Seeing an ordinary man stumble is funny in itself,' he wrote, 'so what is one to say to a white-cloaked monarch falling?'[41]

In what remained of his eventful stay in America, Azm went to the University of California to attend a ceremony granting an honourary PhD to UN Secretary-General Dag Hammarskjold, and was taken on a tour of Hollywood Boulevard and Beverly Hills, two places that apparently failed to impress him.[42] He expressed deep admiration for US civilian airplanes, which went at a 'record-breaking' 650 kilometres per hour, and the infrastructure of San Francisco, especially when he learned that it had been burned almost to the ground in 1905 only to be rebuilt by its own people. He complained of the US cuisine, 'which was not suitable for the United States as a world power', noting that when it comes to hospitality, Americans are no match for the Russians. Prices in the USA were astronomically high, noted Azm, making particular reference to a New York restaurant that served meals at cost of $17 a plate. Wrapping up his impressions of the country, Azm described its people as suffering from a 'superiority complex' that had emerged after the Second World War, noting, 'They viewed people and governments with the attitude of a master, for who heads should bow. They were surprised how a small country like ours would think twice before answering to their beck and call, and then ultimately, refuse to obey orders from the United States.'[43]

The Malki Affair

While Azm was touring Europe, a political assassination rocked the troubled scene in Damascus, eliminating whatever minimal hope the USA still had at mending relations with Syria. On 22 April 1955, the Deputy Chief-of-Staff Colonel Adnan al-Malki, a handsome and charismatic 37-year-old officer from Damascus, was gunned down at a football match. Before security had the chance to arrest his assassin, the young man, named Yunis Abdul Rahim, pointed the gun towards his own head and committed suicide. The army, having kept a low profile since the ousting of Shishakli, went into immediate frenzy, claiming that Malki had been shot because of his Arab nationalistic views, and opposition to the USA. Malki had been a natural leader very popular within the officer class, rumoured to be a secret member of the Baath Party. He had great admiration for Nasser and reportedly had planned to launch a coup in January 1955, to bring down the Fares al-Khoury government if it continued to obstruct Egyptian foreign policy towards Iraq. Abdul Hamid Sarraj, a 30-year-old Nasser enthusiast, appointed to the post of Intelligence Director only one month earlier, was charged with investigating the Malki murder. It was revealed that the assassin was a member of the SSNP, which strove for the unity of Greater Syria and frowned upon the newfound relationship with Egypt. According to SSNP ideology, Egypt was part of North Africa, rather than the Syrian nation, and therefore, an unnatural ally for the Syrian government. A witch hunt ensued, striking at anybody with the slightest record of anti-Egyptian sentiment, bringing scores of SSNP members, and certain affiliates of Hashemite Iraq, to the dungeons of the Syrian Deuxième Bureau.

Malki's relations with the Baath were not as cordial as many believed; he had fallen out with the party after it failed to secure a parliamentary seat for his brother Riad, a Baathist attorney, during the elections of 1954. Additionally he had brought two anti-Baath officers, Amin Nfuri and Ahmad Abdul Karim to the General Staff of the Syrian Army, in the immediate post-Shishakli era. What was certain was his dislike for the USA and Israel, explaining why his assassins were immediately coloured as pro-American. A total of 150 SSNP members were arrested, including Juliette al-Mir, the widow of party founder Antune Saadeh, and, in the trial that ensued, officers tried to draw a direct link between Malki's murder and US aspirations in Syria. Issam Mahayri, the party's secretary-general, was accused of having planned a trip to the USA, to meet with State Department officials. The US connection was reportedly made through Hisham Sharabi, a party member and professor at Georgetown University, who had written to the party's executive council, advocating better relations between the SSNP and the Eisenhower administration.[44]

During the trials, in addition to the accusation against Sharabi, it was reported that the SSNP had contacted the US Embassy in Damascus and provided them with daily reports on anti-US activity of the Communist Party and the Muslim Brotherhood. When the bill of indictment was released in June 1955, it charged party members with murder, disobedience within the army, contacting a foreign power, and exposing Syria to hostile acts by planning for revolution. Prime Minister Asali appeared before the Syrian Parliament days after the murder, saying that the conspirators 'had thrown themselves at the feet of a foreign state, seeking its help and support in order to make an unethical coup in order to seize power'. Ordinary Syrians as well as politically-driven journalists speculated that this 'foreign power' was none other than the USA. The fact that Syria had just signed the defence pact with Egypt made it all the more reasonable for the USA to want to force the Syrians to change course. Although Asali did not make explicit reference to the USA, Ambassador Moose made the blunder of publicly announcing that his country had nothing to do with either the SSNP or the Malki affair.[45] This only added to everybody's suspicion that the USA was indeed involved with the entire incident. The Malki affair, the first crime in Syria to attract so much regional and international attention, was eventually closed with several verdicts: banning the SSNP (that was charged with political murder), and sentencing Saadeh's widow to 22 years in jail, while party heavyweights such as Ghassan Jadid and George Abdul-Massih fled to Lebanon.

Conclusion

Today, 55 years on, it is generally accepted that neither the US nor the SSNP were responsible for the elimination of Malki. The decision to kill him was taken personally by Abdul Massih, the party President acting independently from party command, and Colonel Jadid, who competed with Malki for leadership among a rising generation of Syrian officers. What matters within the context of this research is why such a domestic crisis snowballed into a showdown between the USA and its opponents in Syria? Adnan al-Malki was, after all, no Adib Shishakli and no Husni al-Za'im – certainly not a Syrian Gamal Abdul Nasser. The motifs behind his killing were purely personal, apparently, yet in the troubled months of 1955 everybody seemed to believe that the USA would walk the extra mile, resorting to assassinations to wipe out individual opponents in the Syrian arena. Those who did not believe so certainly spoke and acted in such a manner, seeking to use the Malki affair to settle old scores with the USA. It seemed to provide a perfect scapegoat – so hated by the Syrian public, so frantic with Syria's Soviet orientation that it was willing to try anything to prevent Syria from becoming a Soviet satellite.

The chaos in Syria, which had enabled the elimination of Malki in broad daylight at a stadium filled with over 400 spectators, was testimony to how weak and vulnerable the young Republic had become, less than 10-years after achieving its independence from the French. It also spoke volumes of how inflated a perception the Syrians had of themselves, thanks to the constant tug-of-war that had dragged on between Americans, Soviets, Egyptians and Iraqis since 1949. Why would the USA kill someone like Malki, when a more reasonable target like Khaled Bakdash would have done it a much better service in Syrian domestics? Nobody in Syria seemed to be asking that question in April 1955. President Atasi was packing his belongings and preparing to leave the presidential palace in September. Fares al-Khoury, humiliated by his own people for having stood by Iraq and the USA in 1954, was no longer willing to stick his neck out for the West. Sabri al-Asali, although having already decided to nurture relations with Egypt, blamed the SSNP and USA out of necessity, realizing that, unless he spoke a language the angry officers wanted to hear, he would be ejected from power, with little pomp or ceremony. The Baathists wanted to believe that the USA had pushed its opponents, the SSNP, into eliminating Adnan al-Malki. So did the communists and the Muslim Brotherhood, who were glad to see the end of a popular party on the Syrian street, which had competed with them for members and fame since the 1930s. The fact that the murder was linked to the USA was actually not a surprise since, after the cold war, nearly all major attempts in the region were affiliated, one way or another, to the Soviets or Americans – never to the Arabs themselves. What is interesting is trying to create a link between the SSNP and the USA, a creative approach signed off by a combination of grief-stricken junior officers, ambition-driven senior ones, and political parties across the political

spectrum, all with the implicit approval of Gamal Abdul Nasser. All of these
players brilliantly milked the Malki Affair, at the expense of the SSNP and
the USA. Nasser used it to elevate the standing of his allies on the Syrian
street, while the officers themselves trumpeted Malki's assassination to justify
reinforcing themselves forcefully on Syrian politics, having had their wings
clipped since the downfall of Adib al-Shishakli. The officer class, which on the
whole was anti-American, was now telling pro-Western politicians: 'We need
to be informed of everything that happens in this country otherwise, we will
strike again to take matters into our hands, in order to avenge Malki's blood.'

Although many Syrian historians accuse Gamal Abdul Nasser of exploiting
Syria's weakness in the 1950s, a closer look places full blame for what happened,
in terms of heartbreak with the Western world, on President Hashem al-Atasi
and Prime Minister Sabri al-Asali. Atasi had tried to stand up for the West and
Iraq, against the ambitions of Nasser in 1954, but was forced to abandon his
programme after the downfall of Fares al-Khoury. It made no sense for him
to resign, as he had done in 1951, since at the age of 80 there was little fight
left in him. Additionally, the USA was too reluctant to come to his aid, before
Nasser's heroic reputation had snowballed throughout the Arab world. By the
time Khoury left the premiership in 1955, it needed a superhero to stand up
to Nasserism on the streets of Syria, or to preach anything that even sounded
pro-US. Asali on the other hand, not only lacked the gall to pursue a coherent
political programme but was also unable to promote relations with the USA,
because of loss of popularity on the Syrian street. Although popular within
Damascus, mainly among the business community, Asali was frowned upon
throughout all other major Syrian cities, seen as a distant notable, alien from
the agonies of the ordinary Syrian. He compensated for lack of nationwide
popularity by adopting a programme that was attractive to Syrians from all
walks of life, especially the rural youth – who happened to form the backbone
of the Syrian Army.

Syrian–Soviet relations reached their zenith during the years 1954–1956,
mainly because the USA, although firmly anchored as a world superpower,
still knew very little about the Middle East. It also knew very little about
Syria. Eisenhower had never been to the Arab world, and much had changed
for Syria and the region since Dulles last came to Damascus in 1953. The
impact of the Egyptian Revolution, the downfall of Adib al-Shishakli, and the
Gaza raid, had changed the game for friends of the USA. Gaza in particular
muzzled pro-US voices in major capitals around the region, and in their place
the only voices being heard were loud anti-US ones, such as Khaled Bakdash
and Gamal Abdul Nasser. Strangely enough the seasoned John Foster Dulles,

who had worked with Arab politicians since 1919, still tried to sell the Arabs an argument that placed communism as a more direct threat to their lives and security than Zionism. Nobody in the region was willing to buy it. Certain Arab players such as Shishakli had humoured US officials in the early 1950s, trying to get advanced arms out of them, but by 1955 that had proven to be a failed approach. So long as Israel remained in their midst, there was very little pro-Western politicians could say or do to come in defence of the USA against the Soviet Union. If anything, this explains the surge in anti-American sentiment in Syria, which by 1957 led President Shukri al-Quwatli to remark – for the first time in his country's history – that the USA was 'an enemy of Syria'.

11

TIPPING THE BALANCE AT SUEZ

In September 1955, the regional and international community waited with bated breath to see who the Syrians would elect to replace the incumbent President Hashem al-Atasi, the hard-boiled nationalist who had stood up to Nasserism and the USSR since returning to power in early 1954. Iraq was pushing for Rushdi al-Kikhiya, a pro-Western statesman from Aleppo, to run on behalf of the People's Party but he refused, claiming that it would be useless so long as officers had the upper hand in Syrian politics.[1] Moscow's friend Khaled al-Azm presented his candidature as an independent, having had his eyes set on the presidency since 1943, as did Lutfi al-Haffar, a pro-Western merchant turned politician, and former Premier, who was categorically opposed to the rising influence of Nasserism in Syria. He quickly withdrew his candidacy, however, when Syria's former President Shukri al-Quwatli returned home to run for presidential office in an attempt to right the wrongs inflicted on him since his downfall by military coup in 1949.

Quwatli, by now aged 63, was never exactly anti-US, although the USA had helped bring him down right after the Palestine War, objecting to his stance on Tapline and refusal to sign an armistice with Israel. The USA remembered only too well, however, his loud support for the Germans during the Second World War, and his vigorous criticism of the USA during the war of 1948. His historic opposition to the People's Party and the Hashemites did not necessarily mean that he would support the USA this time, raising a large question mark on whether his prolonged residence in Egypt, and excellent personal relationship with Gamal Abdul Nasser, would have a determining say on whether he would make it to the presidency in 1955. If forced to choose between Quwatli and Azm, however, the USA would certainly have favoured the former, given that since he premiered as a member of parliament back in 1936, Quwatli had shown no extreme fondness of the Soviet Union. He had maintained cordial relations with the Communist Party in the 1940s, but back then, the cold war had not unfolded and it certainly did not make him an agent of International Communism. A devout Muslim, he ranked among the Damascene statesmen who wrote off Communist Party members as heretics and unbelievers, yet found much common ground with Nasser, despite a perfect relationship with the Egyptian President's predecessor, King Farouk.

A two-third majority of the 142-member parliament was required for victory, and, during the first round of elections, Quwatli won 89, Azm 42, and 6 invalid votes were cast, calling for a second round. This time Quwatli won 91, Azm 41 – five were blank, and two were declared invalid. Amusingly, one pro-Iraqi deputy, whose identity was never revealed, scribbled the name of Nuri al-Said on his ballot paper.[2] Although Quwatli tried to keep a distance from both the USSR and USA, his orientation was made clear when, on 10 September, less than one week after coming to office, Syria made an official request for arms from the USA, to be paid on a reimbursable basis.[3] Ambassador Moose sent a strongly worded telegram to the State Department, advising immediate action to ensure Quwatli remained firmly anchored to the Western bloc. Dulles was equally optimistic about Quwatli, lobbying to give the ageing statesman the benefit of the doubt.[4] What encouraged the US Secretary was a statement made by Quwatli, early in the new regime, expressing 'determination to eradicate communism, extremism, and leftist thoughts', noting however that he needed time to achieve that, due to the strong leftist trend in the Syrian Army.[5] Significantly, the Baath Party withdrew from the Asali cabinet, shortly after Quwatli was re-elected, while Azm, branded by Syrian dailies as the 'red millionaire' suffered a heart attack, forcing the pro-Egyptian Prime Minister to resign on 6 September 1955. Quwatli, also wanting to stand at arm's length from Egypt, called on the independent Lutfi al-Haffar, somewhat of a reward for having withdrawn his presidential candidature, to form a government, but the Baath refused to deal with Haffar, based on his pro-Western and anti-Egyptian views. Quwatli then tried his hand with an old opponent, Rushdi al-Kikhiya, who once again refused, claiming that his cabinet would be incapacitated by the officers.[6] Although Abdul Nasser advised Quwatli to bring Asali in for another round, the Syrian President refused, insisting that new blood be injected into the Syrian system and calling on the independent attorney Said al-Ghazzi to form a government. Ghazzi, after all had an unblemished past, and was linked neither to the USA nor to the Russians. A respected attorney, he managed to create a cabinet of national unity, giving four seats to the People's Party, delivering a cabinet policy statement that pledged to uphold neutrality in the cold war.[7] It did contain two clauses that were appeasing to Nasser; pledging to uphold the military pact with Egypt, and saying no to the dreaded Baghdad Pact.

The Ghazzi government did not last for more than nine months and failed to thwart – or even minimize – Soviet influence in Syria. On the contrary, due to the rising influence of Nasser, relations were improved with the Soviet Union and during this period the Russian Mission in Damascus was upgraded to a fully accredited Embassy. Additionally, when a decorated veteran of the Syrian Revolt of 1925, Mohammad Ashmar, was awarded the Stalin Peace Prize, Prime Minister Ghazzi could not but call to congratulate him. Joseph Alsop, a US journalist visiting Syria in May 1956, commented that real power in Syria, during the brief tenure of Said al-Ghazzi, 'lay in the strongly assorted but highly effective combination of Egyptian political leadership, Saudi Arabian bribe money, and communist organizational talent'. Due to this reality, many historians accredit Ghazzi with moving Syrian–Russian relations forward, and distancing Damascus from Washington DC. A closer look at Ghazzi's choice of ministers, however, and the fact that during his tenure, arms were requested from the USA, paints a very different image of the man. Most telling of his early orientation and that of the Syrian President was the lifting of a ban against selling Syrian wheat to Western Europe – mainly France – infuriating the Baathists and Communists. Students from both parties stormed and occupied the Ministry of Economy, demanding that the government change course and forcing Ghazzi to resign from office that summer, against the wishes of the Syrian President. Unable to find a brave independent willing to take the job of Prime Minister, Quwatli had no choice but to call on Sabri al-Asali – again – to form a government, under advice from the new Egyptian Ambassador to Syria, Mahmud Riad.

Asali resorted to all his previous tactics, moving the country back with full force towards Egypt, and giving the anti-US Baath Party the portfolios of Foreign Affairs and Economy. The dramatic rise in their power is testimony to the deteriorating popularity of the USA since only a few months earlier, the Baath had got nothing more than the technical Ministry of Health in Asali's first cabinet. Before accepting Asali's offer, the Baathisti's demanded that the Prime Minister pledge to formally and immediately begin talks aimed at a 'theoretical union' between Syria and Egypt. Asali immediately complied, and, when reading his cabinet policy statement on 27 June 1956, he said, 'We shall embark on a consolidation of our ties with Egypt through immediate talks which we hope will lead to a common policy to which other liberated Arab countries will be invited to adhere, so that we can achieve a comprehensive Arab unity.' Twenty-four hours later, at the urging of the Baath, 3,000 students from Damascus University – many of whom had helped bring down Ghazzi earlier that same month – petitioned the Syrian Parliament, demanding immediate union with Nasser's Egypt. A three-man ministerial delegation, headed by Asali himself, headed to Cairo to commence on talks with Gamal Abdul Nasser. It included Interior Minister Ahmad Qanbar and Foreign Minister Salah al-Bitar. The Baath Party trumpeted the visit as the beginning of the end of US influence in the Arab world, although Nasser himself was originally reluctant to the idea of a union with Syria, a country he had never visited. Five days before the Syrian Prime Minister left for Egypt, however, he received a visit from the Soviet Foreign Minister Dmitri Shepilov in Damascus. The former editor of *Pravada* was given a warm welcome in the Syrian capital, greeted by elementary and secondary school children carrying white flowers, as Soviet and Syrian flags flew. After meeting Quwatli, Shepilov remarked that the USSR was a 'sincere and honest friend, without greed or private designs and with no desire to usurp the riches of others'. He offered long-term, low-interest development loans in Syria and expressed a desire for wide cultural exchange with Damascus. Then, shortly afterwards, on 3 July, the Syrians officially recognized the People's Republic of China – seemingly sending off one message after another to the USA – that the era of Syrian–US engagement was now history. Egypt had made a similar recognition of Beijing less than two months earlier, on 16 May 1956.

The Suez Canal crisis

Amidst the increased activity of the Soviet Union and Egypt in Syria, and the increasing inability of the USA to do anything to confront it, Gamal Abdul Nasser nationalized the Suez Canal Company in a historic speech in Alexandria on 26 July 1956. The Canal, opened in 1869 and operated by the Universal Company of the Suez Maritime Canal, had taken ten years to build by the Egyptian and French governments. Due to heavy debt, Egypt had sold its share to the British government of Benjamin Disraeli in 1875 – 44 per cent for less than £4 million. After the 1882 invasion of Egypt, the British government got full control both of Egypt and its Canal – an asset that proved to be of tremendous use during the Second World War and its aftermath.[8] The Canal was the shortest ocean link between the Mediterranean and Indian Ocean, and had proven vital for Britain's trade with the Far East. Now, it was proving all the more useful due to the vast potential of Middle East oil, in addition to its geostrategic importance. It operated a vast military complex at the Canal, where 80,000 British troops were stationed, much to the displeasure of Nasser and the hard-headed Free Officers who came with him to power in 1952. Shortly before the revolution, the Egyptian government had abrogated the Anglo-Egyptian Treaty of 1936, which granted the British an additional 20-year lease on the Canal, and due to Nasser's troubled relations with London, it was clear by mid-1956 that was he was about to strike at them in Suez.[9] British Prime Minister Anthony Eden saw another Mussolini in Nasser, and tried to enlist President Eisenhower's support for an early offensive against him, which ended in vain, mainly because of Nasser's relationship with Saudi Arabia. Although they agreed on practically nothing else, the Saudis and Egyptians were united in opposing the Baghdad Pact – although for very different reasons. Nasser wanting to ride the horse of Arab nationalism, while Saudi Arabia wanting to limit Hashemite influence in the Arab world. Eisenhower feared that coming to Britain's call would anger King Saud, America's other ally, whose support in the cold war was vital, thanks to the huge potential of Saudi oilfields. Henry Kissinger, who closely observed US diplomacy in 1950 before becoming his country's Secretary of State, wrote: 'Great Britain would have preferred to overthrow Nasser. America, however uncomfortable with the Czech deal, thought it was wiser to propitiate him.'[10]

In his Alexandria speech, Nasser announced that all assets of the Suez Canal Company had been frozen by the Egyptian Government, and that stockholders would be paid the price of their shares according to the day's closing price on the Paris Stock Exchange. The ostensible reason for his nationalization was in response to the World Bank turning down his request for financial assistance to build the Aswan High Dam, which in turn was a response to the September 1955 arms deal with Czechoslovakia.[11] Syria had begun its own talks with the World Bank back in 1954, for long-term financial loans, which dragged well into the Quwatli era. Sixty-eight per cent of the Syrian budget, after all, was allocated to the Syrian Army, explaining a dire national need for additional money in order to carry out much needed developmental projects. After a year-long survey of the situation in Syria, the World Bank had proposed a $23 million five-year development plan, advising investment in agriculture and endorsing two large-scale irrigation projects, one in Yusuf Pasha on the Euphrates and the other in the Ghab Swamp. The Syrians had requested $530 million, explaining why in January 1956 the loan proposal was withdrawn and Damascus terminated the licence of the World Bank office in Syria.

The USA adopted a wait-and-see approach to see how their allies in Britain would respond following Nasser's 26 July nationalization speech. MPs were furious with Prime Minister Eden, claiming that unless immediate action was taken, Nasser would snowball into another Hitler and citing how appeasement of the Fuhrer at Munich back in 1938 had only magnified his territorial ambitions. Eden commented on Nasser saying: 'His relations with the Soviets are much closer than he admits to us. Certainly we should accept, I think, that a policy of appeasement will not bring nothing in Egypt. Our best chance is to show that it pays to be our friend.'[12] On 1 August, a meeting was held at 10 Downing Street, attended by Eden, his Foreign Secretary Selwyn Lloyd, US Ambassador Robert Murphy, and French Foreign Minister Christian Pineau. Three months later, France, Great Britain and Israel met at Sevres, near Paris, and agreed that Israel would invade Egypt, while Paris and London would interfere, with the ostensible aim of separating the warring factions, instructing both parties to withdraw to a distance of 16 kilometres from either side of the Canal. Nasser would then be declared unfit to administer Suez, which would be placed under Anglo-French management once again. The USA was not included in the plan – which proved to be a fatal error on Eden's part, thinking that because of Nasser's relationship with Moscow, the USA would never lift a finger to protect him. The USA, apparently, had other plans – mainly to see Great Britain walk out of the Arab world, which it had co-controlled since the 1940s, in anticipation of establishing US dominance in the Middle East and North Africa.

As a result of US caution, war did begin on 29 October, and Nasser officially requested US support on 1 December, 1956.[13] The 1 November Soviet invasion of Hungary, intended to clamp down on a rebellion against Stalinist rule, played nicely into Nasser's hands. A revolt had broken out in Budapest on 23 October, prompting 17 divisions to march into Hungary through the east, eight days later – an act that was vigorously condemned by the USA. Nasser reasoned that Eisenhower would not want to look like a hypocrite, turning a blind eye to the British–Israel–French invasion of Egypt while condemning the Russian invasion of Hungary. Investing in the Hungary crisis actually worked, and Eisenhower did in fact apply the needed pressure on Tel Aviv, London and Paris to end the war, which although a military defeat for Egypt, did Nasser a dramatic service in terms of political gain and popularity. Overnight, the man was transformed into a living legend throughout the Arab world, and nowhere was his reputation boosted as much as Damascus. During his nationalization speech, Nasser had sent a direct and very public message to his fans in Syria, when he said:

Today, compatriots, I turn towards the brothers, to you in Syria, dear Syria, sister Syria, who decided to unite with us – a union free, dignified, and grand, in order that we may together consolidate the principles of

freedom, dignity, and prestige that we may build Arab nationalism and
Arab unity together ...

Massive demonstrations broke out in favour of Nasser in every city across Syria,
while Prime Minister Asali called his government into open session to study the
crisis in Egypt. President Quwatli for his part phoned the Egyptian leader and
placed 'all of Syria's resources, both governmental and public, at the disposal
of sister Egypt!' Young Syrians volunteered to fight alongside the Egyptian
Army at Suez. One of them, a young naval officer named Jules Jammal, was
killed when he crashed himself into a French warship, for which he was forever
immortalized in both Syria and Egypt. The Syrian Army was called into full
alert, ready to enter the war on orders from President Quwatli. Meanwhile,
British pipelines running through the Syrian dessert were sabotaged, while
the ambassadors of both London and Paris were requested to depart from
Damascus. Cairo Radio proudly announced, 'The Syrian people have found in
Gamal Abdul Nasser the leader they have been waiting for and the commander
they have been hoping for. The people on the street worship Gamal Abdul
Nasser.'[14]

On 30 October, Shukri al-Quwatli landed in Moscow for a prearranged
trip, which was nevertheless the first ever for a Syrian President to the Soviet
Union. He frantically appealed to Soviet leaders, shouting: 'They want to
destroy Egypt!' Calmly, Nikita Khrushchev asked him what was expected
of the Soviet Union, to which he replied, 'Send in the large Red Army that
defeated Hitler!' The Moscow trip, which actually failed to halt the Suez War,
caught the USA off-guard. Here was a Syrian president not only cuddling
up to countries in the Eastern Bloc, but visiting the Kremlin itself. Looking
back at Quwatli's record since returning to Syria and assuming the presidency in 1955, the Americans found a very troubling character, closely allied
not only to Egypt, but apparently, to top officials in the USSR as well. After
returning from Moscow, the Syrian President declared, obviously carried away
by the Russian's warm reception, that, 'Thousands of Soviet Muslims have
announced their readiness to come to the Middle East to rid the Holy Land of
imperialist aggression'.[15] Under his tenure, not only had Syria established full
diplomatic ties with the USSR, but similar exchanges were made with China,
Czechoslovakia and Romania.[16] Not only had 17 deputies gone to Moscow in
1955, but now so had the President of the Republic himself, accompanied by
none other than the notorious head of the Communist Party, Khaled Bakdash.
Something serious had to be done about Syria, the Eisenhower Administration
reasoned – and quickly – before the country transformed into a fully fledged

Soviet satellite. International news wires carried photos of Quwatli meeting with Soviet Defence Minister Marshal Georgy Zhukov, Chief-of-Staff Marshal Sokolovsky and his Assistant, General Antonov.[17]

Back to coups and counter-coups

One of the few Arabs who was unimpressed by Nasser's 1956 victory was Prime Minister Nuri al-Said of Iraq. Coinciding with daily reports reaching him from Iraq's military attaché in Damascus, Abdul Mutalib Amin, about the rise of Nasserist influence in Syria were rumours of Russians delivering arms to Syrian officers east of Aleppo and in the ancient city of Palmyra. He fully agreed with John Foster Dulles that containing communism in Syria should be a high priority for all players in the Arab world, wanting to see an end to the Quwatli regime. Nuri Pasha had never been on good terms with President Quwatli, who had drowned Hashemite ambitions in Syria as far back as 1943, and orchestrated his country's strong alliance with Egypt and Saudi Arabia after returning to power in 1955.

The Iraqi political class was divided on what to do with Syria. Former Prime Minister Fadil al-Jamali was a strong advocate of the union, while Deputy Prime Minister Ahmad Mukhtar Baban wanted nothing to do with the Syrians anymore, claiming that the political class in Damascus was always eager to milk Iraqi officials for money, but never willing to walk the extra mile to materialize union with Baghdad. Pro-union officials such as Nazem al-Qudsi and Rushdi al-Kikhiya had briefly pushed for union, only to abandon the project once deprived of their military supporter, Colonel Sami al-Hinnawi, back in 1949. He admired the activism of the Egyptian Ambassador Mahmud Riad, who 'behaved like the French High Commissioner in Damascus' and overshadowed Iraq's own representative, Colonel Amin – a colourless yet highly intelligent figure, by most accounts. Additionally, while Iraq was always generous with money for union advocates, and occasional technical or military advice from Colonel Amin, it never involved itself directly in Syria and never got its own troops involved in any of the espionage coups and revolutions, not wanting to embarrass itself before the wider Arab public should the coup be foiled by Syrian intelligence. Why bother, when many Syrians were willing to do the dirty work on its behalf? At one point, when a governmental delegation from Damascus visited Baghdad, Nuri al-Said ordered that a secret service team follow them at a distance, to report on their every activity. Heading the delegation was Farzat Mamlouk, a well-known Iraqi sympathizer. When meeting Nuri Pasha at one of his palaces, Mamlouk told him: 'I have to tell you Pasha, that I am very upset at having Iraqi security follow-us all around Baghdad to report on our meetings. Why trouble the poor fellows, Your Excellency, when I am with the Syrian delegation. I will gladly report to you on all their activities.'[18] When Deputy Chief-of-Staff Major-General Ghazzi al-Daghistani was brought to court in Baghdad after the Iraqi revolution of 1958, accused of meddling in Syrian domestics, he famously testified to members of the Supreme Military Court: 'Iraqi governments have made it a principle to interfere in the internal affairs of Syria, from the time of Husni al-Za'im, if not earlier ...'[19] At one point, Colonel Amin had drawn up a plan with ambitious Syrian officers, code-named Operation X, and delivered it to his superior Daghistani and Iraqi Chief-of-Staff, Rafiq Arif, who flatly rejected it. Among other things, it called for a concentrated air strike against government posts in Damascus, Aleppo and Homs, aimed at bringing down the Quwatli regime. By 1956, however, it seemed reasonable for the Iraqis to try to break the pro-Egyptian Quwatli government, with the backing of the USA and Great Britain, who were both equally distressed and had absolutely no clue on how to handle the situation in Syria.

When meeting French officials in Paris in mid-1956, John Foster Dulles acknowledged that Syria was now 'the closest thing to a Soviet satellite' in the Middle East.[20] Events in the region were moving fast – too fast said Dulles – making the Secretary of State 'obliged to make decisions' related to the situation in Damascus.[21] Meanwhile, Vice President Nixon was advising Dulles that a 'thorough re-examination' of US policy towards Syria was needed, calling also on the National Security Council for 'urgent review' of its policies towards Damascus.[22] Dulles responded that the Soviets have 'opened a new front in the Middle East. Although our aims and our military assistance to the Middle East states could not be sufficient to enable these states to halt Russian invasion, US arms and assistance could have immense political impact in the area.'[23] The British for their part had a grim view of Dulles' approach to Syria, reporting: 'He had never known his advisors, especially on the intelligence side, so divided as they were now on Syria. Half of them thought Syria was gone for good, to the Soviet camp. The other half thought she could be rescued. He did not know what to think. It was clear he was moving in the direction of being less averse to, if not wholly favouring, a *coup d'état* by the Iraqis. He said he was afraid that some day it might not be a question of Iraq making a coup in Syria, but Syrian Communists making a coup in Iraq.'[24] Strangely enough, having barely shaken off the bad publicity from the Malki Affair, regardless of how authentic the accusations had been, the USA became entangled – again – in yet another clandestine operation in Syria. This time, however, unlike the case in 1949, involvement was not direct and certainly not involved at a micro-level. It was the Iraqis that were mandated to do the dirty work for the USA and see to it that International Communism be completely rooted out from Damascus.

King Faisal of Iraq called for a senior meeting at the royal palace in Baghdad to discuss the prospects of regime change in Syria, taking the cue from the USA. Crown Prince Abdul Illah was present, along with Abdullah Bakr, Burhan al-Din Bashayan, Ahmad Mukhtar Baban, Ghazzi al-Daghistani and Chief-of-Staff Rafiq Arif. The Iraqi monarch reviewed the situation in Syria with his top officials, who came forward with a list of Syrian officers able and willing to stage a coup in Syria in favour of Iraq and the USA. Ironically, the Iraqis decided on none other than their former arch-enemy Adib al-Shishakli, who had torpedoed the Syrian–Iraqi union back in 1949, and who since leaving office in 1954 had spent his exile divided between Saudi Arabia, Lebanon and Western Europe. Things had changed dramatically since then, however, with Shishakli now willing to work with any regional heavyweight ready to support his return to Damascus. An Iraqi delegation headed off to Switzerland to meet the former Syrian President, who not only encouraged the idea of a coup, but expressed an immediate interest in carrying it out, claiming that given all the domestic problems Syria was facing, it was a golden opportunity to bring the officers back to power. Shishakli asked for 30,000 Iraqi Dinars as a first instalment to prepare for the coup, demanding that the amount be paid to him in Beirut.[25] Eventually, according to Shishakli's former Police Chief Ibrahim al-Husseini, Shishakli expected no less than $300 million to be paid to Syria by the USA.[26] Who else could be better for the job, the Iraqis reasoned, than the coup-master who had seized power twice in Syria, back in 1949 and 1951? If Shishakli could not do the job, then nobody could.

The Iraqis then decided to look for other ambitious officers who shared in Shishakli's lust for power and were willing to work for a foreign nation. The recruitment requirements, one conspirator recalled, were 'a belief that Syria had no business in stronger relations with the Soviet Union or Gamal Abdul Nasser. They did not have to be necessarily pro-Iraq, but nevertheless, willing to work with Iraq to bring about this strategic objective: a communist-free Syria.' Those approached by Iraqi proxies were unaware that the USA was behind the proposed coup, but understood that some Western power, probably Great Britain, supported it, due to its relationship with the Baghdad government. Within Iraq itself, the conspirators found Mohammad Safa, head of the Syrian fugitive officer community in Baghdad. A former officer himself, Safa had tried in vain to bring Shishakli down back in 1953, while being bankrolled by the Iraqi government. He was now projected as a potential ally to work with him for the aim of bringing down Shukri al-Quwatli. Another conspirator brought into the plot was Shishakli's brother Captain Salah, a former member of the SSNP who was *persona non grata* in Damascus both for his association with the Shishakli regime and his membership in the SSNP, banned since the assassination of Adnan al-Malki. A third heavyweight was Ghassan Jadid, the SSNP leader banished from Syria with a bounty on his head, blamed directly for the Malki affair. Within Syria, their contact man was Mikhael Ilyan, a notable and wealthy moneylender from Aleppo and personal friend of Iraq's Crown Prince. Although a former minister and associate of Quwatli, Ilyan longed for improved relations between Damascus and Baghdad, worrying that this was becoming increasingly difficult due to the rise in Nasser's popularity, especially after Suez. If union could not be achieved through democratic means, Ilyan reasoned, then perhaps a military coup was not such a bad idea if it guaranteed a once-and-for-all termination of Soviet and Nasserist influence in Syria. On 1 July 1956, he met with Archibald Roosevelt of the CIA and Wilbur Crane Eveland, the former staff member of the National Security Council, now working also with the CIA. During the meeting, which took place in Damascus, Roosevelt asked Ilyan: 'What would be needed to give the Syrian conservatives enough control to purge the communists and leftist sympathizers?' Ilyan began writing out a long list of potential targets that needed to be removed from top positions in the Syrian government and army. Eveland asked, 'Could these things be done with US money and assets alone?' Ilyan nodded affirmatively, 'without question!'[27] He then asked for half a million Syrian pounds, (approximately $167,000.)

Shishakli arrived in Beirut as planned in July 1956, shortly before the Suez War. The SSNP, of which he had been a member in the 1940s, provided him with a costume, bodyguard and driver, along with different residences to stay in to avoid being spotted by Lebanese officials. He immediately summoned two of his former protégés from Syria, Burhan Adham and Hamdi Salih, to test their pulse on the prospects of a coup. Eventually he was joined by two members of the SSNP, Said Takkidine and Ghassan Jadid. The coup leaders decided that the SSNP would provide technical and military training for Syrian rebels at the Dhur Shwayr village in Mount Lebanon, the birthplace of Antune Saadeh. After six weeks of military training, they would cross the border into Syria, to team with comrades from within, then infiltrate through the Syrian capital, assassinating Akram Hawrani, Khaled Bakdash and Abdul Hamid Sarraj, the three strongest supporters of the Russians and Egyptians. Prime Minister Asali would be forced to step down and be replaced by a member of the People's Party, who would immediately commence on union talks with Iraq. Shishakli warned against violence, citing how he had avoided bloodshed back in 1951, claiming that this would trigger off a chain reaction that would be difficult to contain.[28] Daghistani then handed him the money, 10,000 Iraqi Dinars. The Syrian leader frowned, reminding his Iraqi interlocutor that the agreement had been for 30,000 Iraqi Dinars. Daghistani promised full delivery upon accomplishment of mission. Shishakli reluctantly took the money then to the absolute shock of the Iraqis, completely disappeared. He vacated his earlier residence in Paris and departed for Latin America, for an unknown destination – later discovered to be Brazil. The reasons for Shishakli's walk-out are unclear. Some claim that he never trusted the Iraqis in the first place, but wanted to see how serious they were at bringing him to power – never forgiving them, however, for supporting the coup that brought him down in 1954. Others believe that the Syrian officers with whom Shishakli conferred in Beirut returned to Damascus and reported on their meeting to Abdul Hamid Sarraj. Shishakli therefore, backed out of the entire plot, fearing that the intelligence chief would take revenge on the Shishakli clan in his native Hama. A third argument holds that far from being a gambler, Shishakli was a wise officer who would not carry out a military operation unless absolutely certain that the outcome was in his favour. He therefore decided to back-out, realizing that the time was simply not ripe for a *coup d'état* in Syria.

The Iraqi government formally informed both the USA and Great Britain of its entire encounter with the former Syrian President. The British, eager to see regime change in Syria, were furious with both Quwatli and Nasser, who not only confronted them in Suez, but in March 1956 had also prompted King Hussein of Jordan to dismiss his British Army Commander, John Bagot Glubb, known in the Middle East as Glubb Pasha. As a result, an Anglo-American–Iraqi Intelligence Committee was established in the summer of 1956, aimed at bringing down the regime in Damascus, if not through Shishakli then through some other Syrian figure who was willing to engage in covert activity against Shukri al-Quwatli. The nature of their contribution to the attempted coup (codenamed Operation Straggle), is unknown, although by all accounts they did give advice and send money to the Syrian rebels.[29] Mikhael Ilyan was charged with explaining the coup strategy to the US Embassy in Damascus, and by all accounts the staff at first were not too enthusiastic about it, fearing that if it failed repercussions could lead to a surge in pro-Communist and pro-Nasserist activity all throughout Syria.[30] Dulles came short of bluntly admitting his government's desire to topple the Syrian administration, saying: 'We understand that conservative elements in Syria, dissatisfied with the present situation, are considering steps which might be taken to bring about an improvement. We are endeavoring to obtain more information about the activities of these conservative elements. We will be happy to discuss the Syrian situation further.'[31] His brother Allen, who was director of the CIA during the hot summer of 1956, echoed this approach: 'Syria is in a critical condition where a communist coup might be pulled off. An overthrow of the Syrian government could result in a Syrian invitation to Moscow to send troops into Syria ostensibly to protect Syria from Israel. This would lead to Syria becoming a Soviet base of operations in the area of support of Egypt.'[32]

With Shishakli out of the operation, the Iraqis singled out individual Syrian politicians from different walks of life, broadly grouped as pro-West, to carry out the coup in Syria. Masterminding the event would be Mikhael Ilyan, due to his immediate and direct access to the royal palace in Baghdad. Supporting him were Adnan al-Atasi, the son of President Hashem al-Atasi who married a Turk, and was a ranking member of the People's Party and a former Ambassador to France, as well as Munir al-Ajlani, an eternal supporter of Syrian–Iraqi union who had studied at the Sorbonne and worked as a professor at Damascus University. He had tried and failed to pull off a Jordanian coup during the early years of Adib al-Shishakli, only to be arrested and discharged from his post as Minister of Education. Also involved in the plot was the journalist Sami Kabbara, editor of the anti-Quwatli daily *al-Nidal*, Adel Ajlani, an MP from Damascus, and Hasan al-Atrash, the veteran Druze leader who had facilitated the Allied invasion of Syria to fight off Vichy in 1941. The poet Badawi al-Jabal, a member of the National Party, was brought into the affair, as was Haile Surour, a Bedouin leader from Umm al-Jimal, next to the Syrian–Jordanian borders. The respected Syrian notables, many of them sitting parliamentarians with excellent ties to both Prime Minister Asali and President Quwatli, surely realized that such a massive operation could not simply be a product of Iraqi ambitions. It was certain to everybody involved that the Great Powers were behind Operation Straggle, explaining why they asked for the astronomical sum of 1 million Iraqi Dinars, and no less than 20,000 weapons, in addition to training and air cover by the Iraqi Army.[33] It was generally believed that the Iraqi Army would only intervene in the crisis if the communists came to the support of Quwatli. At the end of the day, the rebels got no more than 2,000 weapons, and 100,000 Dinars. Part of the money was put forth directly by the US State Department. It was distributed down to the smallest detail, under the watchful eye of the Iraqi attaché, Abdul Mutalib Amin. In one example, the owner of a coffee shop in Hama was given SP 50 – an advance payment on drinks to be served to young officers loyal to Shishakli who would visit his café to discuss coup attempts – a generally observed ritual in Syrian politics.[34]

Hasan al-Atrash, although instrumental in the coup, was none too pleased at dealing with Salah Shishakli, given that his brother had mercilessly hit the Druze Mountain during his final months in power back in 1953–1954. At the end of the day, however, the Druze did obtain 500 rifles to use in the insurgency, while the Bedouins working with Haile Surour got 300. They were expected to arouse civil disturbances in their respective districts, while officers raised the siren of rebellion in Hama, as SSNP paratroopers crossed the border from Lebanon, to carry out their target assassinations. Reportedly it was decided that Asali would be replaced by Subhi al-Omari, a former officer in the army of King Faisal who had fought in Maysaloun back in 1920 and had helped create the Iraqi Army. President Quwatli, however, would not be harmed, due to his generally observed status as father of Syrian independence. He would be given an ultimatum by the rebels, however, and forced to choose between his job and his relationship with the Soviet Union and Gamal Abdul Nasser. If he agreed to distance himself from leftist orientations in Syria, then he would be kept in his honourific post as President of the Republic. Atrash grumbled, 'Did they think that I could take on the whole Syrian Army with 500 rifles?'[35]

The date of the coup was scheduled for 28 October 1956 but the conspirators decided to postpone it so it would not coincide with the Tripartite Attack on Egypt, not wanting to be branded as Israeli accomplices by the Syrian street.[36] Reportedly, Ilyan came knocking on the door of CIA operative Eveland shouting: 'Last night, the Israelis invaded Egypt and are right now heading for the Suez Canal. How could you have asked us to overthrow our government at the exact same moment when Israel started a war with an Arab state?'[37] The postponement gave Syrian Intelligence ample time to investigate unconfirmed reports about arms streaming through the border into Syria. When stockpiles of weapons were indeed uncovered in the Druze Mountain, Abdul Hamid Sarraj was furious, sending his men on a hunting campaign, picking up any person with the slightest connection to the Iraqi conspiracy, regardless of how senior his government post. Instructions were sent to the Speaker of Parliament, ordering that the immunity of Deputies such as Munir al-Ajlani and Adnan al-Atasi be lifted immediately, to facilitate their arrest on the charge of 'high treason.' On 22 December, the Bill of Indictment handed over the names of 47 Syrians, all involved in Operation Straggle, accused of treachery for siding with the USA, Great Britain and Iraq, against their own country. First on the list was Adib al-Shishakli. On 8 January 1957, the trial of these men opened at the main auditorium of the Syrian University and lasted for five weeks, headed by General Afif al-Bizreh, a decorated war officer believed to have a strong communist background, who, in the summer of 1957, was to become Chief-of-Staff of the Syrian Army. Nineteen of the accused had already fled the scene, while those who stayed behind were locked up at the infamous Mezzeh Prison, where, according to Munir al-Ajlani, they were tortured 'and treated like animals'. Ghassan Jadid, a leading name in the Iraqi conspiracy, was gunned down before the verdicts were released, by an agent of the Syrian intelligence, Izzat Shath on a busy street in Ras Beirut, on 19 February 1957. The long awaited verdicts were finally released on 8 March 1957, sending shockwaves throughout Syria and the Arab world. Big names like Adnan al-Atasi, Munir al-Ajlani and Adib al-Shishakli, were sentenced to death while others attracted sentences of up to 22 years in prison. Had they been executed as planned, not only would Syria have been deprived of some of its brightest figures, and what remained of pro-West sympathies in the country would have suffered a deadly blow. A troubled Iraq asked the USA to interfere and commute the death sentences to life imprisonment, a request backed by both Lebanon and Jordan.[38] It was reasoned that if Hashem al-Atasi's son was going to be executed, then nobody's life was safe anymore in Syria. Khaled al-Azm wanted to abrogate the verdicts altogether, while Quwatli preferred transforming them either into life imprisonment or a shorter sentence with hard labour.[39]

The verdicts were eventually revoked, not by Iraq, but by Saudi Arabia's King Saud.[40] The pro-Nasser organ of the Baath Party, *al-Baath*, ran the headline: 'Pardoning the criminals is a crime'.[41] The arrested politicians remained in jail even after Syria and Egypt merged to form the United Arab Republic (UAR) in 1958, only to be released under house arrest in Alexandria in 1960. They were eventually brought back into public life when the UAR was dissolved in 1961 but by then their reputations had been ruined, as had their lives and political careers. Adnan al-Atasi was not even allowed to take part in his father's funeral in December 1960, during the heyday of the UAR, testimony to just how angry the leftists were with his pro-Americanism and anti-Nasserism.[42] Although all the politicians involved spent what remained of their lives defending themselves, claiming that no conspiracy was involved and no Americans, Iraqis or British had contacted them to bring down the regime in Damascus, the author was able to get a confession out of Munir al-Ajlani, 40-years after Operation Straggle. When pressed on the topic of the Iraqi conspiracy in 1996, the ageing Ajlani took a long pause, closed his eyes, and said:

> We were young, ambitious, and wild. Perhaps we overdid it. Yes we were planning to launch a coup to change things in Syria. They wanted to

place me [as] Prime Minister and to make Subhi al-Omari, the Minister of Defense. Now in looking back, I tell you that we were wrong, because what you called 'The Iraqi conspiracy' actually gave the leftists a *carte blanch* to strike us, all of us ... the moderates in Syria, with tremendous force. We were never able to rise from the ashes after 1956. We heard rumours back then that Abdul Nasser said, 'See the sons of these big landowning families in Syria? I will crush them with my boot!' We were not trying to bring the Americans to Syria. We were only trying to prevent the Russians from coming to Syria. I am sure you realise the major difference between the two. Were the Americans involved with the Iraqi affair in 1956? To tell you the truth, I don't remember meeting any American official during the planning for the entire event. Some of my comrades, however, may have met with the Americans.

He continued,

We were never traitors – may God forbid – on the contrary we were trying to achieve what was best for Syria. We thought this was the best way to prevent the country from becoming 100 per cent Russian. At the end of the day, what actually prevented Syria from becoming a satellite to the Soviet Union was not us, but Nasser himself, who crushed the Syrian Communist Party after creating union in 1958. The Americans tried to bring down the Communists through planning coups in the 1950s. That failed. They then tried to fund the opposition abroad, reportedly paying Mohammad Safa and his people (in Baghdad) up to USD 3 million. That too failed. They then withdrew their ambassador and began to accuse the Syrians of meddling in the affairs of Jordan, Lebanon, and Turkey, calling on them to strike back, claiming that this was supported by Article 64 of the UN Charter: Self-Defence. When that failed as well, they realised that the best way to root out communism was to bring Gamal Abdul Nasser to Syria. He certainly will achieve what Syrians like us failed at doing. And they were right. He did![43]

The Iraqi conspiracy forced Asali to reshuffle his cabinet on 31 December, expelling ministers associated with Ajlani and the People's Party, and bringing in Khaled al-Azm as Minister of Defense. It was a devastating blow to anybody associated with the West and pressured those on middle ground to take sides or suffer the same fate as Munir al-Ajlani and his associates. Ajlani's wife, the daughter of former president Taj al-Din al-Hasani, recalls visiting

President Shukri al-Quwatli at the presidential palace while her husband was in jail in 1956. Quwatli was sweetness itself, she recalled, describing Ajlani as an old friend and neighbour, who did not deserve the fate he was provided. Quwatli had just began to promise to do his best to secure his release when a Sudanese waiter walked in, bringing the president's coffee. Quwatli's tone suddenly changed, she said, and he snapped, 'But nobody is above the law, not even Dr Ajlani. I am a man of justice, and we will not interfere with the court verdicts. Your husband is convicted of high treason, and only the courts will have a final say in this!' When the waiter exited, Quwatli changed yet again and apologized, telling Ajlani, 'Please forgive me Madame, but spies are all around me at the Palace.'[44] It was a miserable fate for a man who only ten years ago had been hailed as the father of Syrian Independence. He was being spied upon within his own palace, unable to even verbally express support for an old colleague who he had worked with since the 1930s, because of the rising trend in Nasserism and the belief that everything nasty occurring in Syria was the doing of the USA. When returning to office, Quwatli tried to right the wrongs done to his relationship with the USA, through pledging to combat International Communism. In exchange, he needed US support to keep ambitious officers at bay and prevent the repetition of a similar scenario to 1949. Rather than empower the ageing President, the USA only watched as he fought back against the communist giant at his doorsteps, and at home, manifested through men like Akram al-Hawrani, Khaled Bakdash and Salah al-Bitar. With no help whatsoever, apart from lip service from John Foster Dulles, Quwatli had no choice but to 'head East' towards Moscow in 1956, laying the grounds for the famous summer of 1957, when, shortly after Syria and the USSR signed a long-term economic and military agreement, relations between Syria and the USA hit rock bottom over what has been called, 'The Stone Affair'.

12

THE STONE AFFAIR

As Syrians were preparing to go to the public trial of those implicated in Operation Straggle, President Eisenhower announced his doctrine to the US Congress on 5 January 1957. Under the Eisenhower Doctrine, any country could request US economic aid and military assistance if it was being threatened by armed aggression from another state, presumably, a communist nation from the Eastern Bloc. Eisenhower pledged that the US government would 'secure and protect the territorial integrity and political independence of such nations, requesting such aid against overt armed aggression from any nation controlled by international communism'. His approach was born out of a hard-felt reality that the Soviets were going to invest in the Suez crisis and the Damascus trials, and now had ground, naval and air forces on the frontiers of the Middle East, in Bulgaria, Ukraine, the Black Sea, the Caucasus and Central Asia. The Soviet invasion of Hungary was testimony that the USSR was willing to resort to unorthodox means, and 'brute force with lack of moral restraint' to achieve its aims in the Middle East, making US action all the more obligatory.[1] Speaking to the Joint Sessions of the Foreign Relations and Armed Services Commission of the Senate, Secretary Dulles echoed a similar approach saying, 'I can assure you that the leaders of International Communism will take every risk they dare in order to win the Middle East'. Eisenhower sought congressional authority to use the armed forces to protect any Middle East state requesting assistance provided it was under threat from the Russians. He offered a total of $200 million to strengthen the internal security and promote orderly governments in the Levant. This was approved by a joint resolution of the Senate and House on 9 March, and on 12 March the President sent James P. Richards, his newly appointed Special Assistant for Middle East Affairs (and former Chairman of the House Foreign Affairs Committee) to the region, to explain the doctrine to Arab leaders. Naturally, Damascus was not on his travel agenda. Twelve days later, the USA formally joined the Baghdad Pact. Syrian Foreign Minister Khaled al-Azm described the Eisenhower Doctrine as 'the biggest threat to the Middle East'.[2]

Two trends began to emerge in the USA after the Suez War. One was to moderate Syria via Egypt, and the other, to curb the radicalization of Egypt, through bringing Syria back into the Western camp. The British advised the USA to 'seduce rather than rape' radicals in the Middle East, making a clear argument in favour of moderating Egypt, their prime nemesis, via Syria, with whom they still had at least a working relationship despite the tension over Suez.[3] A daily stream of reports was coming from the US Embassy in Damascus, but none were the slightest bit assuring to the Eisenhower White House. On 4 September 1956, 17 Soviet ministers came to Syria, touring the countryside and meeting with villagers, promoting communist views to ordinary Syrians. On 1 October, the Russian news agency TASS opened an office in Damascus, while earlier, in May 1957, Quwatli and Asali had publicly declared they had supported the Baathist Riad al-Malki (Adnan's brother) in the by-elections for the Syrian Parliament, who had run against the Muslim Brotherhood chief Mustapha al-Sibai.[4] In February 1957, a senior Arab meeting took place in Cairo, attended by Quwatli, King Hussein of Jordan and King Saud, aimed at formulating a united response to the Eisenhower Doctrine. While Jordan and Saudi Arabia were eager to back their US ally, the Syrians and Egyptians were reluctant, for obvious reasons, given the history of bad blood between their capitals and Washington DC. In order to unite the Arabs behind the doctrine, the USA called on its trusted ally, King Saud, to mend broken fences in the Middle East and establish himself as a unanimous chief of the Arab community, speaking on their behalf with the Western world. Saud was a clever man, although he had no formal education, who realized that the USA wanted to use him to counterbalance Nasser's rising influence in the region. In turn, he wanted the USA to help him outdo the royal family in Baghdad. But before establishing himself as the Arab leader Eisenhower wanted him to be, Saud had to overcome petty rivalries with both Jordan and Iraq. The two Hashemite dynasties had been at odds with the House of Saud since the 1925 expulsion of Sharif Hussein from the Kingdom of the Hijaz, a military feat carried out by Saud's father against the great-grandfather of the current monarchs of Amman and Baghdad, Hussein and Faisal. In tribal Arab politics, such a matter was essential to the development of relations in the Arabian Gulf, regardless of how old it had become and whether its original players were still around to make claim to lost territory. On 28 April 1957, King Hussein visited Riyadh, and King Saud reciprocated with a visit to Amman on 8 June. On 11 May, he landed in Baghdad for the first visit ever by a Saudi monarch to Iraq. In a joint communiqué with the young King of Iraq, Saud denounced Zionism and Communism, signalling the launch of a new era in Saudi–Iraqi-Jordanian relations, which was bound to serve the Eisenhower Doctrine well. On 3 July, the Iraqi government dispatched Ibrahim al-Suwayyil as its first Ambassador to Saudi Arabia.

The Syrians watched these developments with some alarm; those who had relied on patronage of the Saudis to combat Iraqi influence in Syria were distressed, as were those who had taken money from the Iraqis to bring down pro-Saudi regimes since the 1940s. Leftists were naturally furious with the sudden alliance of pro-Western kings taking place all around them, apparently with complete disregard of their leadership and of that of Gamal Abdul Nasser. Baath Party founder Michel Aflaq barked that 'Saudi Arabia is no longer a neutral state!'[5] The Damascus daily al-Nasr suddenly accused Saud of interfering in Syrian affairs, while Khaled al-Azm accused the Monarch of 'siding with imperialism' against Syria. King Saud, taken aback and furious with the Syrian response, withdrew his Ambassador from Syria and froze Syrian assets in Saudi Arabia.[6] The Saudi Monarch felt personally humiliated by the Syrians, especially considering President Shukri al-Quwatli was a close personal family friend of his late father.[7] When exiled from Syria in 1941, it was King Abdul-Aziz who had mediated on Quwatli's behalf with the British and USA, allowing for his return despite the ostensible Nazi connection, and when the Syrian President was toppled in 1949 it was the Saudis who made it a condition that they would never recognize Husni al-Za'im unless he preserved the life and dignity of Shukri al-Quwatli. The fact that Quwatli allowed the crisis with Saudi Arabia to snowball, against his own wishes, was testimony to how weak the President had become in standing up to leftist tendencies in Syria. On 28 June, Akram al-Hawrani accused the Saudis of organizing a coup in Syria, 'aimed at replacing the current regime with one that would come to an understanding with American imperialism'.[8] Quwatli put in a tremendous personal effort and intervened, calling on Sabri al-Asali to issue a public apology to King Saud, stressing that views of the Syrian press and certain parliamentarians do not express the views of Syrian officialdom. Saud's virtues were praised, in fact exaggerated, and a government order shutting down the communist periodical al-Sarkha was issued by Quwatli himself. Syria's decision not to cross the King of Saudi Arabia was to prove vital and wise in the months to come, since it was Saud who came to the aid of Damascus when relations hit rock-bottom with the USA in August–September 1957, preventing regime change – or as some described it, 'Suez in reverse' – an all-out US war on Syria.

Syrian–US relations plummet

As the Syrian–Saudi schism began to repair, other developments surfaced within Syria, showing resistance to the alliance of pro-Western states that was emerging in the neighbourhood. In early August, Khaled al-Azm visited Moscow, where he signed long-term economic and military agreements with the Soviet Union, causing alarm bells to ring at the US Embassy in Damascus. On 12 August 1957, the Syrians announced that a plot had been discovered in their midst, aimed at regime change in Damascus, carried out by three officials at the US Embassy. They were identified as Lt. Colonel Robert Malloy, the Military Attaché, Francis Jetton, the Vice Consul, and Howard Stone, the Second Secretary, who had recently been appointed to Syria after serving in Sudan. Only 33, Stone was already a legend within the CIA, having helped topple the Iranian government in 1953.[9] Ambassador James Moose had been recalled to the USA in late June, and a successor had not yet been named, meaning the US Embassy in Damascus was now left in the hands of junior officials, who were no match for the diplomatic heavyweights at the Russian embassy next door on Abu Rummaneh Street. Salah al-Din al-Tarazi, Secretary General of the Foreign Minister, called on the Embassy staff and advised them to pack up and leave within a grace period of 24 hours, effectively declaring them unwelcome. The Damascus daily *al-Nasr* opened with an inflammatory front page editorial the next morning, stating, 'American imperialism has no intention of letting Syria alone, securing the means of its safety, and letting it attain its natural aims by means unanimously approved by its people. American imperialism is working continuously to hatch an un-interrupted chain of plots, despite the continued failure which awaits all links of this criminal chain.'[10]

It seemed absurd, almost abstract, for such a crisis to emerge, two years after the Malki affair, seven months after Operation Straggle. Howard Stone had a notorious record for covert intelligence activity in Iran, Guatemala and Sudan, labelled by the Syrian press as a 'coup mastermind' who had tried to launch a revolt in Damascus, aimed yet again at restoring Adib al-Shishakli to power, along with his former Police Chief Ibrahim al-Husseini. Reportedly, under the watchful eye of the USA the two men had visited Syria in disguise on fake Syrian passports provided by the CIA, sometime in the first half of 1957, meeting with certain officers to discuss the chances of a coup, much in the same manner as they had done in 1956.[11] The now expelled US diplomats, who had orchestrated Shishakli's brief visit, had also met with potential officers for the job, including Quwatli's loyalist and former military assistant Suheil al-Ashi. The choice of accomplices could not have been more careless, since all of them returned to report the coup attempt either directly to the President himself, or to his Intelligence chief, Abdul Hamid Sarraj. Infuriated by Sarraj's expulsion of the three diplomats, Molloy decided to leave Syria in style, sending a strongly worded message to the Quwatli government. As he was escorted to the Lebanese border by Syrian police, he threw the Syrian motorcycle off the road, shouting, 'Colonel Sarraj and his commie friends should be told that Molloy will beat the shit out of them with one hand tied behind his back if they ever cross his path again!'[12]

At first, US officialdom was taken completely aback by the Syrian declaration, with many in the State Department believing that Syria was bluffing with the sole purpose of diverting attention away from the recent verdicts of the Iraqi conspiracy.[13] *The New York Times* headlined that these were empty accusations, typical of a communist state, asking, 'Can the US and Syria's pro-western neighbours tolerate a Soviet satellite – or something very much like one – in the heart of the Middle East?' On 19 August, a 'crisis meeting' was held at the White House to discuss the situation in Syria, attended by President Eisenhower, John Foster Dulles and British Ambassador Sir Harold Caccia. The USA formally decided to reciprocate by expelling the Syrian Ambassador to Washington, Farid Zayn al-Din, and members of his staff – fully aware that now there would be no American, British or French diplomats in the Syrian capital. The last two had been expelled during the Suez War, meaning that Damascus would become a vast playing field for members of the Russian Embassy to Syria. The British, Eisenhower noted, could take no similar action back in 1956, because of the burden of Suez, but Washington could not stand back and see its diplomats being humiliated without coming to their defence. The strategy that emerged from the White House meeting was to minimize damage caused by the diplomatic crisis, and maximize gain by using it to further isolate the Quwatli administration. Dulles proposed sending immediate US aid to Arab countries surrounding Syria to avert a communist takeover, which was automatically approved by the President.[14] The two men nevertheless acknowledged that the crisis, coming just days after Azm's triumphant visit to Moscow, was 'very disturbing'. The only solution, they argued, was to now treat Syria as an outlaw state, to call on its Arab neighbours to refuse doing business with it, and to effectively, 'quarantine the government' in Damascus.[15] Days after his government expelled the US diplomats, Quwatli appointed Afif al-Bizreh, the military judge of the Iraqi conspiracy trials, as Chief-of-Staff of the Syrian Army. *The New York Times* described Bizreh as a 'ranking communist' given that he had received advanced military training in Moscow and had strongly supported the SCP in both words and actions since the mid-1950s.[16] Born in 1914 in Sidon, Lebanon, Bizreh had risen to the ranks of the French-created Troupes Spéciales under the French mandate, deserting to join Syrian rebels during the 1945 bombing of Damascus. He was one of the founding fathers of the modern Syria Army who brilliantly served during the Palestine War of 1948, and worked briefly on the armistice talks with Husni al-Za'im during the summer of 1949. Tall, conniving and dark (both in skin colour and character), he was an unattractive figure by most accounts, who had boundless ambition and was willing to go to great lengths to see Syria neatly allied with the Eastern Bloc, with no interference from the USA. Tawfiq Nizam al-Din, who had succeeded Shawkat Shuqayr as Chief-of-Staff one year earlier, had apparently been retired from his job because he refused to dismiss officers implicated in anti-Egyptian conduct.[17] Bizreh did not hesitate to sign off the dismissal warrants, endearing himself to the military strongman of Syria, Abdul Hamid Sarraj.

On 23 August, 'a special handling category for cables and memoranda concerning sensitive aspects of policy or operations related to the situation in Syria' was established by the US State Department. Eisenhower then dispatched the Deputy Undersecretary of State for Administration, Loy W. Henderson, to Turkey to start building a fortress around the Syrian regime, punishing it for coming too close to the Soviet Union. Henderson had famously co-drafted the Truman Doctrine and had played an instrumental role in bringing down Iranian Prime Minister Mossadeq in 1954, explaining why his presence in the region raised tensions between Damascus and Washington to new heights. Prior to his departure, Dulles instructed Henderson to refrain from any action that would involve a Turkish or Israeli attack on Syria, seeing that this would scare off the Arabs, and ensure no action was taken that could not be justified under Article 51 of the UN Charter, being self defence. He explained:

> In your discussions you should of course bear in mind US policy of supporting the principles of the UN and opposing unprovoked military intervention in any country. At the same time the United States must be fully alert to obvious dangers of a situation in which Syria, under increasing Soviet influence, is receiving large amounts of military goods, obviously exceeding those required for Syria's defensive needs. We must take into account any legitimate military planning required by Syria's neighbors to be prepared to protect themselves from any Syrian aggression.[18]

In Istanbul, Henderson conferred with Prime Minister Menderes, a loyal ally in the fight against communism, and both King Saud and King Hussein, who came to meet him. He then went to Beirut for a meeting with President Camille Chamoun, heading back to Turkey to meet with King Faisal II of Iraq. With great intention, both Cairo and Damascus were bypassed during his trip to the region, since they were the subject of his talks, prompting Egyptian Radio to describe him as 'an expert in coups who had come to the region to isolate and lay siege to sister Syria'. While speaking to these Arab leaders, the US diplomat said Washington 'was prepared to give appropriate support to Syria's Muslim neighbours in case Syrian provocations would force them to take some kind of defensive action'. The USA was not, he stressed, 'urging any particular action' but felt that these countries 'could best decide among themselves what they could and should do'. Upon returning to the USA on 5 September, Henderson reported that there was 'deep concern' in the Middle East over the communist trend in Damascus, describing the country as 'a victim of International Communism' which has 'become a base for further threatening the independence and integrity of the region'. The following day, US arms arrived in Jordan, Iraq and Lebanon to defend these states against possible Syrian aggression. The policy was to 'expose the pretensions of the present Syrian regime' so that 'good Arab nationalists' could stand up to Shukri al-Quwatli, denouncing him and his government 'for what they are – namely communists and communist stooges'.[19] Dulles even spoke to Chief-of-Staff Twining on 21 August, telling him to prepare for the worst should the Arab initiative fail, warning: 'We are thinking of the possibility of fairly drastic action.'[20] He then spoke to his British counterpart Selwyn Lloyd, adding, 'It seems to use that there is now little hope for correction from within. We must perhaps be prepared to take some serious risks to avoid even greater risks and dangers later on.' British Prime Minister Harold Macmillan commented, 'The Americans are taking it very seriously and talking about the most drastic measures – Suez in reverse. If it were not serious, it would be rather comic!'[21] Other world leaders shared a similar view, including Indian Prime Minister Jawaharlal Nehru, who described the Syrian–US crisis as 'dangerous and explosive.'[22] Showing just how serious his country was, Eisenhower authorized the transfer of American aircraft from Western Europe to American airbases in Adana, Turkey, and ordered the Sixth Fleet into the Mediterranean, placing it on high alert for the possibility of an offensive on Syria. He then commented, 'All we can do is to make sure that the Soviets cannot come in, and give assurances to that effect, and also, give military aid to our allies'.[23] The Syrians cried foul play – without directly criticizing Eisenhower – only reminding him that back in October 1956, during the Soviet invasion of Hungary, he had said, 'Military force was not a justifiable means for settling disputes'.[24]

Although a military option seemed very much on the table in August 1957, the USA eventually abandoned the idea and decided to call on King Saud to save the explosive situation in Syria. Dulles wrote to him saying:

> We believe that it is highly preferable that Syria's neighbours should be able to deal with this problem without the necessity for any outside intervention. In view of the special position of Your Majesty as Keeper of the Holy Places of Islam, I trust that you will exert your great influence to the end that the atheistic creed of communism will not be entrenched at a key position in the Muslim world.[25]

One problem that Henderson encountered was hearing one thing from Arab leaders in private, but something completely different in public, where they all rallied in favour of Syria, fearing the wrath of their own constituencies.[26] King Saud responded to Dulles' letter on 25 August, flatly refusing to apply any pressure on Quwatli, and placing full blame for the crisis on the USA.[27] Iraqi Foreign Minister Ali Mumtaz said that he would clearly veto any US intervention in Syria while Iraq's new Prime Minister Ali Jawdat al-Ayyubi went to great lengths at harmonizing his country's relations with Damascus, to mend broken fences left behind by Nuri al-Said who had resigned from office earlier that summer. Ayyubi, who had been Prime Minister during the Atasi presidency, ordered that the jam imposed on broadcasts from Damascus Radio be lifted, and signalled his readiness to take part at the September 1957 Damascus International Fair, sending his Economy Minister Nadim al-Pachachi to represent the Iraqi government. This was not the kind of attitude the US government expected from countries that it considered allies, who supposedly, were under threat of a communist take-over from Syria. Henderson described both Ayyubi and Mumtaz as 'feeble and weak' while an angry Dulles commented that 'it might be desirable that Nuri Pasha should go back (to power)'.[28] Additionally, important Iraqi periodicals such as *al-Bilad* and *al-Zaman* expressed strong support for Syria and loudly criticized Henderson during his trip.[29] For his part, King Hussein excused himself from confrontation by heading off to a summer vacation in Italy and Spain, causing Eisenhower to remark, 'Contrary to what we had been led to believe, Jordan did not want to join any move against Syria'.[30]

Reporting the situation to Macmillan, Dulles wrote:

> There is nothing that looks particularly attractive and the choice of policy will be hard. We are not completely satisfied with any of the alternatives which thus far have been suggested. We are continuing to explore other

possibilities. Loy Henderson has the impression that the Turks are desperately serious about the situation and I don't think either of our governments wants to try and impose what could be another Munich.

Indeed, the Turks were frantic because of the situation in Syria, fearing a communist spill-over into their own country. This was made clear at another senior meeting at the White House, attended by Eisenhower, Dulles, Assistant Secretary of State William Rountree, Chief-of-Staff Nathan Twining, General James F. Whisenand, General Charles Cabell, the Deputy Director of the CIA, Robert Cutler, the National Security Advisor and General Andrew Goodpaster, the Defense Liaison Officer to the president. This was the top brass of the US army who had known only too well how important it was to have Turkey on their side, and on NATO's, since 1952, as well as how difficult it was for them to digest a Syria controlled by the communists.[31] These men saw the crisis with Syria in broad cold war terms, not as a problem between Syria and the USA, but rather, as a potential confrontation between the USA and USSR, giving very little regard to what the Syrians were saying during the entire crisis (mainly, repeated claims that they were nowhere close to becoming a Soviet satellite). By referring to Munich in his talks with the British Prime Minister, Dulles struck a particularly raw nerve in London, reminding Macmillan how his predecessor Neville Chamberlain had failed to halt Adolf Hitler's territorial ambitions at the Munich Conference of 1938. At the White House meeting, Dulles made a similar argument, drawing parallels between Nikita Khrushchev and the German Fuhrer saying that he was 'crude and impulsive, more like Hitler than any other Russian leader we have previously seen'. As his guest in 1956, Quwatli was now portrayed as though he had stood in the presence of Hitler himself. If the Soviets manage to transform the Quwatli's state into a communist regime, he added, 'success would get into Khrushchev's head, and we might find ourselves with a series of incidents like the experience we had with Hitler'.[32] While the Second World War parallel sold well with the American officers, Eisenhower was unimpressed, calling for a hands-on contingency plan to deal with Quwatli. He pushed for the 'holy war' argument, saying that if the right strings were pulled, King Saud could be talked into applying serious pressure on Syria to prevent atheist communists from taking over Muslim Syria. On 10 September, the outcomes of the White House meeting, which had 'reached at the highest level of the US Government, were delivered to the US Embassy in Turkey. Dulles instructed the Ambassador to convey them orally to Menderes, 'under absolute secrecy'.[33]

The following are some of the most important points reached by the US officials:[34]

- The United States judges that Syria has become, or is about to become, a base for military and subversive activities in the Near East, designed to destroy the independence of those countries and to subject them to Soviet Communist domination.

- If the aggressive spirit, which is being inculcated into Syria by means of Soviet arms, propaganda, etc., should, or seems likely, manifest itself in actual deeds – and some such manifestations have already occurred in Lebanon (in reference to a series of bombings that were blamed on Damascus) the United States would hold that a case existed for individual or collective self-defense under Article 51 of the United Nations Charter and that there would be no violation of Article I of the NATO Treaty.

- The United States believes, however, that Israel should, irrespective of provocations other than large-scale invasion, show restraint so as not to unite and inflame the Arab world against Israel and in support of Syria on the theory that Israel has aggressive purposes and territorial ambitions.

- The United States further believes that Turkey should act other than in required reinforcements of Arab defensive actions.

- If Syria's Muslim neighbours should consider their security endangered by the threat of Syrian aggression and should request from the United States economic assistance and military supplies in connection with a concrete plan effectively to meet such aggression, the US would give prompt and sympathetic consideration to such a request. If any or more of Syria's Arab neighbours, responding to provocations, should act pursuant to Article 51 of the Charter, the United States would, upon request, and pursuant to the Middle East Resolutions, extend such countries economic assistance and military supplies; it would support such countries if attacked in the UNSC or the GA (General Assembly).

- If any of Syria's Arab neighbours were physically attacked by the Sino-Soviet bloc, the United States, upon request, would be prepared to use its own armed forces to assist any such nation or nations against such armed aggression.

- If hostilities between Iraq and Syria should result in the closing of the pipelines and the cutting off of revenues from Iraq, the United States would, as a temporary emergency measure, help to mitigate the financial consequences of this to Iraq.

- If any of Syria's neighbours should become involved in hostilities with Syria, it is a precondition to any US support that it be made clear that such hostilities are not for the purpose of impairing political independence or the territory of Syria, but are merely for the purpose of restoring Syria to the Syrians.
- The US will continue to deploy the Sixth Fleet in the Eastern Mediterranean.
- The US has consulted with the UK which is in complete agreement with this position.

It was made very clear that these 16 points were not to be leaked to a troublesome Congress, which would make implementation a headache for Eisenhower and Dulles. The President's speechwriter Emmet John Hughes wrote to the Undersecretary of State Christian Herter saying that he had reviewed 'some recent, clumsy, clandestine American attempt to spur Turkish forces to do some vague kind of battle with Syria'.[35] As a result of US approval, 50,000 Turkish troops were indeed sent to the borders with Syria, shocking Quwatli, who placed his own army on high alert.[36] Dulles reminded General Twining that the US Army should be constantly prepared, adding that the situation 'had a considerable amount of danger in it'.[37] While the Turks were amassing on the borders with Syria, the intelligence community prepared a report on Syria and presented it to President Eisenhower. It read:

> In the absence of forceful intervention from outside Syria, the presently dominant coalition probably will be able to maintain control for some time. No opposition group within the country, civilian or military, is likely to challenge the coalition effectively. Some groups within the country may hope for intervention from the outside.[38]

For their part the Syrians, who had watched in bewilderment as the world debated their future, said very little during the entire ordeal, trying hard to downplay the crisis with Eisenhower. The Foreign Ministry's Secretary General reminded journalists at a press conference in early September that 'three officials at the American Embassy, and not the American government' were responsible for the coup attempt in Damascus.[39] Even the outspoken Salah al-Bitar seemed to lay low that summer, politely remarking, 'We hope that Henderson's visit to the Middle East enables President Eisenhower to become familiar with the real developments in the Middle East. Syria is open to all visitors and seekers of the truth.'[40] He added, 'We will not impede the tasks of this envoy'. On 9 September, Bizreh called an unusual press conference, stressing four major points that Syria wanted the world to hear:

1. Syrian-Turkish relations were cordial and Damascus wanted them to remain as such.
2. Syria would never permit foreign military bases on its territory, be they American or Russian.
3. There were no Soviet officials, officers, or technicians operating out of bases on Syrian territory.
4. Syria would never become a communist state.[41]

One week later, a yet even more unusual sign came out of Damascus, this time via a press conference held by none other than the intelligence chief, Abdul Hamid Sarraj, who not only rarely gave interviews, but was rarely even seen in public, fearing for his life ever since the SSNP ordeal in 1955. The fact that he was calling members of the press corps into an urgent meeting at his office meant that he had something important – very important – to say. Sarraj defended himself before an army of reporters, saying that by no means was either he or Bizreh members of the SCP, describing his comrade as a 'true nationalist' who wanted what was in Syria's best interest. All of what was being said about both them, he added, was fabrication by anti-Syrian media both in the Arab world and international community, asking journalists to double-check their facts before 'firing accusations left and right' about the political background of Syrian officials.[42]

Just as the Syrians seemed to be downplaying the crisis, the Kremlin decided to step in with full force, investing in the gridlock to score points against the USA. Andrei Gromyko, who had replaced Shepilov as Foreign Minister in June, came to the aid of Quwatli, asking, 'How would Turkey like it if troops of a foreign state [in reference to the Soviet Union] were concentrated on her borders?' He questioned why the USA had not taken the matter to the UN, then adding, 'It would be dangerous for Turkey to be guided by the advice of those who want to compel her to carry out their adventurous plans for unleashing war in the Near East'. Soviet Premier Bulganin then sent a note to Prime Minister Menderes warning: 'The Soviet Union cannot remain indifferent to these events.'[43] To make himself well understood, Bulganin sent the cruiser Zhdanov and destroyer Svobodny to the Syrian port city of Lattakia, in response to the presence of the Sixth Fleet, and to Turkish reinforcements on the Syrian border. Moscow then fired with a note to Washington, London and Paris:

> It is difficult to assess such a position of the government of the USA in any way other than as proof for the fact that the US is not the least interested in the lessening of tensions in the Near and Middle East and in the presenting to the people of this area the opportunity to live in peace and quiet and to themselves determine their domestic and foreign policy.[44]

Dulles commented that the Soviets were getting 'pretty nasty' while *The Washington Post*, reflecting on the Eisenhower Administration's response, scoffed back, writing: 'The new Russian proposal for a pledge of non-interference in the Middle East reflects the magnanimity of the thief who has just stolen the chickens.'[45] Dulles even replied to his Soviet counterpart's remarks, accusing him of 'deliberate falsifications'. Yet suddenly and miraculously, right after the Russian intervention, both verbally and militarily the crisis came to a sudden and absolute halt between Syria and the USA. On 10 September, Dulles held a press conference, downplaying all previous tension by basically saying that the Eisenhower doctrine, which pledged to punish communist-dominated states, does not really apply to Syria:

> The situation internally in Syria is not entirely clear and fluctuates somewhat. While I have not discussed this with the President I would think that in a situation which is still somewhat borderline the President would not make a finding unless there were other events which called for it so that the finding would be contemporaneous with the other events. Now, as you know, there are in the world some of these borderline situations. There are some countries which are, beyond the peradventure of doubt, under the domination of international communism and others where it is not so clear. In cases where it is not entirely clear, and where the situation is somewhat obscure from the standpoint of who is exercising authority at the moment, I think that the President would not make the findings (that Syria has 100 per cent shifted into the Communist Bloc) until it was of practical significance to do it, rather than an academic exercise.

Coinciding with the State Secretary's sudden and somewhat incoherent remarks was an unexpected visit by King Saud to Damascus, where he was greeted and embraced in Arab fashion by President Quwatli. Members of the diplomatic community were present at Damascus International Airport, including the US chargé d'affaires, but he was given no special attention by the Saudi monarch, who preferred to concentrate on his Syrian host, a message well understood by the USA. Saud thundered: 'Saudi Arabia will not stand with hands folded in the event of any aggression against Syria,' adding:

On this occasion I would like to declare without obscurity and ambiguity, and with all sincerity for which I am known by my Syrian brothers, that I denounce any aggression against Syria and any other Arab country, from wherever it comes. I shall resist with my Syrian brothers any aggression committed against their independence whatever its source may be. I do not think any Arab will sink so low as to harm another Arab.[46]

Coinciding with the King's speech were similar statements by Saudi Arabia's Envoy to the UN Ahmad al-Shuqayri, who stated:

Who is in power and who is not in power in Syria is the concern of Syria alone. We are not here to deal with the change of government. This domestic realm of internal affairs must remain immune. As for the arms deal with Russia we see no valid justification to interfere. Saudi Arabia shall stand by Syria in the defence of its sovereignty and independence.[47]

Shukri al-Quwatli could not hold back a smile – this was a passport to security for Syria, coming from none other than the doyen of the Arab community. Politicians of all stripes and colours, even the hostile Baath leaders, came out to praise King Saud, hailing him for having led the campaign in favour of their country. The conservative Education Minister Hani al-Sibaii said that the royal visit 'was beneficial to us and will remove the harm facing Syria', while Justice Minister Maamoun al-Kuzbari added, 'His Majesty's attitude towards the recent plot against Syria and the generous feelings and noble effort helped repeal harm from Syria'. Before landing in Syria, Saud had stopped briefly in Lebanon where, in addition to President Chamoun, he met Sheikh Abdullah Salim al-Sabah of Kuwait, who was spending his summer in the town of Shtura, next to the Syrian–Lebanese border. Using his charm, Saud elicited a statement out of al-Sabah, strongly endorsing Syria and 'brother Shukri al-Quwatli.' With encouraging words coming from both Saudi Arabia and Kuwait, the safekeepers of Arab oil, other Arab states quickly followed suit. The Speaker of the Iraqi Parliament, Jamil al-Madfai, immediately commented, 'Any aggression against Syria would be aggression against Iraq and every Arab country' while the Jordanian Prime Minister Samir al-Rifaii added, 'Israel and Zionism, rather than Communism, are the Arab world's number one enemy.'[48] A few days later, on 1 October, King Hussein opened the Jordanian Parliament by speaking at length about the crisis in Syria, assuring President Quwatli that the government and public in Amman stood firmly behind the people of Syria. Before departing from Damascus, King Saud sent note to the US President, ultimately urging him not to worry about Syria and emphasizing that the country was nowhere close to becoming a Soviet satellite. The entire stand-off, he added, (by now known as The Stone Affair), had been exaggerated by the governments of both Damascus and Washington DC.[49] Apparently both needed to magnify The Stone Affair for very different reasons. The Syrians wanted it to end the meddling of ambitious officers and neighbours, who were constantly plotting for regime change in Damascus. The Americans needed it to show the world that they were willing to go to great lengths, if the need were to arise, to standup to international communism. Had Eisenhower or Bulganin been foolish, then perhaps, a third World War would have erupted from Damascus. *The New York Times* covered the entire crisis at length in the summer of 1957, never for once implying that the Syrians might have been right in their accusations at the Eisenhower Administration. On 17 August, *The New York Times* published an editorial stating: 'There are numerous theories about why the Syrians struck at the United States. One is that they acted at the instigation of the Soviet Union. Another is that the government manufactured an anti-US spy story to distract public attention from the signing of Syria's negotiations with Moscow.'[50]

13

THE UNITED ARAB REPUBLIC

Their policy reversals following King Saud's initiative revealed the 'flabbiness' of Syria's neighbours, according to Secretary Dulles.[1] Coinciding with a complete reversal of any plans for regime change in Syria, politicians in Damascus suddenly began to speak a new language, clearly no longer interested in being at odds with the US government. Their country had been on the verge of a political and military earthquake, and everybody was glad that the dark clouds had receded ... Foreign Ministry Secretary General Salah al-Din al-Tarazi addressed the Arab press saying that relations had indeed begun to improve between Syria and the USA, thanks to the 'relentless' efforts of the Saudi king. Meanwhile, the ageing Ihsan al-Jabiri, Chairman of the Foreign Relations Committee at the Syrian Parliament, said that contrary to what had been discussed in August, Syria would file no complaint against the USA at the UN.[2] There was no need for such a complaint, he explained, now that the drums of war had silenced. Similar remarks echoed across the political spectrum in Syria, including the disbanded SSNP, expressing appreciation for Quwatli and Sabri al-Asali's 'wise' handling of the crisis with the USA, a tone which implied that the crisis was history. Even the 'red millionaire' Khaled al-Azm came out with a remarkable statement, testifying that his country was still communist free, yet, in another statement aimed at reaching the ears of Dwight Eisenhower, Azm said:

> We have obtained arms for the defence of our country. We have also obtained aid for promoting prosperity of our people. Thereby we are banishing the ghost of communism, which is a system unsustainable for our country. I affirm that these plans of ours will not lead us to communism. Rather, it is poverty and economic domination which would do that.

When Russia agreed to grant us economic aid, it thereby combated communism in our country.[3]

Then came a carefully crafted statement from the Syrian Embassy in Ankara, dated 3 October 1957, theoretically ending all tension with the Turkish Republic. It read: 'Syria's only desire is to see the existence of good relations between the two countries. The only country from which Syria expects an attack is Israel. We have no anxieties about any other country.'[4] Additionally there was no crisis mood, or mode, felt on the streets of Syria. Apart from one military checkpoint near the border with Jordan, soldiers were not found on street corners, martial law was not imposed, nor was there a call on reserve troops in the Syrian Army. On 12 October, the two Soviet warships, which had helped change the US attitude, sailed back home from the port of Lattakia.[5] The US chargé d'affaires in Syria, Robert Strong, put an end to doubt when he implicitly announced that Dulles' policy of isolating Syria, toppling the regime in Damascus or changing its behaviour had all ultimately and collectively failed. 'The best we can hope for,' he noted, 'would be genuine neutrality. No one in Syria can bring Syria back to the western camp under any foreseeable circumstances. We cannot do that by ourselves.'[6] Eisenhower himself admitted, rather timidly on 3 October, that the situation in Syria 'seems to have solidified to some extent' adding that the original alarm of Syria's neighbours 'seems to have quieted'.[7] Rumour in Damascus had it that Foreign Minister Salah al-Bitar was due to arrive in Washington for meetings with Dulles. The USA announced that President Eisenhower had named a new Ambassador to Syria, Charles W. Yost, a career diplomat from New York, to fill the post that had been vacant since James Moose was recalled in June 1957. The new Princeton-trained Ambassador raised hopes the conspiracy-filled days of Ambassador Moose – which began under President Shishakli and lasted under both Presidents Atasi and Quwatli, climaxing with the Malki affair and Operation Straggle – were finally over.[8]

The only person not satisfied with the new situation in Damascus was Gamal Abdul Nasser. For the first time since he had ventured onto the Syrian scene in 1954, a crisis had been solved in Damascus without any consultation or the slightest interference from Cairo. King Saud had intentionally drowned everything Nasser had been working for since the Egyptian Revolution of 1952: pan-Arab leadership for the Egyptian President. Nasser had carefully crushed anyone and everything that stood in his path, from respectable elderly statesmen such as Fares al-Khoury in Damascus to pro-US ones such as Nuri al-Said in Baghdad. Never for a second had he regretted his actions, nor had he looked back at what his thunder had left behind in any country, making use of major events like the

1955 Israeli raid on Gaza to consolidate his power in Egypt. He suddenly found himself left out from Syria, of all places, thanks to the diplomatic initiative of the Saudi king. For years, Nasser had focused on Nuri al-Said, seeing him as his only rival for pan-Arab leadership. Saud was always regarded as an inexperienced monarch, a temporary one in fact, who would ultimately fail at filling the over-sized shoes of his father, Abdul-Aziz. His tenure, Nasser believed, would be only temporary and sooner or later the Saudi throne would fall to his brother, the seasoned and powerful Foreign Minister, Prince Faisal. When Nasser agreed to sign the defence pact with Syria and Saudi Arabia back in 1955, he had hoped that Egypt would dominate the two countries due to the soft leaderships that were in power in Damascus and Riyadh. Saud, however, astutely assessed Nasser's worth from the outset, and fully understood the political and demographic weight of Egypt. He was careful to never cross Nasser, but nevertheless worked slowly and delicately to prop himself as an alternative Arab leader, playing the powerful, rich and wise mediator between Oriental and Occidental worlds. Saud's moment of opportunity came in the summer of 1957, when Quwatli, an old friend of the Saudi Kingdom, came to blows with the Eisenhower White House, which happened to enjoy strong and strategic relations with Riyadh. He knew very well that he now had an advantage over Nasser, having the ears of decision-makers in Washington DC and therefore great leverage to solve the Syrian–US crisis. At one level, the Saudi initiative could be read in terms of Arab–Arab affairs, a point in favour of Saudi Arabia against Egypt. At another, the situation could be analysed in cold war terms: a victory for the US proxy in the Middle East, over that of the Soviet Union. Caught in the middle, Syria therefore could theoretically be considered as having taken a baby step back towards the pro-Western camp of 'moderate' Arab states.

Speaking publicly, nobody in their right mind could criticize the Saudi initiative, not even somebody with Nasser's charismatic appeal, since this would have been perceived as anti-Syrian by the Egyptian leader's Syrian audience. Nasser did give an interview to the Associated Press, however, trying to position himself as an alternate interlocutor for the USA, stating that he did not mind meeting President Eisenhower. When asked if he hoped to mediate in the Syrian–US crisis, Nasser quickly replied that mediation would never work, calling for a direct meeting between Shukri al-Quwatli and Eisenhower to solve pending problems between the two countries.[9] On 11 September, however, Nasser called on his two Syrian proxies Abdul Hamid Sarraj and Afif al-Bizreh, to visit him in Cairo. They had long talks with Egyptian Chief-of-Staff Abdul Hakim Amer and General Hafez Ismail of the Joint Syrian–Egyptian Command, the details of which were never released. There are no written minutes for these meetings and no mention of them could be found either in Egyptian or Syrian archives. With the exception of Sarraj, all participants in the Cairo talks have taken its secret with them to the grave. Sarraj himself, aged 85 at the time of writing in 2010, has to date refused to give any interview about his active years in the Syrian Intelligence. What we do know is that less than one month after the two men returned from Cairo, Nasser launched a grand public relations stunt, landing 2,000 Egyptian troops in Lattakia, to 'defend sister Syria' against US and Turkish aggression. Logic disavowed such a dramatic move, since the snow-balling crisis between Syria and both countries had ended last September. To ordinary Syrians watching Nasser's men march through the coastal city, how-ever, logic did not really matter. What mattered to them was that Nasser – their heroic champion since the Suez Crisis – was coming to their aid, with the entire coat of arms of the mighty Egyptian Army. If anything, this made age-ing politicians such as Shukri al-Quwatli, and distant monarchs such as King Saud, look silly and weak before an overwhelmingly pro-Nasser Syrian populace. This single event helped elevate leftist orientations in Syria as never since 1956, securing for Akram al-Hawrani, for example, a staunch Nasserist, re-election as Speaker of Parliament on 14 October, 24 hours after the Egyptian landing. His opponent Nazem al-Qudsi, the AUB-trained leader of the People's Party, was badly defeated within the Syrian Chamber. The Egyptian daily *al-Ahram* drew a link between Nasser's move and the Syrian–Egyptian defence agreement signed under President Atasi, saying that the Egyptian leader had proved it to be 'more than ink on paper; it is a reality'.[10] By all accounts, Quwatli was taken off guard by the Egyptian stunt but was by no means in a position to question or chal-lenge.[11] The Syrian President only made public a telephone conversation he had with King Saud, inviting Saudi Arabia to send troops to Syria as well. It was too late, however. The Nasserist craze, which led to the creation of a union two months later, had already electrified the Republic, making the events of January 1958 fairly predictable.

On January 1958, a group of Syrian officers, 14 in total, drove up to Damascus airport by night, boarding a plane headed for Cairo. Heading the delegation was none other than Chief-of-Staff Afif al-Bizreh, who sternly spoke to unde-cided officers among the group, saying, 'Men, there are two roads ahead of you. One leads to Mezzeh. The other leads to Cairo!' (Mezzeh was the location of the notorious prison created by the French which housed political dissidents in the post-1946 era). Either these officers carried out the job as planned, trav-elled to Cairo to plead for union with Gamal Abdul Nasser's Egypt, or faced a lifetime in jail for disobeying orders. The delegation included a wide vari-ety of pro-Soviet officers, ranging from Mustapha Hamdun, a Baathist who had helped bring down Shishakli, to Amin al-Hafez, a Nasserist who was to become President of the Republic after the Baath Revolution in 1963.

Amin Nfuri, a prominent Sarraj loyalist, was left in Damascus to deliver a note to President Quwatli and Defence Minister Azm, explaining why the officers had travelled to Cairo with no passports and no authorization from the Syrian government. 'They went to demand union with President Nasser, a policy endorsed and embraced by Prime Minister Asali's cabinet', replied Colonel Nfuri. Quwatli was once again cornered. Throughout his entire political life, which started while he was a young man in the Arab underground under the Ottoman Turks, Quwatli had dreamed of Arab unity. Now in old age, this union seemed finally within reach. Forbidding the officers would have obstructed a lifetime dream for the Syrian president. Additionally, he knew quite well from his encounter with Husni al-Za'im how painful it was to confront ambitious officers in the Syrian Army, who would have toppled him in a breeze in 1958, just as they had done back in 1949. Azm, however, was furious with the officer dictate, calling on Quwatli to banish them all and refuse them entry back into Syria for having taken such a drastic move without higher authorization and in total disregard of constitutional procedure and elected government. A veteran industrial and economic heavyweight, Azm had watched the steady rise of socialist policies in Egypt since Nasser came to power in 1952. He feared, with good reason, that if union were made in such a swift manner, similar policies incompatible with Syria's economic system would be enforced in Damascus. He also worried that Nasser would eradicate the multi-party system that had characterized Syrian political life since the 1930s, just as he had done in Egypt, arguing that this would be destructive for the country's healthy political environment. At the end of the day, Quwatli got his way and decided to put his full weight behind the Syrian officers in Cairo. Upon arriving in Egypt, Nasser had refused to greet them, claiming that they had no authorization from the Syrian president. Quwatli gave them the legitimacy they needed, sending Foreign Minister Salah al-Bitar to back them up in the negotiations, then travelling to Cairo himself in February to sign off the UAR.

When the new US Ambassador Yost arrived in Damascus and presented his credentials to Quwatli on 16 January 1958, the Syrian leader was effectively leading a caretaker government, preparing to retire from politics and make way for Nasser to assume full control of Syria. The US Embassy in Damascus was reclassified as a Consulate on 25 February, and relocated to Cairo, along with all other foreign embassies in the UAR. An entire era seemed to be coming to an end. Dulles was grounded with colon cancer, which he had developed in 1956, and had temporarily left the State Department, only to retire in April 1958 and die in May, at the age of 71. For his part, Eisenhower remained in office until 1961, forced to step down by the 22nd Amendment to the US Constitution, which prevented him from staying at the Oval Office for more than two terms. He endorsed his own Vice President Republican Richard Nixon, against John F. Kennedy, and gave his final address to the nation, riddled with cold war rhetoric, on 17 January 1961. Much of what Eisenhower said reflected his line of thought during the troubled summer months of 1957, when his relationship with Syria was at an all-time low. 'We face a hostile ideology global in scope, atheistic in character, ruthless in purpose and insidious in method,' he said. Only an alert and knowledgeable citizenry, he added, could 'compel the proper meshing of the huge industrial and military machinery of defence with our peaceful methods and goals, so that security and liberty may prosper together'. The UAR press reported his farewell address with more than a pinch of salt, glad to see the end of the war general although acknowledging that it was Eisenhower's resolve that had saved Egypt during the Suez War of 1956. He died of congestive failure in March 1969, at the age of 79. America's new Envoy to Damascus, Yost, was quickly replaced by a Consul in Damascus, Ridgway B. Knights, who remained in the job until the break-up of the Syrian–Egyptian union, rising to the rank of Ambassador in December 1961, during the era of President Kennedy.

As for the Syrians, Shukri al-Quwatli was given the honourific title of 'First Arab Citizen' for stepping down from presidential office in 1958, and spent much of the UAR period divided between Lebanon and Europe. He quickly realized the folly of having handed Syria to Nasser on a platter, and lived to regret it, furious with Nasser's socialist policies, his confiscation of land and private property, and the Egyptian leader's decision to abrogate Syrian celebrations on 17 April, the date of Independence. When he raised the issue with Nasser, the latter calmly replied that 'Citizens of the United Arab Republic have only one national day and it is the day of the Egyptian Revolution, 23 July, 1952.' Quwatli argued that this was a major mistake, reminding Nasser that 'people have memories that you cannot erase that easily. I am afraid for this union that we created; I feel it will not last.' Nasser promised him that it would last for 100 years but it fell short by 97 years, dramatically collapsing at the hands of Syrian officers on 28 September 1961. The rebels in Syria toyed with the idea of restoring Quwatli to office, acting as if the Nasser era had never passed, but the idea never materialized, largely due to Quwatli's old age – he was by then 70. He died at a hospital in Beirut on 30 June 1967, three weeks after the Arab–Israeli war that led to the occupation of the Syrian Golan. His body was returned to Damascus, where he received a hero's funeral and was hailed as the founding father of the Syrian Republic.

Depending on whom one talks to in Syria, the UAR – an indirect result of the Syrian–US crisis of 1957 – is either remembered with romanticism and nostalgia, or nothing but bitter regret. Most Syrians view it as the short-lived achievement of a lifelong dream, while some regard it as the ultimate success of US foreign policy in the Middle East. Eisenhower had placed Syria on his country's priority list in the mid-1950s, when all of a sudden Syria came under the direct threat of communism. That was practically why the USA had funded the Syrian opposition, which according to Munir al-Ajlani, had received no less than $3 million from the US government. It explains why the USA got itself involved with the Malki affair, Operation Straggle and The Stone Affair, ruining its reputation in the eyes of ordinary Syrians. The radicalization of the 1950s only silenced pro-US politicians such as Fares al-Khoury and gave rise to loud US critics like Akram al-Hawrani, Afif al-Bizreh and Abdul Hamid Sarraj. When all of that failed to curb the communist tide in Syria, the USA reasoned, as the chargé d'affaires Robert Strong had said, that they would not be able to do it on their own. Gamal Abdul Nasser showed up in 1958 to do the dirty work, striking at the SCP and forcing the outspoken Khaled Bakdash into exile in Eastern Europe. What Eisenhower and Dulles had failed to achieve in 1954–1957, Nasser managed to do within a matter of days, in March 1958. By no means can the man be accused of being a US stooge, regardless of his early flirtations with Eisenhower, yet, 50 years after the UAR, it is safe to claim that the Syrian–Egyptian union served America's cold war interests in the Middle East, sheltering Syria from a communist takeover.

NOTES

Wilsonian Principles and Shattered Dreams

1. The first US President to mention Syria in public was Dwight Eisenhower during a press conference on strained bilateral relations on 21 August 1957. See Chapter 12.
2. Ambrosius, *Woodrow Wilson and the American Diplomatic Tradition,* pp. 64–78.
3. Interview with George Lathkani, a former soldier in the Ottoman Army, during the First World War, conducted in Damascus on 6 November 1996.
4. Mu'awiya was the founder of the Umayyad Dynasty who ruled from Damascus, during the heyday of the Muslim Empire, from 661 to 680.
5. Tibawi, *A Modern History of Syria, Including Lebanon and Palestine,* p. 77.
6. Lathkani, 6 November 1996.
7. Russell, *The First Modern Arab State,* pp. 31–32.
8. Ibid.
9. Ibid.
10. Qasmiyah, *al-Hukuma al-Arabiya,* p. 85.
11. Ibid, p. 86.
12. Qasmiyah, p. 95.
13. Ibid.
14. Qasmiyah, p. 86.
15. Ibid.
16. Zein, *Struggle for Arab Independence,* pp. 248–251.
17. Text of the petition found in Box 112 at the Syrian National Archive Museum, entitled, 'King Faisal I in France, 1919'.
18. Tibawi, *A Modern History of Syria, Including Lebanon and Palestine,* p. 78.
19. Qasmiyah, p. 45.
20. Andelman, *A Shattered Peace,* p. 61.
21. Ibid, p. 62.
22. Ibid, p. 63.

23. Qasmiyah, p. 101.
24. Ibid. Wilson's aid, Colonel House, channelled the request to John J. Pershing, commander of US troops in Europe, who complied with the Emir's wish.
25. Penrose, *That They May Have Life*, p. 41.
26. Khoury, *Awraq Fares al-Khoury*, pp. 70–71. Fares al-Khoury used to call Daniel Bliss, 'a brilliant devil'.
27. Interview with Colette Khury, granddaughter of Fares al-Khoury, 11 October 2008.
28. Zein, *Struggle for Arab Independence*, pp. 249–250.
29. Ibid, p. 33.
30. Ibid.
31. Ibid.
32. Qasmiyah, *al-Hukuma al-Arabiya,* p. 115.
33. Ibid.
34. Ibid.
35. Russell, p. 90.
36. Qasmiyah, p. 115. For full findings of the commission, see Fares al-Khoury's memoirs, volume 1, pp. 69–71 and Qasmiyah's *al-Hukuma al-Arabiya*, pp. 118–119.
37. Interview with Munir al-Ajlani, 10 April 1999.
38. Ibid.
39. Wilson was good friends with several prominent American Zionists like Louis Lipsky, Louis Brandeis, Felix Frankfurter and Stephan Wise, a Rabbi. When Wise asked him about how he would react to Arab resentment of the Balfour Declaration, Wilson pointed to the trash bin next to his desk and said, 'Is not that basket capacious enough for all their protests?' Suleiman, *Arabs in America*, p. 227.
40. Ibid, p. 231.
41. Christison, *Perceptions of Palestine*, p. 27.
42. Interview with Ajlani, 10 April 1999. Ajlani would later become a protégé of Shahbandar and close ally in the late 1930s.
43. Weizmann, *Letters and Papers*, pp. 197–206.
44. Ibid, p. 210.
45. Smith, *Palestine and the Arab-Israeli Conflict*, p. 80.
46. Ibid.
47. Mack, *A Prince of Our Disorder*, 260. Shortly after the deal was signed, *The Jewish Chronicle* wrote of the Faisal–Weizmann Agreement, 'A complete understanding between the Emir and Dr Weizmann was arrived at on all points'.
48. Barbour, *Palestine, Star or Crescent*, p. 100, quoting an article in *News Chronicle*, 9 July 1937.
49. Andelman, *A Shattered Peace*, p. 70.
50. Ibid.
51. Christison, p. 33.
52. *Washington Post*, 30/9/1920.
53. FO 371/5039, Walter Taylor Report, 21 February 1920.
54. Lawrence, *Seven Pillars of Wisdom*, p. 56.
55. Interview with Ajlani, 10 April 1999.
56. Andelman, p. 67.
57. Ibid, p. 68.

Crane in Damascus Again

1. *La Reveil*, 5 August 1920.
2. Polier and Wise, *The Personal Letters of Stephan Wise*, p. 187. Stuart Knee, Professor of History at the University of Charleston, remarked 'The stuff of which great men are made was manifestly missing in Harding. Unlike Wilson, a molder of foreign policy, the Republican was manipulated by his associates whose doctrinaire attitudes of non-involvement succeeded in gaining a preeminence not to be forfeited for nearly two decades' *Journal of American Studies for Turkey*, Issue 5, 1997, 3–18.
3. *New York Times*, 28 July 1920.
4. Ibid.
5. Interview with Munir al-Ajlani on 10 April 1999.
6. USNA Syria, 890d.000/100, Telegram to Secretary of State, 13 April 1922.
7. Ibid.
8. Nickoley, who channelled messages back and forth between Shahbandar and Crane, was the man to admit women into the Schools of Medicine, Pharmacy and Dentistry, at AUB.
9. Interview with Ajlani, 10 April 1999.
10. Hakim, *Muzakarat*, pp. 55–56. Uthman Sharabati, a respected merchant who developed an early admiration for the USA, sent his son Ahmad to study engineering at AUB and MIT. He eventually returned to Syria, becoming Minister of Defence in 1948, and business agent for General Motors in Damascus.
11. Khoury, *Syria and the French Mandate*, pp. 122–123.
12. Hakim. In addition to a monthly salary of 360 SP, which was a staggering amount for Syria, Haqqi al-Azm received 8,500 SP annually to spend on entertainment, 6,000 SP for travel, and 400 SP for newspaper subscriptions – and bribes. This money was often used to 'reward' journalists for writing about the new ruler of Damascus and his French patron, Henri Gouraud. Haqqi al-Azm, a wealthy man in his own right, came from an aristocratic Syrian family, and was married to a widowed cousin of King Ahmad Fouad I of Egypt.
13. Interview with Ajlani, 10 April 1999.
14. Ibn Taymiyyah was a renowned Muslim scholar who grew up in Harran, what is now modern Turkey, and moved to Damascus during the Mongol invasion, in 1268, then ruled by the Mamluk dynasty of Egypt. He is buried in Damascus and known as 'Sheikh al-Islam'.
15. USNA Syria, 890d.00/120 and FO 371/4442, vol. 7846, 8 April 1922.
16. The conversation between Naziq al-Abid and Charles Crane can be found in the private papers of Munir al-Ajlani, who went on to become a private aid, and hardcore loyalist, of Shahbandar in the late 1930s. Given their third-person narration, they might be somewhat inaccurate although when discussing them with Ajlani, 75 years later, he attested that they were very precise, indeed 'coming from the lion's mouth'. In his memoirs, Hasan al-Hakim, another Shahbandar loyalist, makes mention of the Crane–Shahbandar–Abid meeting.

17. USNA Syria, 890d.00/120.

18. *New York Times*, 25 May 1922.

19. Ibid. The article gave a brief biography of Crane, saying that he had 'made a fortune in the manufacturing of bath tubs and sanitary fittings'.

20. Ibid.

21. *New York Times*, 27 May 1922.

22. Ibid.

23. Khoury, pp. 123–124.

24. The *New York Times*, 14 May 1922.

25. Ibid.

26. The *New York Times*, 26 May 1922. Crane told French lawmakers that continued occupation would cost them around 1 billion francs per year, and needed an army of 100,000 men.

27. Khoury, p. 141.

28. Charles Crane died in 1939, one year before Shahbandar was murdered in Damascus. He distanced himself from Syrian affairs as of 1922, however, and there is no record of any contact between him and any Syrian national during the years 1922–1939.

29. Interview with Ajlani, 10 April 1999. Ajlani's statement, however, could not be verified by any of the American or Syrian sources from the Mandate years. It nevertheless is difficult to believe, given the USA's isolationist policies in the 1920s and Coolidge's absolute distance from the Arab world.

The Rocky 1920s

1. Interview with Ajlani, 10 April 1999. Shahbandar would write letters on a periodic basis to congressmen and State Department officials, obtaining their addresses from friends at the AUB.

2. Weizmann, *Trial and Error*, pp. 431–432. This view was shared by heavyweight American Zionist leaders, such as Rabbi Stephen Wise who once wrote, 'I really am inclined to [believe] ... that there is a cabal in the State Department deliberately and, I am afraid, effectively working against those Zionist interests, which are precious to some of us.' See Melvin Urofsky, *American Zionism from Herzl to the Holocaust*, p. 408.

3. Manuel, *The Realities of American-Palestine Relations,* p. 172.

4. The Syrian–Palestinian Congress was founded in Geneva in November 1921 and included leading nationalists in exile such as Prince Shakib Arslan, Rashid Rida and Shukri al-Quwatli. It was bankrolled by the Hashemite family in Arabia and Prince Michel Lutfallah, a wealthy Lebanese immigrant based in Cairo, who served as its co-chair with Shahbandar.

5. Shahbandar had actually tried in the past, also in vain, to contact President Harding via handwritten correspondence, sent through AUB. See *The New York Times*, 1 September 1921.

6. Ibid, 19 May 1922. A copy of the letter was sent to the League of Nations in Geneva.
7. De Novo, *American Interests and Policies in the Middle East 1900–1939*, p. 323.
8. Rayyes, *al-Kitab al-Zahabi*, pp. 167–169.
9. Moubayed, *The Politics of Damascus*, pp. 53–68 and Khoury, *Syria and the French Mandate*, p. 178.
10. Hakim, *Muzakarat*, pp. 283–284.
11. De Novo, *American Interests and Policies in the Middle East 1900–1939*, p. 326.
12. Khoury, *Syria and the French Mandate*, p. 179.
13. *The New York Times*, 30 October 1925.
14. Ibid, p. 325.
15. J.H. Kelley Jr to Kellogg, DS 890d.00/283, 2 November 1925.
16. Ibid.
17. Knabenshue to Kellogg, DS 890d.00/27, 8 November 1925.
18. De Novo, p. 326.
19. Ibid.
20. Knabenshue to Kellogg, DS 890.99/348, 25 January 1926.
21. De Novo, p. 326. The ships were eventually withdrawn on 6 December 1926, but an agreement was reached with the US Navy where they were placed on standby, awaiting any instructions to return from Knabenshue.
22. Khoury, *Syria and the French Mandate*, p. 397.
23. Ibid.
24. PRO 371/4055, vol. 16974, 1 July 1933.
25. Ibid.
26. Thompson, *Colonial Citizens*, p. 197.
27. Ibid. By 1922, Damascus, Beirut and Aleppo had three or four cinemas each. By 1932, 10 out of 12 cinemas had sound projectors in Syria, immediately after the invention of 'talkies'.
28. Thompson, p. 198.
29. Ibid, p. 198. See also Qassab Hasan, *Hadith Dimashqi*, p. 213.
30. The influence remained strong for decades and when Syrian Television was established in 1960, a young actor named Duraid Lahham became number one in his own right, creating a character that looked, walked and acted like Charlie Chaplin, called Ghawar al-Tawsheh.
31. Lathkani, 6 November 1996.
32. Ibid.
33. Thompson, p. 198.
34. Ibid.
35. *Al-Shaab*, 5 March 1933.
36. Roosevelt, *Great Speeches*, p. 17.
37. *Al-Ayyam*, 30 July 1932.
38. See Moubayed, *Steel & Silk* (Cune Press, 2005).
39. Teddy Roosevelt was also uncle of Eleanor, the wife of FDR who in 1933 became First Lady of the USA.
40. Interview with Munir al-Ajlani, 9 August 1999.
41. Ibid and see also *al-Shaab*, 28 March 1933.

42. Klare, *Blood and Oil*, pp. 31–36.
43. Saikal, *Islam and the West*, pp. 46–48.

The Road to Washington Runs Through Berlin

1. Interview with Ajlani, 9 August 1999. See also, Moubayed, *The Politics of Damascus 1920–1946*, Dar Tlass, 1999.
2. Spears, *Fulfillment of a Mission*, p. 70.
3. Khoury, *Syria and the French Mandate*, p. 565.
4. Munir al-Ajlani, then a rising politician in the upper echelons of power in Damascus, was present at the meeting and recalls, 'The Nazis were bluffing. They had no intention to help us out but as the popular saying in Arabic goes, he who is sinking tries to float by holding on to a straw!'
5. PRO 371/2837 vol. 27291, Gardner to FO, 9 April 1941.
6. Khoury, p. 591 and Moubayed, *The George Washington of Syria*, p. 141. See also, The Papers of Nazih Mu'ayyad al-Azm (file # 245), 15 April 1941 at the Center of Historical Documents in Damascus.
7. Interview with Ajlani, 9 April 1999.
8. Ibid.
9. Yahil, *The Holocaust: The Fate of European Jewry*, p. 676. The Mufti also requested that German help end Jewish immigration to Palestine.
10. Davidson, *America's Palestine: Popular and Official Perceptions from Balfour to Israeli Statehood*, p. 239.
11. Among the prominent Syrian nationalists who took part in the Palestinian uprising was Fawzi al-Qawikji, a guerilla leader from the Great Syrian Revolt of 1925–1927.
12. Lewis, *Semites and Anti-Semites: An Inquiry into Conflict and Prejudice*, pp. 150–151.
13. Lewis, *The Jews of Islam*, p. 190.
14. Yisraeli, *The Palestine Problem in German Politics*, p. 310.
15. Ibid.
16. Interview with Ajlani, 9 August 1999. Dawalibi told the story to Ajlani, when they were both living in Saudi Arabia in the 1990s, and Ajlani mentioned it to the author.
17. Ibid.
18. Ibid. Ajlani claimed, 'This was 100 per cent untrue. Hitler never uttered such words against the Arabs. All of his speeches are readily available; historians can return to the archives to check!'
19. Ibid.
20. *The New York Times*, 13 October 1937.
21. Spears, *Fulfillment of a Mission*, p. 1.
22. Khani, *Jihad Shukri al-Quwatli*, p. 170 and Hull, *The Memoirs of Cordell Hull*, vol. 2, p. 1543.
23. Spears, pp. 169–170.
24. Mardam Bey, *Syria's Quest for Independence*, p. 75.

25. Khani, p. 170.
26. Ibid.
27. Ibid.
28. Ibid.
29. Interview with Suhail al-Ashi, 13 August 2001.
30. Mardam Bey, *Syria's Quest,* p. 76.
31. Ibid.
32. Moubayed, *The George Washington of Syria,* p. 151.
33. FO 371/1/1995 vol. 27330, Gardner to FO, 44 May, 1942.
34. Ibid.
35. Interview with Hassan al-Quwatli, 16 July 1999.
36. Mardam Bey, *Syria's Quest,* p. 83.
37. Moubayed, *The George Washington of Syria,* p. 198.
38. Mardam Bey, *Syria's Quest for Independence,* p. 140 and *al-Inshaa,* 13 December 1944.
39. Ibid, p. 149.
40. Ibid.
41. *The London Times,* 24 August 1920.
42. Mardam Bey, *Syria's Quest,* p. 188.
43. Quwatli had sent messages requesting to attend the UN Conference to the USA, Great Britain, the USSR and China. His ambassador to London, Najib Armanazi, had discussed the matter at length with the Soviet Ambassador and so had his representative in Cairo, Assem al-Naili. Great Britain's Minister to Syria and Lebanon, Sir Edward Spears, had also raised the matter before the House of Commons. See Mardam Bey, *Syria's Quest,* pp. 88–89.
44. Interview with Ashi, 13 August 2001.
45. Minutes of the Quwatli–Churchill Summit can be found in Nasuh Babil, *Sahafa wa Siyasa fi Souriya* (Journalism and Politics in Syria), Moubayed, *The George Washington of Syria,* and Khani, *Jihad Shukri al-Quwatli,* pp. 170–173.
46. Ibid.
47. Ibid, pp. 182–183.
48. 190.
49. Dallek, *Franklin D. Roosevelt and American Foreign Policy, 1932–1945,* p. 520.
50. Khabbaz and Haddad, *Fares al-Khoury,* p. 134.

Free at Last

1. Interview with Ashi, 13 August 2001.
2. Interview with Ajlani, 9 August 1999. Ajlani was a one-time protégé of Mardam Bey who held office as Minister of Education in the 1940s.
3. Ibid.

4. Back then, Mardam Bey was Abdul Rahman Shahbandar's assistant at the Foreign Ministry.
5. *The New York Times*, 3 October 1941.
6. Interview with Ajlani, 9 August 1999. When becoming his country's ambassador to Yemen, shortly after the Second World War, Wadsworth was to establish the country's first golf club.
7. Eventually, Jacobson was the man to arrange for the first meeting between Truman and Weizmann in 1948, and the USA became the first country to recognize Israel.
8. Oshinsky, *The American Presidency*, pp. 365–380. Truman's mother Martha Ellen Young Truman was to die during his presidency in 1947 while Quwatli's mother was to die only days after he was deposed in 1949, when the Syrian leader was in jail.
9. Eventually, Jacobson was the man to arrange the first meeting between Truman and Weizmann in 1948, and the USA became the first country to recognize Israel.
10. Mardam Bey, *Syria's Quest*, p. 207.
11. Ibid, p. 201.
12. Ibid.
13. Ibid, p. 213.
14. Earlier in November 1943, the French had arrested the President and Prime Minister of Lebanon, along with members of the Lebanese government, and planned on repeating the same scene in Syria.
15. Mardam Bey, *Syria's Quest*, p. 216.
16. Interview with Abdullah Khani, 6 December 2001.
17. Mardam Bey, p. 217.
18. Ibid.
19. Moubayed, *George Washington of Syria*, p. 185.
20. Ibid, p. 217.
21. Mardam Bey, p. 220.
22. Ibid.
23. Roger Louis, *The British Empire in the Middle East*, p. 164.
24. Interview with Ajlani, 9 August 1999.
25. 225.
26. Ibid, p. 186.
27. Ibid.
28. *Al-Ayyam*, 6 July 1945.
29. Ibid, 6 August 1945.
30. Ibid.
31. Moubayed, *Politics of Damascus*, p. 212.
32. Hahn, *The United States, Great Britain, and Egypt*, p. 21.
33. Wadsworth died of cancer in 1958, the year Syria signed union with Gamal Abdul Nasser's Egypt, less than one month before he was scheduled to retire from the Department of State on his 65th birthday.

The Syrian Mussolini

1. Conversation between Ambassador Robert Keeley and Ambassador Imad Moustapha in Washington DC on 22 January 2006.
2. Ibid.
3. Interview with Abdul Ghani al-Otari, 28 September 2002.
4. Lesch, *Syria and the United States*, p. 17.
5. Ibid.
6. Truman, *Memoirs 2*, p. 158.
7. Torrey, *Syrian Politics and the Military*, p. 103.
8. Conversation between Ambassador Robert Keeley and Ambassador Imad Moustapha in Washington DC on 22 January 2006.
9. Copeland, *The Game of Nations*, p. 42.
10. Ibid, pp. 49–60.
11. Ibid, p. 42.
12. Rabinovich, *The Road not Taken*, p. 85.
13. FO 371/75529, E4–72, 28 March 1949.
14. Interview with Abdullah al-Khani, 6 December 2008.
15. Rabinovich, p. 84.
16. Ibid.
17. Ibid, p. 86.
18. Ibid.
19. Ibid.
20. USNA, 350 Syria 3144.0501.
21. Rabinovich, p. 86.
22. Ibid, p. 19.
23. Ibid, p. 94.
24. Conversation between Ambassador Robert Keeley and Ambassador Imad Moustapha in Washington DC on 22 January 2006.
25. Tarazi reportedly wept when commissioned by al-Za'im to join the armistice talks, convinced that his country must not recognize the new State of Israel (Interview with Ashi, 16 July 2002).
26. Rabinovich, p. 68.
27. Interview with Haitham Kaylani, 17 July 2002.
28. Ibid, p. 69.
29. Interview with Kaylani.
30. Interview with General Husni al-Za'im *al-Inkilab* newspaper, 20 August 1949.
31. Ibid.
32. Ibid, p. 69.
33. Ibid, p. 70.
34. Conversation between Ambassador Robert Keeley and Ambassador Imad Moustapha in Washington DC on 22 January 2006.
35. Copeland, *Game of Nations,* p. 43.

36. Antune Saadeh, the charismatic head of the SSNP, came to Syria in the summer of 1949 fleeing an arrest warrant from Lebanese authorities. He wanted to use al-Za'im to get rid of Prime Minister Riad al-Sulh of Lebanon, who was a staunch Quwatli ally, and al-Za'im wanted to use him to bring down the Lebanese government because it was the only one in the Middle East that refused to deal with him after the coup of March 1949. Al-Za'im gave him asylum, and presented him with his personal side arm as a token trust, then handed him over to Lebanese authorities, where he was executed after a mock trial, on 8 July 1949. For more see *8 Tammuz: Qadiyat Muhakamet Antune Saadeh wa Idamuh* (8 July: The Trial and Execution of Antune Saadeh) by Antoine Boutros, Beirut 2002.

37. *The New York Times*, 18 August 1949.

The Rise of Colonel Shishakli

1. Interview with Ajlani, 9 August 1999.
2. Ibid.
3. Damascus Radio, 14 August 1949.
4. Interview with Ajlani, 9 August 1999.
5. Ibid.
6. Interview with Haitham Kaylani, 11 July 2003.
7. Sanders, *The United States and Arab nationalism*, p. 21.
8. Ibid.
9. Ibid, p. 14.
10. Ashour, Ghazoul, Reda-Mekdashi, Arab Women Writers, p. 501.
11. Tarazi's book, *Araii wa Mashairi* (My Thoughts and Feelings) was published in Damascus in 1939 with an introduction by Syrian poet Khalil Mardam Bey, author of the Syrian National Anthem.
12. Thompson, *Colonial Citizens*, p. 241.
13. Ibid. For more on both women, see Buthaina Shaaban, *Both Left and Right Handed*, p. 43.
14. Sanders, *The United States and Arab Nationalism*, p. 14.
15. Ibid.
16. Ibid, p. 15.
17. Lesch, *Syria and the United States*, p. 21.
18. Sanders, *The United States*, p. 15.
19. Ibid.
20. Even pro-American politicians such as ex-Prime Minister Husni al-Barazi, who was Shishakli's cousin, had no respect for Selu. In his memoirs, Barazi describes him as 'weak, both in character, politics, and honour'. See Husni al-Barazi *Memoirs – Oral History Project*, Middle East Studies at AUB (1969).
21. *Al-Nidal*, 31 October 1950.
22. Ibid.

23. Interview with Abdul Qadir Qaddura, former speaker of the Syrian Parliament, 1 October 2009.
24. Hahn, *Caught in the Middle East*, p. 135.
25. Ibid.
26. Ibid, p. 26.
27. Ibid, p. 31.
28. Ibid, p. 141.
29. Ibid.

Ike Comes to Damascus

1. Interview with Abdul Ghani al-Otari, 6 January 2002.
2. Interview with Abdullah al-Khani, 11 April 2009.
3. Interview with Otari, 6 January 2002.
4. Ibid.
5. Nielsen, *The Radical Lives of Helen Keller*, p. 106.
6. Ibid, p. 107.
7. Interview with Otari, 6 January 2002.
8. Interview with Ajlani, 9 August 1999.
9. Interview with Abdul Ghani Otari, 6 January 2002.
10. *Al-Ayyam*, 1 March 1953.
11. Interview with Otari, 6 January 2002.
12. Ambrose, *Eisenhower*, pp. 234–235.
13. Review of *al-Nidal, al-Ayyam, al-Qabas* (October 1952–January 1953).
14. Interview with Colette Khoury, 11 April 2009.
15. Interview with Ajlani, 9 August 1999.
16. DeNovo, *American Interests and Policies in the Middle East*, p. 365.
17. *New York Times*, 23 January 1953.
18. Ibid.
19. *New York Times*, 19 January 1953.
20. FO 371/104966.
21. Sanders, p. 35.
22. Al-Ayyam, 16 May 1953.
23. Ibid.
24. Lesch, *Syria and the United States*, p. 32.
25. Ibid, see also Sanders, p. 53.
26. Lesch, p. 32.
27. *Al-Ayyam*, 16 May 1953, see also *TIME*, 25 May 1953, p. 29.
28. USNA, Secretary of Defence, Charles E. Wilson to JFD, 8 September 1953. 611.83/9–853, RG59.
29. The school was eventually founded in 1956 and named the Damascus Community School (DCS). The President of the Board was the sitting US Ambassador to Syria. The school remained open non-stop until the Arab–Israeli war of 1967, where it

closed its doors temporarily, then reopened until September 2008, when it was closed again after US troops stormed into Syrian territory to ostensibly strike at a member of al-Qaeda, during the final stages of the George W. Bush Administration. It was founded on a large plot of land in the posh Abu Rummaneh district, through agreement between the State Department and the then Syrian Foreign Minister Salah al-Din al-Bitar – ironically, one of the two founding fathers of the Baath Party.

30. John Foster Dulles to Eisenhower, 18 May 1953, Ann Whitman Files, Dulles-Herter Series, Box 1, DDEL.
31. Sanders, *The United States and Arab Nationalism*, p. 24.
32. Ibid.
33. Lesch, *Syria and the United States,* p. 42.
34. Lesch, p. 40.
35. Interview with Ajlani, 9 August 1999.
36. Lesch, p. 36.
37. *The New York Times*, 21 November 1953.
38. Lesch, *Syria and the United States*, p. 37.
39. *The New York Times*, 29 October 1953.
40. USNA, US Embassy to US State Department, 9 November 1953, 611.83/11–953, RG59.
41. Abu-Jaber, Faiz, 'Eisenhower, Israel, and the Jordan Valley Authority Scheme', *Middle East Forum*, vol. XLI, no 2, 1969, pp. 51–63.
42. *Al-Inshaa, al-Ayyam, and al-Shaab*, 31 October 1953.
43. Interview with Abdul Qadir Qaddura, former speaker of the Syrian Parliament, 1 October 2009.
44. Lesch, p. 56.
45. FO 371 (111137 PRO) British Embassy, Damascus, 12 February 1954.

Turning Back the Clock

1. PRO 371/110785, British Embassy in Damascus, 30 June 1954.
2. PRO 371/110787, British Embassy in Damascus, 1 March 1954.
3. Seale, *The Struggle for Syria*, p. 196.
4. *The New York Times*, 5 March 1954.
5. Seale, p. 171.
6. Ibid, pp. 169–170.
7. Lesch, p. 48.
8. Ibid.
9. Ibid.
10. *Al-Ayyam*, 4 September 1954, *al-Nidal*, 3 September 1954, and *al-Inshaa*, 6 September 1954.
11. Ibid. See also *Forward Magazine*, June 2008 and *LIFE Magazine*, 27 September 1954.
12. *The New York Times*, 10 September 1954.

13. Each seat in the Syrian Parliament was supposedly to represent 30,000 Syrians, at a time when Syria's population was a total 4.2 million people. Any literate male over the age of 30 could stand for office, and any Syrian over the age of 18 could vote. Additionally, women with an elementary school certificate could also vote, thanks to a 1949 law passed by President Husni al-Za'im. See Seale, p. 172.
14. Interview with Ajlani, 9 August 1999.
15. Ibid.
16. Ibid.
17. *Al-Musawwar*, 5 December 1954.
18. Torrey, *Syrian Politics and the Military*, p. 270.
19. Turkey had received US aid since 1947, participated in the Korean War, and Seale, p. 217.
20. Ibid.
21. Seale, p. 169.
22. Seale, p. 219.
23. PRO 371/115945 British Embassy in Damascus, 10 March 1955.
24. *Al-Jumhuriyya*, 6 February 1955.

Ropes of Sand

1. Seale, p. 166.
2. Lesch, *The United States*, p. 64.
3. Ibid, p. 165.
4. BBC, 14 April 1954.
5. *Al-Rai al-Aam*, 7 March 1955 – Signing the pact on behalf of the Syrian government was Foreign Minister Khaled al-Azm. See also, Azm, *Muzakarat*, vol. 2, pp. 391–401.
6. *Al-Mukhtar*, Interview with Sabri al-Asali, 22 December 1955.
7. Interview with Munir al-Ajlani, 9 August 1999.
8. Ibid. Sharett heard news of the spy ring on Israeli Radio and reportedly shouted at one of his aides, 'Is this true? It cannot be true! I am the Prime Minister here and I did not order it!'
9. Seale, pp. 234–235. According to Major Salim, Egypt had only six working planes, while 30 were grounded to airports, in desperate need of spare parts. Tank ammunition could last for only one hour, while 96 per cent of Egyptian tanks were in need of 'major repair'.
10. Seale, p. 254.
11. Interview with Munir al-Ajlani, 9 August 1999.
12. Husni al-Barazi Memoirs – Oral History Project, Middle East Studies at AUB, 1969.
13. Lesch, *The United States*, p. 65.
14. Ibid, p. 75.
15. Telegram from Department of State to US Embassy in Damascus, 13 April 1955.

16. Ibid, pp. 65–66.
17. Sanders, *The United States and Arab Nationalism*, p. 28.
18. Lesch, *Syria and the United States*, p. 75.
19. Ibid, p. 67.
20. Cairo Radio, 29 March 1955.
21. Lesch, *The United States and Syria*, p. 64.
22. Seale, *The Struggle for Syria,* p. 235.
23. Interview with Abdul Wahab Homad, 21 July 1999.
24. Seale, *The Struggle for Syria*, p. 253.
25. Ibid.
26. Sanders, *The United States,* p. 31.
27. Ibid, p. 32.
28. Ibid.
29. Ibid.
30. Patrick Wilkinson (Baghdad) to FO, 1531/47/56, 14 July 1956. See also, John Coulson (Washington) to FO, Telegram 327, April 1956, 121273V1075/107.
31. PRO 371/128223, British Embassy in Beirut, 25 July 1957.
32. Sanders, p. 29.
33. Azm, *Muzakarat,* vol. 2, 414. During Azm's visit to Paris, rumour spread in Damascus that he had received ex-President Shishakli, by now a symbol of pro-Americanism, at his hotel. Azm quickly denied, accused the Deputy Iraqi Foreign Minister Burhan al-Din Bashayan of spreading the rumour through the Iraqi Embassy in Damascus, to foil his endeavour in Paris.
34. Stevenson's grandfather Aldai E. Stevenson had been Vice President to Grover Garfield in 1893–1987 while his great-grandfather had been campaign manager to President Abraham Lincoln. Azm's ancestors, however, had been the eighteenth century governors of Ottoman Damascus.
35. Trained at Princeton University as an attorney, Stevenson had began his career at a prestigious law firm in Chicago, and in 1945, served as Assistant to Undersecretary of State Archibald MacLeish. During his tenure at the UN (May 1945-February 1946) he had met and admired Syria's delegate, Fares al-Khoury. The two men met again when Stevenson came to Syria after being defeated in the presidential race and discussed issues related to the Middle East at large, Syria and Palestine in particular. Interview with Abdul-Wahab Homad, 11 July 2000.
36. Azm, *Muzakarat,* vol. 2, p. 414. The conversation turned tense, Azm explained, when it came to the Arab–Israeli conflict and the future of the Palestinians. Azm asked Stevenson to bring a map of the world, and then asked him to locate Israel on the map, while taking off his glasses. Humoured, the US statesman complied, and succeeded with difficulty. 'You cannot spot this country if you remove your eyeglasses for it is nothing but a spot in an Arabian ocean. You the Americans leave the Arabs and support this small state, small in size, large in danger', he said.

37. Stevenson ran for office against Eisenhower and was defeated in 1956. He made another attempt against John F. Kennedy but was also defeated in 1961.

38. Ibid, p. 432.

39. Ibid, p. 357.

40. Azm decided to write the Dutch Ambassador a strongly worded letter, accusing him of seeking revenge for loud words spoken by the Syrian delegation at Bandung, criticizing the Dutch Empire. Zayn al-Din laughed, 'These tactics work in the Syrian Parliament not here.' Azm replied angrily, 'You know how things are done here in the United States; you handle it!' The next day, the Filipino diplomat Carlos Peña Rómulo was also cut short by the speaker, leading Azm to conclude that this was a US plan aimed at muzzling all countries of the Third World. Azm, *Muzakarat*, vol. 2, p. 466.

41. Ibid, p. 491.

42. Azm spoke to Arab students twice, at the university and during a reception in Los Angeles, on how advanced Syria had become 'especially in social reforms, mainly in relation to unveiling, but also in athletics and education'. Azm, p. 432.

43. Syria's UN Ambassador Rafiq al-Asha took Azm for a night out in New York. Azm recalls amazement with prices, claiming that the cheapest item on the menu cost $5, while the most expensive was lobster, which cost $17 a plate. Asha's salary, Azm added, was only SP 1,200, meaning that two thirds of it would be spent that evening on 12 guests. Azm humourously writes that he decided to 'devour' his Ambassador's salary, but said to himself, 'If only Salah al-Bitar (the Baath co-founder) becomes Foreign Minister and comes to America. He would reconsider slashing the salaries of the Foreign Ministry'. Cutting back on expenses was in fact being heavily debated at the Syrian Parliament by head of the Budget Committee Salah al-Bitar and his Baath colleague, Akram al-Hawrani. He wraps up saying, 'My wish was granted [when Bitar became Foreign Minister in 1956] but unfortunately, salaries remained low at the Ministry'.

44. BBC, no 601, 6 September 1955. Sharabi was a Palestinian scholar who had studied philosophy at AUB and undertaken his graduate and post-graduate studies at the University of Chicago, working in the 1940s as Editor-in-Chief of the SSNP periodical *al-Jeel al-Jadid* (The New Generation) before returning to the USA after the execution of Saadeh in 1949.

45. Seale, *The Struggle for Syria*, p. 69.

Tipping the Balance at Suez

1. Interview with Abdul Wahab Homad, 21 July 1999.

2. Seale, p. 252.

3. Interview with Homad, 21 July 1999.

4. Lesch, p. 84.

5. Ibid.

6. Ibid.

7. Ali Buzzo became Minister of Economy, Rashad Barmada became Minister of Defence, Rizqallah Antaki became Minister of Finance, while Abdul Wahab Homad became

Minister of Agriculture. In the polarized world of Syrian politics, all of them were mild enthusiasts of the USA and firm opponents of the USSR.

8. Turner, *Suez 1956: The First Oil War*, pp. 21–24.
9. Butler, *Britain and Empire*, p. 111.
10. Kissinger, *Diplomacy*, p. 528.
11. Ibid, p. 529.
12. PRO 371/121271 – British Foreign Office, 5 March 1956.
13. Love, *Suez: The Twice Fought War*, pp. 557–558.
14. BBC, 28 July 1956.
15. Seale, *The Struggle for Syria*, p. 288.
16. *Al-Ahram*, 19 February 1956.
17. PRO 371/121867 – British Embassy in Moscow, 5 November 1956.
18. Interview with Abdul Qadir Qaddura, ex-speaker of the Syrian Parliament, 23 July 2009.
19. Seale, *The Struggle for Syria*, p. 266.
20. PRO 371/115469, British Embassy in Paris, 26 October 1955.
21. Lesch, p. 80.
22. Ibid.
23. Ibid.
24. PRO 371/115469, United Kingdom Delegation Meeting of Foreign Ministers in Geneva, 28 October 1955.
25. Seale, pp. 270–271.
26. Blum, *Killing Hope*, p. 88.
27. Blum, pp. 85–86.
28. Seale, pp. 271–271.
29. Seale, p. 273.
30. PRO 371/115954 – British Embassy in Washington, 27 October 1956.
31. Lesch, p. 96.
32. Ibid.
33. Seale, p. 273.
34. Ibid.
35. Seale, p. 788.
36. Interview with Ajlani, 9 August 1999.
37. Blum, p. 87.
38. PRO 371/128221. Among those to intervene on behalf of the arrested Syrians was the Lebanese Deputy Hamid Franjiyieh and the Maronite Patriarch. See Azm, *Muzakarat*, vol. 2, p. 495.
39. Azm, *Muzakarat*, vol. 2, p. 494.
40. Interview with Ajlani, 9 August 1999.
41. Azm, pp. 295–296.
42. Interview with Ridwan al-Atasi, 25 January 2008.
43. Interview with Ajlani, 9 August 1999.
44. Interview with Inaam al-Hasani, 1 September 2000.

The Stone Affair

1. *New York Times*, 21 August 1957.
2. Azm, *Muzakarat*, vol. 2, p. 498.
3. PRO 371/115954, British Foreign Office, 28 October 1955.
4. *Al-Hayat*, 8 May 1957.
5. PRO 371/128223, British Embassy in Beirut, 20 June 1957.
6. PRO 371/128223, British Embassy in Beirut, 27 June 1957.
7. During Quwatli's 1945 meeting with Winston Churchill, he had famously said, 'This man, Abdul-Aziz, is my best friend on the face of this earth'.
8. *The Daily Star*, 29 June 1957.
9. Blum, *Killing Hope*, p. 88. Stone had been transferred to the US State Department at the request of top CIA officials Archibald and his cousin, Kermit Roosevelt, the grandsons of former President Teddy Roosevelt.
10. Al-Nasr, 15 August 1957.
11. Blum, *Killing Hope*, p. 88.
12. Ibid.
13. Eisenhower, *The White House Years*, p. 196. The US State Department described the Syrian claim as a 'complete fabrication'.
14. Lesch, pp. 138–139.
15. *New York Times*, 22 August, 1957.
16. *New York Times*, 17 August, 1957.
17. Seale, p. 295.
18. Lesch, p. 148.
19. PRO 371/1282224, MacMillan to Dulles, 23 August 1957.
20. Lesch, p. 141.
21. MacMillan, *Riding the Storm*, pp. 279–280.
22. *Al-Ayyam*, 2 September 1957.
23. Eisenhower, *Waging Peace*, pp. 198–199.
24. Ibid, p. 198.
25. Lesch, p. 142.
26. The British Ambassador to Turkey was unimpressed with Eisenhower's envoy, remarking that Henderson came to the region 'inadequately briefed and rather devoid of ideas'. PRO 371/128224, British Embassy in Turkey, 25 August 1957.
27. Ibid, p. 147. The State Department wrote back to its Embassy in Saudi Arabia saying: 'We find it very disappointing' claiming that only Saud 'had the political and moral authority ... to facilitate generating pressure designed to isolate Syria and to work towards improvement of situation in that country'.
28. PRO 371/127743, British Embassy in Beirut, 31 August 1957.
29. PRO 371/128234 – British Embassy in Baghdad, 29 August 1957.
30. Eisenhower, pp. 200–2001.
31. General Whisenand had served Assistant Deputy Director of the Air Force on the Joint Strategic Plans Committee and in 1954, Commander of the 388th Fighter Bomber Wing. When summoned to discuss the situation in Syria, he had just been

appointed Deputy Director of Plans in the Office of the Deputy Chief of Staff for Operations.

32. *New York Times*, 15 September 1957.
33. Lesch, p. 155.
34. Lesch, pp. 154–156.
35. Hughes, *The Ordeal of Power*, pp. 253–254.
36. Eisenhower, p. 203.
37. Lesch, p. 156.
38. Ibid, p. 157.
39. *Al-Ayyam*, 4 September 1957.
40. Ibid, 22 August 1957.
41. *Al-Qabas*, 9 September 1957.
42. Ibid, 16 September 1957.
43. Lesch, p. 163.
44. Smolansky, *The Soviet Union and the Arab East under Khrushchev*, pp. 59–74.
45. *Washington Post*, 6 September 1957. Dulles noted that these were 'perhaps the bitterest attacks ever made by a Soviet official on the United States'.
46. *Al-Hayat*, 27 September 1957.
47. Shuqayri was a Palestinian attorney who had served on Syria's mission to the UN in 1945, then worked as Ambassador for Saudi Arabia before becoming the first Chairman of the Palestinian Liberation Organisation (PLO) in 1964, brought to the job with the backing of President Nasser, four years before Yasser Arafat.
48. PRO 371/1282227, British Embassy in Baghdad, 16 September 1957.
49. *New York Times*, 15 September 1957.
50. *New York Times*, 17 August 1957.

The United Arab Republic

1. PRO 371/128228, British Delegation to the United Nations, 17 September 1957.
2. PRO 371/128228, British Embassy in Beirut, 17 September 1957.
3. Lesch, p. 191.
4. PRO 371/128231, British Embassy in Ankara, 4 October 1957.
5. Mackintosh, *Strategy and Tactics of Soviet Foreign Policy*, p. 227.
6. Lesch, p. 191.
7. *New York Times*, 4 October 1957.
8. After having travelled extensively in Europe, visiting the USSR, Germany, Austria and Poland, Charles Yost was brought into the Foreign Service in 1930 by Secretary of State Robert Lansing, the uncle of John Foster Dulles.
9. *Al-Ayyam*, 27 September 1957.
10. *Al-Ahram*, 14 October 1957.
11. PRO 371/128231, British Embassy in Beirut, 18 October 1957.

BIBLIOGRAPHY

Interviews

Abdul Ghani al-Otari (Publisher of Al-Dunia Magazine in the 1940s and 1950s) – Damascus, 6 January 2002

Abdul Qadir Qaddura (Baath Party leader, Former Speaker of Parliament) – Damascus, 23 July 2009

Abdul Raouf al-Kassem (Former Syrian Prime Minister) – Damascus, 6 April 2002

Abdul Wahab Homad (People's Party leader, cabinet minister, MP) – Damascus, 21 July 1999

Abdullah al-Khani (Secretary General of the Presidential Palace 1943–1958) – Damascus, 6 December 2008 and 11 April 2009

Colette Khoury (Novelist, MP, granddaughter of Prime Minister Fares al-Khoury) – 11 April 2009

George Lathkani (Officer in the Ottoman Army during World War I) – Damascus, 6 November 1997

Haitham Kaylani (Ambassador, retired officer in the Syrian Army) – Damascus, 11 July 2003

Inaam Taj al-Din al-Hasani (Daughter of President Hasani) – Beirut, 1 September 2000

Jimmy Carter (Former US President) – Damascus, 25 December 2008

Mansour Sultan al-Atrash (Baath Party leader, Parliament Speaker, son of Sultan Pasha al-Atrash) – Damascus, 26 February 2001

Mohammad al-Imadi (Minister of Economy) – Damascus, 23 October 2010

Munir al-Ajlani (Cabinet Minister, MP) – Beirut, 9 August 1999

Ridwan al-Atasi (Grandson of President Hashem al-Atasi) – Damascus, 25 January 2008

Shaker al-Fahham (Baath Party founder, cabinet minister, MP) – Damascus, 10 March 2002

Suheil al-Ashi (Former military aid to President Shukri al-Quwatli) – Damascus, 15 July 2002

Tayseer al-Saadi (Pioneer of Syrian theatre, radio and TV) – Damascus, 11 November 2010

Newspapers & Magazines

Al-Ahram (Cairo)
Al-Ayyam (Damascus)
Al-Baath (Damascus)
Al-Hayat (Beirut)
Alif Bae (Damascus)
Al-Inqilab (Damascus)
Al-Inshaa (Damascus)
Al-Jumhuriyya (Cairo)
Al-Mukhtar (Cairo)
Al-Muwsawwar (Cairo)
Al-Nasr (Damascus)
Al-Qabas (Damascus)
Al-Rai al-Aam (Damascus)
Al-Shaab (Aleppo)
Al-Souri al-Jadid (Homs)
Annahar (Beirut)
Barada (Damascus)
Dimashq al-Masaa (Damascus)
Forward Magazine (Damascus)
LIFE Magazine
The Daily Star (Beirut)
The London Times (London)
The New York Times (New York)
The Washington Post (Washington DC)

Official Records

Assad National Library – Damascus
Bibliothèque Nationale de France – Paris, France
French Centre of Diplomatic Archives – Nantes, France
National Documents Museum – Damascus
Office of the Historian – US Department of State
Public Records Office (PRO) – London
US National Archives (USNA)

Dissertations

Abu al-Shamat, Hania, 'Syria: an improbable democracy,' MA dissertation, American University of Beirut, 1999.
Atiyah, Najla Wadih, 'The attitude of the Lebanese Sunnis towards the state of Lebanon,' PhD dissertation, University of London, 1973.
Drewry, James, 'An analysis of the 1949 coups d'etat in Syria in light of Fertile Crescent unity,' American University of Beirut, 1960.
Ismail, Thuraya, 'Myths and realities,' MA dissertation, London School of Economics (LSE), 2002.

Landis, Joshua, 'Nationalism and the politics of za'ma: The collapse of republican Syria 1945–1949,' PhD dissertation, Princeton University, 1997.

Mufarrij, Fou'ad, 'Syria and Lebanon under the French Mandate,' MA dissertation, American University of Beirut, 1935.

Nashabi, Hisham, 'The political parties in Syria 1918–1933,' MA dissertation, American University of Beirut, 1952.

Tomeh, Ramez George, 'Landowners and political power in Damascus 1858–1958,' American University of Beirut, 1997.

Books and Articles in English

Abd-Allah, Umar, *The Islamic Struggle in Syria* (Berkley, 1983).

Abu-Jaber, Faiz, 'Eisenhower, Israel, and the Jordan Valley authorities' scheme' *Middle East Forum*, vol. XLI, no 2, 1969.

Ambrose, Stephen, *Eisenhower: President and Soldier* (New York, 1991).

Ambrosius, Lloyd, *Woodrow Wilson and the American Diplomatic Tradition: The Treaty Fight in Perspective* (Cambridge, 1990).

Andelman, David, *A Shattered Peace: Versailles 1919 and the Price We Pay Today* (New Jersey, 2008).

Barazi, Husni, *Memoirs of Prime Minister Husni al-Barazi*, Oral History Project at the Middle East Studies Center at the American University of Beirut (Beirut, 1969).

Batatu, Hanna, *Syria's Peasantry: The Descendants of Its Lesser Rural Notables and Their Politics* (New Jersey, 1999).

Ben Gurion, David, *My Talks with Arab Leaders* (Jerusalem, 1972).

Blum, William, *Killing Hope: US Military and CIA Interventions Since World War II* (London, 2003).

Bregman, Ahron, Tahri, Jihan, *The Fifty Years War: Israel and the Arabs* (London, 1998).

Butler, Lawrence J, *Britain and Empire Adjusting to a Post-Imperial World* (London, 2002).

Carlton, Alford, 'The Syrian coup d'etat of 1949' *Middle East Journal,* vol. I, 1950.

Christison, Kathleen, *Perceptions of Palestine: Their Influence on US Middle East policy* (California, 1999).

Churchill, Winston, *The Churchill-Eisenhower Correspondence 1953–1955* (North Carolina, 1990).

Cleveland, William, *A History of the Middle East* (Colorado, 2000).

—— *The Making of an Arab Nationalist: Ottomanism and Arabism in the Life and Thought of Sati, al-Husri* (New Jersey, 1971).

Commins, David, *Historical Dictionary of Syria* (Maryland, 1996).

Dallek, Robert, *Franklin D. Roosevelt and American Foreign Policy, 1932–1945* (Oxford, 1995).

Davidson, Lawrence, *America's Palestine: Popular and Official Perceptions from Balfour to Israeli Statehood* (Florida, 2001).

Dawn, Ernest, *From Ottomanism to Arabism: Essays on the Origins of Arab Nationalism* (Illinois, 1973).

DeNovo, John, *American Interests and Policies in the Middle East 1900–1939* (Minnesota, 1963).

Devlin, John, *The Baath Party: A History from Its Origins to 1966* (California, 1976).

Eisenhower, Dwight, *Mandate for Change 1953–1956: The White House Years* (London, 1963).

Eisenhower, Dwight, *Waging Peace 1956–1961: The White House Years* (London, 1966).

Gouraud, Henri, *La France en Syrie* (Paris, 1922).

Hahn, Peter, *Caught in the Middle East: US Policy toward the Arab-Israeli Conflict, 1945–1961* (North Carolina, 2004).

Hoover, Herbert, *The Memoirs of Herbert Hoover: The Cabinet and Presidency* (London, 1952).

Hughes, Emmet John, *The Ordeal of Power: A Political Memoir of the Eisenhower Years* (New York, 1963).

Hull, Cordell, *Memoirs*, 2-volumes (London, 1948).

Immerman, Richard, *John Foster Dulles: Piety, Pragmatism, and Power in us Foreign Policy* (Maryland, 1999).

Khoury, Philip, *Syria and the French Mandate* (New Jersey, 1987).

—— *Urban Notables and Arab Nationalism: The Politics of Damascus 1860–1920* (Cambridge, 1983).

Kissinger, Henry, *Diplomacy* (New York, 1994).

Lawrence, T. E. *Seven Pillars of Wisdom* (London, 1935).

Lesch, David W., *Syria and the United States: Eisenhower's Cold War in the Middle East* (Colorado, 1992).

Lewis, Bernard, *Jews of Islam* (Connecticut, 2002).

Louis, William Roger, *The British Empire in the Middle East, 1945–1951: Arab Nationalism, the United States, and Postwar Imperialism* (Gloucestershire, 1986).

Love, Kennett, *Suez: The Twice Fought War* (New York, 1969).

Mack, John E., *A Prince of our Disorder: The life of TE Lawrence* (Massachusetts, 1998).

Mackintosh, Malcolm, *Strategy and Tactics of the Soviet Union* (London, 1963).

Macmillan, Harold, *Riding the Storm* (London, 1971).

Manuel, Frank Edward, *The Realities of Palestine-American Relations* (Connecticut, 1975).

Maoz, Moshe, *Modern Syria: From Ottoman Rule to Pivotal Role in The Middle East* (Sussex, 1999).

Mardam Bey, Salma, *Syria's Quest for Independence* (London, 1994).

Moubayed, Sami, *Damascus between Democracy and Dictatorship* (Maryland, 2000).

—— *The George Washington of Syria: The Rise and Fall of Shukri al-Quwatli* (Beirut, 2005).

—— *The Politics of Damascus 1920–1946: Urban Notables and the French Mandate* (Damascus, 1998).

—— *Steel and Silk: Men and Women Who Shaped Syria 1900–2000* (Seattle, 2006).

Nielsen, Kim, *The Radical Lives of Helen Keller* (New York, 2004).

Nixon, Richard, *RN: The Memoirs of Richard Nixon* (New York, 1999).

Orofsky, Melvin, *American Zionism from Herzl to the Holocaust* (Nebraska, 1995).

Overndale, Richard, *The Middle East since 1914* (Essex, 1992).

Penrose, Stephen, *That They May Have Life: The Story of the American University of Beirut 1866–1941* (Beirut, 1970).

Rabinovich, Itamar, *The Road Not Taken* (New York, 1991).

Rathmell, Andrew, *Secret War in the Middle East: The Covert Struggle for Syria 1949–1961* (London, 1995).

Roosevelt, Franklin D., *The FDR Memoirs* (New York, 1973).

Russell, Malcolm, *The First Modern Arab State: Syria under Faysal I* (London, 1987).

Saikaly, Samir, 'Abd al-Rahman Shahbandar: the beginnings of a nationalist career,' published *Abhath*, a periodical of the American University of Beirut (Beirut, 1986).

Saikaly, Samir, 'Damascus intellectual life in the opening years of the 20th century,' published in *Intellectual Life in the Arab East 1890–1939* (Beirut, 1981).

Sanders, Bonnie F., *The United States and Arab Nationalism: The Syria Case 1953–1960* (London, 1996).

Sheffer, Gabriel, *Moshe Sharett: Biography of a Political Moderate* (Oxford, 1996).

Shorrock, William, *French Imperialism in the Middle East: The Failure of Policy in Syria and Lebanon*, (Wisconsin, 1976).

Seale, Patrick, *Asad: The Struggle for the Middle East* (London, 1988).

—— *The Struggle for Arab Independence: Riad el-Solh and the Makers of the Modern Middle East* (Cambridge, 2010).

—— *The Struggle for Power in Syria* (London, 1961).

Shaaban, Bouthaina, *Both Right and Left Handed: Arab Women Talk about Their Lives* (London, 1988).

Simon, Reeva, *Iraq between the Two World Wars* (New York, 1986).

Smith, Charles D., *Palestine and the Arab-Israeli Conflict: A History with Documents* (New York, 2009).

Smolansky, Oles, *The Soviet Union and the Arab East under Khrushchev* (Pennsylvania, 1974).

Spears, Edward, *Fulfillment of a Mission: The Spears Mission to Syria and Lebanon, 1941–1944* (London, 1977).

Suleiman, Michael W., *Arabs in America: Building a New Future* (Philadelphia, 1999).

Thompson, Elizabeth, *Colonial Citizens: Rights, Paternal Privilege, and Gender in French Syria and Lebanon* (New York, 1999).

Tibawi, Abdul Latif, *A Modern History of Syria, Including Lebanon and Palestine* (London, 1969).

Truman, Harry, *Memoirs of Harry S. Truman: Years of Trial and Hope* (Massachusetts, 1987).

Torrey, Gordon, *Syrian Politics and the Military* (Ohio, 1964).

Turner, Barry, *Suez 1956: The Inside Story of the First Oil War* (London, 2006).

Van Dam, Nikolaos, *The Struggle for Power in Syria: Politics and Society under Asad and the Baath Party* (London, 1996).

Weizmann, Chaim, *Trial and Error: The Autobiography of Chaim Weizmann* (New York, 1966).

Wise, Stephen, *The Personal Letters of Stephen Wise* (Boston, 1956).

Zeine, Zeine, *Struggle for Arab Independence: Western Diplomacy and the Rise and Fall of Faisal's Kingdom in Syria* (New York, 1977).

Books in Arabic

Abdul Karim, Ahmad, *Hasad* (Harvest), Damascus 1994.

Abdullah, King of Jordan, *Wathaeq Hashemiya* (Hashemite Documents), Amman 1993.

—— *Muzakarati* (My Memoirs), Jerusalem 1945.

Abu Assaf, Amin, *Muzakarat* (Memoirs), Damascus 1990.

Abu Mansour, Fadlallah, *Aaasir Dimashq* (Damascus Storms), Beirut 1959.

Adil, Fouad, *Qusat Souriyya bayn al-intidab wa al-inqilab* (The Story of Syria between the Mandate and Coup), Damascus 2001.

Aflaq, Michel, *Ma'rakat al-Masir al-Wahid* (Battle for One Destiny), Beirut 1958.

Ajlani, Munir, *Difaa al-Doctor Munir al-Ajlani amam al-Mahkama al-Askariya* (Defense of Dr Munir al-Ajlani before the Military Court), Damascus 1957.

Armanazi, Najib, *Muhadarat An Souriyya min al-ihtilal hata al-Jalaa* (Lectures on Syria from Occupation to Emancipation), Cairo 1953.

Arslan, Adil, *Muzakarat al-Ameer Adil Arslan* (Memoirs of Prince Adil Arslan), 3-volumes, Beirut 1972.

Arsuzi, Zaki, *Mashakiluna al-Qawmiya* (Our Nationalist Problems), Damascus 1958.

Atassi, Mohammad Radwan, *Hashem al-Atasi 1873–1960: Hayatuh wa Asruh* (Hashem al-Atasi 1873–1960: His Life and Era), Damascus 2004.

Awad, Walid, *Ashab al-Fakhama Ruassa Lubnan* (Their Excellencies the Presidents of Lebanon), Beirut 2002.

Azm, Abdul Qadir, *al-Usra al-Azmiya* (The Azm Family), Damascus 1951.

Azm, Khaled, *Muzakarat Khaled al-Azm* (The Memoirs of Khaled al-Azm), 3-volumes, Beirut 1973.

Babil, Nasuh, *Sahafa wa Siyasa fi Souriyya* (Journalism and Politics in Syria), London 1988.

Bayhum, Mohammad Jamil, *Fatat al-Sharq fi Hadaret al-Gharb* (Girl of the East in Western Civilization), Beirut 1952.

Bizreh, Afif, *Al-Nasiriya fi Jumlat al-Istimaar al-Hadeeth* (Nasserism and Modern Imperialism), Damascus 1962.

Buayni, Hasan Amin, *Sultan Basha al-Atrash: Masirat Qaid fir Tareekh Umma* (Sultan Pasha al-Atrash: The Struggle of a Leader in the History of a Nation), Damascus 1985.

Dahhan, Sami, *Mohammad Kurd Ali: Hayatuhu wa Atharuhu* (Mohammad Kurd Ali: His Life and Legacy), Damascus 1955.

Dayeh, Jean, *Ghassan Jadid*, London 1990.

Droubi, Ihsan Bayat, *Sami Droubi*, Damascus 1982.

Elias, Joseph, *Tatawur al-Sahafa al-Souriyya fi al-Ahd al-Uthmani* (Development of Syrian Journalism in the Ottoman Era), Beirut 1972.

Elias, Joseph, *Aflaq wa al-Baath* (Aflaq and the Baath), Beirut 1991.

Faris, George, *Man Hum fi al-Aalam al-Arabi* (Who's Who in the Arab World), Damascus 1957.

Farfur, Mohammad Saleh, *Aalam Dimashq fi al-Qarn al-Rabe Ashr lil Hijra* (Damascus Notables in the 14th Century after Hijra), Damascus 1987.

Farhani, Mohammad, *Fares al-Khoury wa ayam la tunas* (Fares Al-Khoury and Unforgettable Days), Beirut 1965.

Hafez, Thurya, *Hafiziyat*, Damascus 1980.

Haffar, Lutfi, *Zikrayat* (Memoirs) 2-volumes, Damascus 1954.

Haffar, Salma, *Lutfi al-Haffar 1891–1968*, London 1997.

Hakim, Daad, *Awrak wa muzakarat Fakhri al-Barudi* (The Papers and Memoirs of Fakhri Al-Barudi), 2-volumes, Damascus 1999.

Hakim, Hasan, *Abdul Rahman Shahbandar: hayatuh wa jihaduh* (Abdul Rahman Shahbandar: His Life and Struggle), Damascus 1989.

—— *Muzakarati 1920–1958: safahat min tarkeekh Souriyya al-Hadeeth* (My Memoirs 1920–1958: Pages from Modern Syrian History), 2-volumes, Beirut 1965.

Hakim, Yusuf, *Souriyya wa al-Ahd al-Faysali* (Syria and the Faisalian Era), Beirut 1965.

—— *Souriyya wa al-Intidab al-Faransi* (Syria and the French Mandate), Beirut 1966.

Hanna, Abdullah, *Abdul Rahman Shahbandar 1879–1940*, Damascus 1989.

Hawrani, Akram, *Muzakarat Akram al-Hawrani* (Memoirs of Akram al-Hawrani), 3-volumes, Cairo 2000.

Husari, Sati, *Yawm Maysaloun* (The Day of Maysaloun), Beirut 1947.

Jeha, Michel, *Mary Ajamy*, London 2001.

Jumaa, Sami, *Awrak min daftar al-Watan* (Pages from Notebook of the Homeland), Damascus 2001.

Jundi, Adham, *Shuhada al-Harb al-Alamiya al-Kubra* (Martyrs of the Great World War), Damascus 1960.

—— *Tareekh al-Thawrat al-Souriyya fi Ahd al-Intidab al-Faransi* (History of Syrian Revolts during the French Mandate), Damascus 1960.

Kasmiyyah, Khayriyah, *al-Hukuma al-Arabiyya fi Dimashq bayn 1918–1920* (The Arab Government in Damascus between 1918 and 1920), Cairo 1971.

—— *al-Rael al-Arabi al-Awal: Awrak Nabih wa Adil al-Azma* (The First Arab Generation: The Papers of Nabih and Adil Al-Azma), Damascus 1990.

—— *Muzakarat Fawzi al-Qawikji 1914–1932* (Memoirs of Fawzi al-Qawikji 1914–1932), Beirut 1975.

—— *Muzakarat Muhsen al-Barazi 1947–1949* (Memoirs of Muhsen al-Barazi 1947–1949), Beirut 1994.

Kawtharani, Wajih, *Wathaeq al-Mutamar al-Arabi al-Awal* (Documents of the First Arab Congress), Beirut 1980.

Kayali, Abdul Rahman, *Al-marahil fi al-intidab al-Faransi wa nidaluna al-watani* (Stages of the French Mandate and Our Nationalist Struggle), Aleppo 1958–1960.

Khalidi, Ghassan, *Al-Hizb al-Qawmi wa Qadiyat al-Malki: Hakika amm itiham* (The Syrian Social Nationalist Party and the Malki Affair: Truth or Accusation?) Beirut 2000.

Khani, Abdullah, *Jihad Shukri al-Quwatli fi sabeel al-istiklal wa al-wihda* (Shukri al-Quwatli's Jihad for Independence and Unity), Beirut 2003.

—— *Souriyya bayn al-democratiya wa al-hukm al-fardi* (Syria between Democracy and Dictatorship), Beirut 2004.

Khayer, Hani, *Adib al-Shishakli: Al-Bidaya wa al-Nihaya* (Adib al-Shishakli: The Start and End), Damascus 1994.

Kurd Ali, *Muzakarat* (Memoirs), Damascus 1949.

Maarouf, Mohammad, *Ayam Ishtuha 1949–1958* (Days That I lived 1949–1958), Beirut 2003.

Mardini, Zuhair, *Al-Ustaz: Qissat Hayat Michel Aflaq* (The Teacher: The Life of Michel Aflaq), London 1988.

Mouallem, Walid, *Souriyya 1918–1958: al-Tahadi wa al-Muwajaha* (Syria 1918–1958: Challenge and Confrontation), Damascus 1985.

Omari, Subhi, *Awrak al-Thawra al-Arabi* (Papers of the Arab Revolt), London 1991.

—— *Lawrence kama ariftahu* (Lawrence as I Knew Him), Beirut 1965.

Otari, Abdul Ghani, *Abquariyat Chamiya* (Damascene Geniuses), Damascus 1986.

—— *Abquariyat min biladi* (Geniuses from My Country), Damascus 1995.

—— *Abquariyat wa Aalam* (Geniuses and Notables), Damascus 1996.

Qadri, Ahmad, *Muzakarat an al-Thawra al-Arabiya al-Kubra* (Memoirs of the Great Arab Revolt), Damascus 1956.

Qassab Hasan, Najat. *Hadeeth Dimashqi 1884–1982* (A Damascene Conversation), Damascus 1988.

—— *Saniou al-Jalaa fi Souriyya* (Makers of Independence in Syria), Damascus 1999.

Quwatli, Shukri, *Shukri al-Quwatli Yukhateb Ummatuh* (Shukri al-Quwatli Speaks to His People), Beirut 1970.

Rihani, Amin, *Faisal al-Awal* (Faisal the First), Beirut 1958.

Rifaii, Shams al-Din, *Tareekh al-Sahafa al-Souriyya 1800–1947* (History of Syrian Journalism 1800–1947), 2-volumes, Cairo 1969.

Sulh, Hilal, *Rajul wa Qadiyya* (A Man and a Cause), Beirut 1996.

Sultan, Ali, *Tareekh Souriyya 1908–1918* (Syrian History 1908–1918), Damascus 1987.

Tarazi, Falak, *Araa wa Mashair* (My Thoughts and Feelings), Damascus, 1939.

Uthman, Hashem, *Al-Ahzab al-Siyasiya fi Souriyya: Al-Siriyya wa al-Alaniyya* (Political Party Life in Syria: Secret and Public), Beirut 2001.

—— *Al-Sahafa al-Souriyya: Madiha wa Hadiruha* (Syrian Journalism: its past and present), Damascus 1997.

Yunis, Abdul Latif, *Muzakarat al-Doctor Abdul Latif Yunis* (Memoirs of Dr. Abdul Latif Yunis), Damascus 1992.

Zakariya, Ghassan, *Al-Sultan al-Ahmar* (The Red Sultan), London 1991.

Zaytun, Nazir, *al-Shaheedan al-Zahrawi wa Sallum* (The two martyrs Zahrawi and Sallum), Damascus 1961.

INDEX OF NAMES